COMPLETE

IDIOT'S
GUIDE® TO

Buying a Piano

by Marty C. Flinn and Jennifer B. Flinn

ALPHA

A member of Penguin Group (USA) Inc.

We dedicate our work to the encouragement of Music Education and the tremendous benefits it brings to those who embrace it. Playing piano enhances the mind of a child, enriches family life, and brings stress relief to adults. Our thanks to all who contribute to this goal.

ALPHA BOOKS

Published by the Penguin Group

Penguin Group (USA) Inc., 375 Hudson Street, New York, New York 10014, USA

Penguin Group (Canada), 90 Eglinton Avenue East, Suite 700, Toronto, Ontario M4P 2Y3, Canada (a division of Pearson Penguin Canada Inc.)

Penguin Books Ltd., 80 Strand, London WC2R 0RL, England

Penguin Ireland, 25 St. Stephen's Green, Dublin 2, Ireland (a division of Penguin Books Ltd.)

Penguin Group (Australia), 250 Camberwell Road, Camberwell, Victoria 3124, Australia (a division of Pearson Australia Group Pty. Ltd.)

Penguin Books India Pvt. Ltd., 11 Community Centre, Panchsheel Park, New Delhi—110 017, India

Penguin Group (NZ), 67 Apollo Drive, Rosedale, North Shore, Auckland 1311, New Zealand (a division of Pearson New Zealand Ltd.)

Penguin Books (South Africa) (Pty.) Ltd., 24 Sturdee Avenue, Rosebank, Johannesburg 2196, South Africa

Penguin Books Ltd., Registered Offices: 80 Strand, London WC2R 0RL, England

International Standard Book Number: 978-1-59257-718-7
Library of Congress Catalog Card Number: 2008922779

10 09 08   8 7 6 5 4 3 2 1

Interpretation of the printing code: The rightmost number of the first series of numbers is the year of the book's printing; the rightmost number of the second series of numbers is the number of the book's printing. For example, a printing code of 08-1 shows that the first printing occurred in 2008.

Printed in the United States of America

Note: This publication contains the opinions and ideas of its authors. It is intended to provide helpful and informative material on the subject matter covered. It is sold with the understanding that the authors and publisher are not engaged in rendering professional services in the book. If the reader requires personal assistance or advice, a competent professional should be consulted.

The authors and publisher specifically disclaim any responsibility for any liability, loss, or risk, personal or otherwise, which is incurred as a consequence, directly or indirectly, of the use and application of any of the contents of this book.

Most Alpha books are available at special quantity discounts for bulk purchases for sales promotions, premiums, fundraising, or educational use. Special books, or book excerpts, can also be created to fit specific needs.

For details, write: Special Markets, Alpha Books, 375 Hudson Street, New York, NY 10014.

Publisher: *Marie Butler-Knight*
Editorial Director: *Mike Sanders*
Senior Managing Editor: *Billy Fields*
Acquisitions Editor: *Tom Stevens*
Development Editors: *Jennifer Moore, Susan Zingraf*
Production Editor: *Megan Douglass*
Copy Editor: *Emily Garner*

Contributing Editor: *Michelle Tullier*
Cartoonist: *Chris Sabatino*
Cover Designer: *Bill Thomas*
Book Designer: *Trina Wurst*
Indexer: *Angie Bess*
Layout: *Ayanna Lacey*
Proofreaders: *Terri Edwards, Mary Hunt*

Contents at a Glance

Contents

Introduction

About 100,000 new pianos are sold in the United States each year. This figure has remained relatively constant for the past 15 years. It includes all new vertical, grand, and digital pianos. The estimated number of used pianos that change hands each year is somewhere between three to five times the number of new instruments. So, as many as half a million pianos change hands each year in the United States!

How do these buyers decide on the pianos they end up purchasing? Their decision-making processes are nearly as varied as the instruments themselves. Nevertheless, several common factors have an influence on the buying process, including …

- Budget.

- Size of piano their space can accommodate.

- Performance capabilities.

- Appearance (the color, finish, and style of the piano).

- Name brand recognition.

- Prestige of a brand or model.

- Recommendations from someone who knows about pianos.

- Connecting with a particular salesperson or dealer.

In this book we help you understand how each of these factors might play into your own decision and we equip you with the knowledge needed to find the right piano for you.

Why We Wrote This Book

The process of buying a piano should be fun and easy. Sadly, over and over again, we have seen customers shop the fun and excitement right out of the process by belaboring it for far too long. We've even had customers take years to make a decision, and then a not so good one at that! The process turns from pleasurable to painful when you lack confidence in your ability to choose the best piano for your needs. Sales demos might seem confusing, and you may fall victim to a salesperson's hype or disreputable tactics. We don't want that to happen to you. So we've written *The Complete Idiot's Guide to Buying a Piano* for several reasons:

- We saw the need for a comprehensive piano-buying guide written by people from within the retail piano sales industry. All other books have been written by piano players or piano technicians. In addition to playing and working on pianos, we have over 44 years of experience in the retail piano business, and so have insights others do not.

◆ We believe that as a buyer of a big-ticket piece of merchandise, you should be armed with enough facts and knowledge to make an intelligent buying decision.

◆ We cannot think of a product so fraught with misinformation and an institution-alized mythology as the piano, and we want to cut through the misconceptions for you.

We are passionate about this stuff, and we stand behind our information with confidence that comes from our many years in the industry. We promise to tell it like it is!

Who This Book Is For

If you are serious about purchasing a piano within the next few days, weeks, or months, then this book is for you. It will help you make a better, more informed purchasing decision.

Beginners and First-Time Buyers

Much of this book's content is for the first-time piano buyer. It's for the parent, grand-parent, aunt, uncle, or family friend buying for a beginner child or family of children. It's for the adult who took piano lessons as a child and now wants to pick it back up. It's even for the 89-year-old neighbor of one of our editors who bought herself a piano after decades of not playing! Whichever situation you find yourself in, we offer enough basic information to help you understand what pianos are all about and how to figure out which one is right for you.

Experienced Players Upgrading

This book is also for the more experienced player. Despite being an upper-intermediate, or advanced player, or even a music teacher, you may not have current knowledge of the models and features available and price tags they come with. Or your confidence as a player may not transfer to confidence as a shopper. Most of this book will be of use to you, but we dedicate Chapter 18 to your unique needs and likely questions. The buyer's guide in the chapters of Part 3 will help you as well. Also, be sure to check out Chapters 16 and 17 for the latest electronic gadgets and gizmos that you can get these days.

Institutional Purchases

This book is also for anyone buying a piano for an institution, such as a school, college or university, house of worship, or commercial venue, including hotels and restaurants. You might be the designated purchasing rep for your institution but know next to nothing about pianos. Or maybe you do know a lot about pianos and have your sights set on particular brand or model or size, but other folks back in your organization control the purse strings. We devote Chapter 20 to you, as well as portions of Chapters 4 and 14, though all chapters of the book contain valuable information relevant to institutional purchases.

Clearly, the needs of a family with a six-year-old beginner are different from those of a teacher or a graduate student in piano performance, but the advice and information needed to make an informed decision is often the same. So, whether beginner or experienced or somewhere in between, this book will answer your questions and guide you through the process.

How to Get the Most Out of This Book

Our goal is to help you focus your energy and resources toward the purchase of a suitable instrument that meets your needs. We want you to spend enough time shopping for a piano that you see a good range of choices, but not so much time that the process becomes a burden for you. Reading this book will save you time when you hit the stores because you'll know what you're looking for and won't waste your time on instruments that don't fit your selection criteria. And you won't lose time or get frustrated by a sales pitch that takes you in the wrong direction or a demo that you don't understand.

Here's an overview of the process we recommend for using this book and other things to complement what you'll learn here:

Step 1: Spend a few hours skimming through this book and highlight, underline, or make notes. Pay special attention to the chapters in Part 1 that help you determine your strategy and appropriate mindset.

Step 2: Spend a couple of hours on the Internet to see what various manufacturers have to offer. (Use Chapter 5 as your guide in this.)

Step 3: Measure your space. Will you need a vertical or grand? If you have room for a grand, just how grand can it be?

Step 4: Make notes about your room's acoustics, including the size of the room, height of the ceiling, type of flooring, and number of windows and drapes.

Step 5: Measure your wallet. Don't mortgage the farm, but don't be too cheap, either. You can get preliminary ideas of pricing in Chapter 2.

Step 6: Identify the dealerships you'll visit and plan your overall shopping attack. Refer to Chapters 3 and 4 for shopping strategies and pitfalls to avoid, and use the shopping comparison forms provided in Appendix B.

Step 7: Visit two to four reputable dealerships, but first study up on the features and benefits of pianos as discussed in the chapters of Part 2, as well as the buyer's guides in Part 3. You'll need this technical and product knowledge to understand what the salespeople are talking about and to know which models you want them to show you.

Step 8: Investigate private-party, used pianos, if you dare. Read Chapter 6 for more about this.

Step 9: Go back on the Internet to confirm information you've collected about the pianos you've seen. Narrow your list down to a short list of best options.

Step 10: Review the chapters in Part 5 of the book to prepare to strike a deal. Go back to the one or two dealerships that offer the pianos that have made it to your short list. Make your final selection and negotiate the price.

Now you're done and can relax. Sit back and enjoy the sound of those tinkling ivories!

How Long It Will Take to Find a Piano

If you plan well and study up, you can accomplish the whole process in one or two weekends. If you drag it out more than a month, or if you visit more than four dealerships, you are probably making the process much harder than it needs to be. You may become confused and fatigued. In this frame of mind, you can fall victim to a strong salesperson with a weak product. And if you involve children in a long, drawn out process, they might be ready to quit lessons before the piano is even delivered!

Extras

Throughout this book, you'll find many tidbits of information in the form of sidebars set apart from the main text. Watch for these to find special tips, facts and figures, anecdotes, and definitions of piano industry jargon.

Key Note _____

These boxes contain quick tips, tactics, and advice.

def•i•ni•tion _____

Here you'll find definitions of piano terminology.

> **Rhythm and News**
>
> These sidebars contain tales, trivia, and anecdotes about the piano shopping experience.

> **B-Sharp**
>
> Watch out for these pitfalls and common mistakes piano buyers make.

Acknowledgments

We would like to thank Mom, Phyllis Walker, for her tireless dedication to making our writing the King's English. And Dad, Donald Walker, for his encouragement and example.

Thanks also to Michelle Tullier for her excellent eye for organization and her contributions to style and editing. You did a great job!

We would like to thank Tom Stevens of Alpha Books who believed in the project enough to sell it to the powers-that-be.

Thanks also to the rest of the editorial staff at Alpha Books for their work in making this book the most useful tool it could be for you, the reader.

We would like to thank two retailers, Keyboard Concepts and Sherman Clay & Co., and the manufacturers we have worked with including: American Sejung ASC, Baldwin, Bösendorfer, C. Bechstein, Estonia, Fazioli, Kawai, Mason & Hamlin, Pearl River, Petrof, Roland, Samick Music Corp. SMC, Schimmel, Schulze Pollmann, Steinway & Sons, Yamaha, and Young Chang for the opportunity to grow in this wonderful thing we call the music business.

We acknowledge the sacrifices of the families of all who work in retail sales, the missed holidays and family occasions (and worked weekends).

And finally, we'd like to thank the many customers we've worked with and learned from over the years.

Trademarks

All terms mentioned in this book that are known to be or are suspected of being trademarks or service marks have been appropriately capitalized. Alpha Books and Penguin Group (USA) Inc. cannot attest to the accuracy of this information. Use of a term in this book should not be regarded as affecting the validity of any trademark or service mark.

As Unbiased as It Gets

The opinions and conclusions we express in this book are our own and are as objective as humanly possible. They come from experience with thousands of real customers and contact with thousands of pianos of every shape, size, brand, and age. They come from hundreds of hours of factory product training and hands-on technical work we've personally performed. Our observations are not those of our employers—past, present, or future. Our observations are not those of any manufacturers we have represented in the past, present, or future. We have not accepted, nor will we consider accepting, any form of support from any manufacturing or retailing entity to influence our opinions or conclusions. We call 'em as we see 'em to give you the inside scoop!

The house lights dim, and the overture begins …

Part 1

Shopping for a Piano

You have the power to make shopping for a piano fun and easy. By equipping yourself with the necessary knowledge and tools, you can make an informed decision and purchase a piano that's right for you and your family, or the institution you represent.

In this part, we help you define what you need in a piano, what to look for, and explain what it's going to cost. We offer strategies to make your shopping process as productive and efficient as possible, while also debunking myths and misconceptions that could trip you up along the way. We also address the pros and cons of shopping on the Internet and buying a used piano instead of new.

The Right Piano

In This Chapter

- Identifying what's important
- Who will play it?
- Measure your space and your budget
- A recommended shopping process

An entire book devoted to buying a piano? That's right! It's easy to become intimidated by the wide array of brands, models, sizes, and prices to choose from, so this book is designed to reduce the anxiety and confusion that often comes part and parcel with a piano purchase. The goal of this book is to help you wade through the many options you'll face and to help you come to a purchasing decision you can feel good about.

A piano is like no other instrument, or any item for that matter, you will purchase. As a musical instrument it should be pleasing to the touch and the ear, and as a piece of furniture—a large one at that—it can enhance the elegance or warmth of a room. A piano is a marvel of both old-fashioned handcrafting and high-tech ingenuity. It has so many intricate, moving parts that your head may spin when trying to learn how it works, let alone when buying one. A piano is expensive, even at the lower-end of the prestige and quality scale. It is, simply, a major purchase, one worthy of research, investigation, and contemplation to ensure you secure the right piano to meet your needs.

Whether you're buying a piano for your home or for an institution, such as a school, group home, or house of worship, for a young beginner or an accomplished player, you want to select the right piano to meet your needs. The best place to start is to identify those needs. In this chapter, we'll help you identify your piano selection criteria, address common concerns about buying a piano for a beginner, and give you some pros and cons of renting versus buying. This chapter concludes with a simple, ten-step process for buying a piano.

With the foundation provided in this chapter, you'll then be ready to continue your education with the rest of the book, where we walk you through pitfalls to avoid, help you understand how pianos work, survey pros and cons of various models and styles, and offer tips for striking a favorable deal.

Determining What's Important

Any major purchase process should start with identifying your selection criteria. So let's look at the factors that will help you decide if a particular piano is right for you or not. Here are three basic questions to help you get at the most critical criteria:

◆ Who will play the piano?

◆ What's the budget?

◆ Where will the piano be located (or fit in your home or other space)?

Who Will Play It?

Is the piano for a child, an adult, various family members, a group of students? Is it a gift for someone else? Will the piano be used for teaching or in an institutional setting, such as accompaniment for a choir? If the piano is for a beginning student, there are several options available. The more advanced the student, teacher, or institutional need, the narrower the choices become, since these situations call for a more professional instrument.

A piano being in tune (the notes sounding in the correct relationship to each other) and at concert pitch (all of the notes are at the international standard tone) is an absolute minimum requirement, for any piano, for any player. For the beginning student, a piano needs to be able to be tuned and should have a consistent touch (each key feeling like its neighbors) across the keyboard. *Ear training* is critical for beginners since they need to learn how each note is supposed to sound. For instance, the middle C note on the piano they play and practice on needs to sound the same as their teacher's middle C note. If it sounds different—if it's at a different pitch—a student can become confused.

Touch training is also critical for beginners. Having each key play like its neighbor is important. Piano keys that are worn or feel irregular add an extra layer of difficulty to learning how to play. If beginners have to remember that they must play certain keys harder to achieve the same volume, they can tire easily and lose interest in playing. There are some notes in western music that are played more often than others, sort of like vowels in language. These commonly played notes will wear faster and more noticeably than the rest of the keys. Technicians can make adjustments to make up for their differences, but only for so long before the keys simply cannot be adjusted further. Not to mention, if the E key sticks every time it is played and so the player has to pull it back up, it will be hard to keep time to the music.

def•i•ni•tion

Ear training is a process by which musicians learn to recognize intervals, melodies, notes, and rhythms. It begins with the first lesson.

Touch training is a set of techniques by which piano students learn to control how loud or soft and how long or short a note sounds.

Today there are thousands of used pianos available that have aged long beyond their useful musical life expectancies. Many of these instruments may have been mediocre to begin with, so today they exhibit little touch consistency, poor tone quality and little or no tuning stability. Their cabinets may be less than inspiring as well, often with broken legs, cigarette burns, drink rings, or cracked key tops. Just because most of the pieces are there and it sort of works does not mean the piano is necessarily good enough to be a practice instrument. The essence of successful beginning piano progress is repetition through regular, daily practice, and that requires a suitable instrument to practice on each and every day.

If you are an advanced player or teacher, or represent an institution with such, you will need to select a piano that matches your more sophisticated needs in touch and tone and one that can stand up to heavier, more

 B-Sharp

Pianos do not improve with age. Cheaply made pianos age even less gracefully!

frequent play. As we describe pianos and their functionality throughout this book, you will find references to features and models that are particularly suitable for institutions. Chapter 20 focuses on special considerations for institutional purchases, while Chapter 18 is devoted to advanced players.

What's the Budget?

Pianos aren't cheap, so price and budget are big considerations. Some families decide they will buy a better instrument after the beginner progresses. Unfortunately, this isn't always the best logic when it comes to buying a piano, and it can actually mean spending more than if you invested in a solid instrument to begin with. Spending more money now on a better instrument can help you avoid a more costly upgrade years down the road if you or the player you're buying for progresses to the upper-intermediate or advanced levels of play. Pianos last a long time, so plan for long-term need.

Beginners are really at the mercy of the piano they must practice on, so it's important that tone and touch are as good as possible from the very start. Plus, after a less expensive starter piano is purchased, the acquisition of an upgraded instrument often doesn't happen, and the student either continues on an inferior piano or loses interest altogether. Advanced players can usually play around the limitations of most pianos and still create something musical, but beginners don't have that ability.

> **B-Sharp**
>
> Resist the temptation to save money by spending only a couple hundred dollars on a *keyboard* instead of buying a piano. A keyboard is a portable electronic unit that often has fewer than a piano's standard 88 keys. Keyboards don't have the same touch or tone as a piano, so they aren't good learning instruments, and many teachers won't accept students who only have a keyboard to practice on.

Pianos that are suitable for beginners come in various price ranges. A new, good entry-level vertical piano will cost in the neighborhood of $2,000, an entry-level grand piano $5,000 or more, and just over $1,500 for a suitable digital piano (more on these different models of pianos later in the book). These are street prices for new pianos, not the manufacturers' suggested retail prices. New pianos much below these prices will likely be unsuitable in performance and serviceability.

We'll discuss pricing in more detail in Chapter 2, but for now, just keep in mind the ballpark of what a good new piano will cost, and later we'll talk about new vs. used pianos. Also, later in this chapter, we'll cover the pros and cons of renting a piano, an approach that can work well for families with serious budget limitations, but that is not without its downside.

Where Will It Fit?

As part of your selection criteria, you will need to identify where you are going to put the piano. Vertical pianos are about five feet wide and two feet deep, and they vary in height from about three feet to five feet. Digital pianos typically have a slightly smaller footprint, usually reaching only four-foot ten inches from side to side and less than two feet in depth. Grand pianos measure about five feet across the front and extend back from the keyboard about four-feet seven-inches to more than nine feet for a concert grand piano.

Determine where you will place your piano and measure that area before you start shopping. Also, take a look at the room's acoustics—the qualities of the space that determine how the piano will sound. These include size of the room, whether the ceilings are vaulted or low, floor coverings such as carpet, wood, or tile, and whether windows have drapes or are uncovered. Thinking about these details will help you and the salesperson narrow down the field of available pianos to those that will best match your space.

Pianos, Children, and Parents

As parents, we throw money, time, attention, love, and care into the pot, stir it for eighteen years, and hope for the best for our children's development. There are no guarantees of success for your child's attempts to learn piano and become a serious player, but learning to play piano will enhance a child's life. We encourage you to consider piano lessons as a critical part of your recipe for your child's development.

Will Your Child Stick with It?

We often hear parents say, "I don't want to spend a lot of money on a piano until I'm sure my child will stick with it." Let's break this statement down to think about what it really means.

"A lot of money …" What does that mean? You now realize that a $200 keyboard will not do the child justice, and you have some idea what beginning-level pianos cost.

"Until I am sure …" The learning curve on piano is steeper than on some other instruments. It will take at least 18 months in the best case scenario for beginners to edge ahead of the learning curve and sound somewhat musical.

"… sure my child will stick with lessons." The decision to have your child take piano lessons and learn to play the piano belongs to you. If you let children quit lessons, they all will. Liberace probably would have quit lessons if his mother had let him. All beginners want to quit lessons. Learning to play an instrument takes work. Anything that takes work requires a lot of commitment.

If your child must "demonstrate" stick-to-it-iveness to you, set a reasonable goal such as six months or one year to practice on a rental piano, then buy a decent piano.

Rhythm and News

Hardly a week goes by that we don't talk to adults who were allowed to quit piano lessons and now wish they could play. Don't let your child be another one to say, "I wish my parents had made me stick with it." You, the parent, can decide that piano lessons and music are going to be a part of your family's traditions and culture. Imagine your child coming home from school and saying, "Mom, Dad, I've tried really hard and I've had several teachers, but I've decided not to study math any longer." You're probably not likely to say, "Okay, Johnny." Adopt piano lessons as a core requirement just like math and social studies. This doesn't mean it can't be fun for your child; however, at times, you will have to encourage your child to stick with it. Usually, children reach a plateau in the learning cycle and want to quit, but a change of teachers, sitting down next to your child to encourage and offer your undivided attention, or allowing the child to choose a song he or she wants to play will often help get over the hump.

The Case for Piano Lessons

Several studies have proven that piano lessons facilitate and enhance synapse development of the nerve cells in the brain. This development benefits spatial relationship reasoning, verbal skills, cognitive memory, hand-eye coordination, and more.

In 1993, Dr. Gordon Shaw, a physicist, and Dr. Frances Rauscher, a psychologist, both at the University of California, Irvine, coined the phrase "The Mozart Effect" to title their research conclusions. Their original experiments tested college students who had listened to 10 minutes of Mozart's Sonata in D Major for Two Pianos compared to those who had ten minutes of silence or relaxation tapes. The Mozart listeners scored significantly higher on a spatial-temporal test than the other two control groups. This type of testing measures the ability to recognize objects as the same or different but also tests the ability to form mental images of physical objects. This is a key to the higher brain function required for mathematics, physics, and engineering.

Their next studies focused on actual brain development. Rauscher and Shaw worked with inner-city preschoolers to see the effect of musical training on brain development. Group 1 was given piano lessons. Group 2 was given computer lessons. Group 3 was given singing lessons. Group 4 was given no lessons, only the standard school curriculum. Six months later, the piano students performed 34 percent better on spatial-temporal ability testing than did the control groups.

The conclusions of these and other studies are that, although the child is born with trillions of neurons in the brain, if these circuits are not connected and stimulated by a child's environment, they are trimmed by the brain and discarded. Patterning, or connection building, begins shortly after conception and continues until at least age 10. The richer and more stimulating the child's world is, the more enhanced the brain network becomes.

Typically, girls are started in traditional piano lessons as early as five, boys at six. This four- or five-year window between then and age ten is critical for many of the brain-building benefits we are discussing. This is not to say that piano lessons aren't good for older children or adults. We see regular success stories with every age group in learning to play. There are just extra benefits to piano lessons for youngsters.

Piano lessons and regular practice teach discipline and build self-esteem. Piano lessons build a work ethic and reinforce the idea that important things are worth working for. Piano lessons and regular practice counter current cultural trends promoting immediacy and instant gratification.

What About Renting a Piano?

Renting a piano is a good first step for some families with budget concerns, though renting is not without its drawbacks. First, the concept of renting shouts "temporary" or "not permanent" to beginners. It can signal a lack of commitment to the project. Also, rental pianos are, by definition, used pianos. Many rental fleets are comprised of aging instruments that were found to be unsaleable as used pianos. In addition, rentals are often neglected in terms of servicing and are inconsistent in their touch. They may have been abused by other renters who didn't have the pride of ownership.

There are cosmetic considerations as well. When you rent a piano, you may have little choice in the appearance of the instrument you will place in your home or on display in an institutional setting. The style, color, and condition is often "what you see is what you get."

B-Sharp

Watch out for the details in a piano rental contract. Many rental programs have minimum lengths of contracts, typically six months. And if you rent for a number of years and then want to buy, be aware that most dealers will credit a maximum of only 12 months of rent toward a purchase.

And, although most rental companies offer some kind of rental credit if and when you decide to purchase a piano from that company, few companies sell the specific piano you rent. So make sure the company has pianos that you might wish to buy down the road.

Another area to be aware of in renting involves your future purchase. While you rent for a year, the prices of the new pianos you might like to buy are rising by as much as 7 percent. Even if you get a rental credit, you are losing ground the longer you put off a purchase. On a $3,500 new instrument, that could relate to a $245 increase in the price.

Often, existing customers with rental credits are not able to extract the lowest possible discount on the purchase price because the salesperson knows he will have to give you your rental credit, yet you cannot buy elsewhere without abandoning your rental credit. For example, if you have been paying $35 per month on your rental for a year, you could receive a $420 credit toward the purchase of a piano. Therefore, a salesperson might try to keep the price on the piano you want to purchase about $400 higher than you might otherwise be able to negotiate.

Steps to Finding the Right Piano

This book will equip you with a great deal of knowledge to support your piano purchase decision. You'll learn which features and materials make a difference in piano quality and longevity, you'll learn about different types of pianos and their pricing and value, and you'll learn how to negotiate and close the best possible deal. All that information is useless, however, without a good battle plan to guide your shopping excursions and buying decisions. We want to launch your shopping process with the following recommended 10 steps:

Step 1: Spend a few hours with this book and highlight, underline, or make notes. Skip the parts that you feel don't pertain to you and hone in on the parts that do.

Step 2: Spend at least a couple of hours conducting research on the Internet. Go to the manufacturers' sites we list in Chapter 5. You will not find prices on those sites, but you will find lots of model specifications and furniture style depictions. Use these to get a feel for what's out there.

Step 3: Measure your space. Know before you go what you have to work with in terms of physical space dimensions. If you can accommodate (and afford!) a grand piano, go for it.

Step 4: Make notes about your piano's future location. Get a concept of your space acoustics, including ceiling height, floor covering, drapes, windows, and more. Is it a live and reverberating room or somewhat dead acoustically? If it's too live, there will be harshness. If it's too dead, there will be no vitality. A small, live room will typically accommodate only a small, mellow piano. A large, soft room can work with a big, bold piano.

Step 5: Measure your wallet. Don't leave the house without a frank discussion with your significant other about your budget limits for this project. You may have to reexamine this subject after some shopping, but start with a concept of what you can afford.

Step 6: Plan which dealerships you will visit. Two to four reputable dealers with multiple lines of pianos should give you a spectrum of instruments to select from. We recommend that you use the shopping comparison lists in Appendix B for the category of piano you are interested in.

Step 7: Investigate private-party pianos, if you dare. Unless you are prepared to make decisions on the spot and employ the help of a qualified, independent piano technician, private-party shopping may not bring you the jewel you are searching for. Used pianos are one-of-a-kind by definition and are subject to immediate sale. Used pianos from private parties will come with no meaningful warranty.

Step 8: Go back to the Internet to confirm information and specifications dealers have given you about the pianos that have made your short list of choices. Try to verify what you were told about parts, construction, country of origin, and other features. Try to ascertain the true Manufacturer's Suggested Retail Price, MSRP, for your choices.

Step 9: Go back to the one or two dealerships you felt the most comfortable with and that had the pianos of most interest to you. Go with the idea that you will make a final selection and finalize the price. Only after you have made an informed choice that you feel comfortable with, should you enter price discussions and negotiations with your salesperson. Expect to get anywhere from 15 to 30 percent off the MSRP on new pianos.

Step 10: Bring it home and enjoy! The kids are happy and practicing, or the school music teacher is playing, or the church chorus has nice accompaniment. You've achieved a happy ending.

If you plan well and study up, you can accomplish all these steps in one or two weekends. But go at your own pace and take the time you believe is necessary. Just keep in mind that if you spend more than thirty days looking around, or if you visit more than four dealerships, you might be making it much harder than it needs to be. This is when you can become susceptible to falling victim to a strong salesperson with a weak product.

The Least You Need to Know

- Evaluate who the piano is for, how much you want to spend, and where it will go to help guide your piano buying process.

- Because touch and ear training are critical for beginners, it's important to buy a decent instrument at the start.

- Pianos do not improve with age; a worn-out old piano can hinder a beginning student's progress.

- Renting a piano can make it hard to negotiate the price if you plan to buy one later.

What Makes a Piano Cost So Much?

In This Chapter

- ◆ Manufacturers and wholesalers
- ◆ What goes into retail dealer mark-up
- ◆ The importance of prepping a new piano
- ◆ Categories and typical price ranges of pianos

Pianos are a marvel of materials and engineering. They are made from fragile and rare materials, yet at the same time they must be built to contain and control the twenty tons of pressure created by the strings within them. They must be able to withstand a range of temperature and humidity conditions in various locations, which often shift with the seasons. To remain in tune and at pitch, a piano's stability and movement (expansion and contraction of the parts) must be measured in mere thousandths of an inch. It's intricacies like these and many others we'll talk about that make pianos cost a lot more than a plastic recorder.

Unlike any other furniture, pianos often display large expanses of unsupported cabinetry, such as grand piano lids and upright piano bottom panels.

It is important that this cabinetry not warp, and the high-gloss finishes reflect completely true and flat surfaces. Pianos need to produce tones that have consistency, beauty, and the ability to sustain. In addition, piano key mechanisms must respond to the lightest touch of a child's small fingers as well as the pounding attack of a concert musician. A piano should perform consistently for at least an entire generation, and often for more.

So to meet all of these requirements and many others, fine pianos must have excellent properties in design, materials, and execution of the crafting and assembly processes. All of this costs the manufacturer, who must pass the expense on to the retailer, who, in turn, has expenses in operating a dealership, which get passed on to you. In this chapter, we will review the various factors in more detail that influence the price you pay for a new piano.

How Manufacturing and Wholesaling Factors Affect Price

First, let's explore several aspects of building a piano that affect its ultimate retail price.

Country of Origin

The country of origin is the single most influential factor affecting the price of a piano. Despite all the automation that has been brought to bear in piano building, the most expensive aspect is still human labor, and making pianos is very labor intensive. Manufacturers of pianos are located across the globe, and the countries with manufacturers offering pricing from lowest to highest are: Mainland China, Indonesia, South Korea, Eastern Europe, Japan, the United States, and Western Europe. There are exceptions, of course, but this is the general trend.

Production Time and Volume

The time spent making a piano and the number of pianos made in a given factory also affect the price. Highly mechanized mass-production can churn out more units faster and can affect economies of scale in materials, manufacturing, and shipping, thereby reducing the per-unit cost. Some piano companies make fewer than 300 pianos per year, likely at a higher price tag each, while others churn out tens of thousands.

Distribution Channel

Whether pianos are sold directly from the factory to the retailer or go through a middleman distributor affects the end price as well. Very few pianos today are sold directly from the factory to a retailer. Nearly every manufacturer utilizes distributorships for regions, continents, or even hemispheres, which then sell the pianos into various markets so they can be sold at retail. In turn, the distributors bear expenses of shipping and receiving the pianos, warranty repair, advertising and promotion, warehousing, and more. They add these expenses along with their profit margins to the wholesale price that is then paid by a retail dealer.

B-Sharp

A common theme among retailers is to include the word *warehouse* or *wholesale* in their store name. However, manufacturers almost never sell directly to retailers or the public.

Inventory Overstocks

Distributors may have some missteps in their buying from manufacturers that can lead to overstocks of certain models or finish and style combinations. Since wholesalers do not plan for, or necessarily want, excessive inventories, it can result in discounts to retailers below and beyond what is typical, and that discount in turn can get passed on to you.

Nature of Materials

The quality and nature of the raw materials in pianos is last in order of significance when it comes to determining price. With a few exceptions, the insides of most pianos are very similar. Strings, tuning pins, and other components are often supplied by common vendors to multiple manufacturers. Of course, when a manufacturer takes advantage of indigenous materials local to its factory, that can help give them an advantage with their material expenses.

Rhythm and News

Acoustic pianos (not digital or electronic) incorporate materials that, in some cases, are becoming scarcer and more costly, for example, hard woods, fine cabinet-grade exotic veneers, buckskin leather (yes, from deer), virgin wool, petroleum products, and foundry casting.

The Retailer's Role in Pricing

The difference between what the retailer pays for the piano from a distributor and what you pay as the consumer might seem excessive. Why so much mark-up? Retailers of pianos face some major expenses, and savvy piano retailers know that there are only a few formulas for growth and financial security of a traditional brick-and-mortar piano store. Stores that follow these formulas for pricing and cost control succeed and stay in business; those that do not are typically destined to fail. Retailers must effectively appropriate the following expenses into their piano prices in order to remain in business for any length of time.

1. **Cost of merchandise.** Most retailers utilize *flooring companies* to finance the enormous cost of inventory on hand at any moment. Typically, retailers pay interest-only on the pianos they have in stock each month until they are sold. When they are sold, the piano's wholesale cost must be paid off on a timely basis. It is not uncommon for a single store to pay $10,000 to $20,000 per month in flooring charges, depending on the value of the inventory, just in interest only on the stock. Some flooring agreements call for a unit to be paid off after a certain length of time, whether it sold or not.

def•i•ni•tion

A **flooring company** is a finance company that extends lines of credit to retail dealers, enabling them to fill their stores with merchandise to sell.

2. **Retail store and warehouse rents.** The value of commercial property in some regions has skyrocketed in recent years. To be competitive and visible, piano retailers have sought larger and higher profile properties to display their wares, but must pay a higher price for doing so.

3. **Salaries, commissions, and employee benefits.** Successful piano sales is a studied and experienced craft. Piano salespeople are typically paid on commission. To attract and keep quality sales personnel, retailers must pay a meaningful portion of the profit to them. (Whatever tiny tidbit of commission your salesperson earns on your sale, he or she has probably earned many times over in the time spent with other customers who didn't buy. For any decent-size retailer, especially those with multiple locations, employees are needed behind the scenes to perform other vital functions. These people include delivery and service coordinators, corporate accounting personnel for bookkeeping, employment and sales tax reporting, banking, merchandise ordering, and other back-office roles. In addition, employee benefits packages are typical in this industry, including paid vacation, along with health and dental coverage.

4. **Retail advertising.** Print ads, Yellow Pages, direct mail, radio, TV, and websites are all used by the industry to create customer traffic in stores. Without marketing and sales promotion outreach, most piano dealerships would not survive. A traditional figure for promotion is 10 percent of sales. So a store with an annual sales budget of $2,000,000, for example, would likely budget to spend about $200,000 a year on promotion.

5. **Moving and technical expenses.** Each piano must be received at a central warehouse, unboxed, unpacked, cleaned, tuned, adjusted, and detailed before it is delivered to the store. If a piano sits in the store longer than a few weeks, which is common, it must be tuned and serviced again. If not being delivered off the sales floor, each piano must go through this process before it is delivered to the customer from a warehouse. Technicians who perform this work have studied for years in their craft, and their time does not come cheaply.

New Piano Preparation

Unlike most manufactured products, pianos do not come out of the box in ready-to-play condition, and this is more of what goes into the retail price you ultimately pay.

For two reasons, new pianos need to be prepared before they are placed on a showroom floor or delivered to a customer's home. First, piano factories simply do not spend enough time on fine adjustments to bring an instrument to its level of engineered perfection. The demands of manufacturing typically preclude hours and hours of effort on a single piano. It's sad but interesting to note that higher-priced instruments rarely receive more fine tuning at the factory than lower-end ones. A common philosophy, even from top-tier companies, is that this finishing work is the responsibility of a dealer.

Second, most of a piano is made from wood, and wood continues to dry, cure, and react to its environment. The journey from a boxed unit at the factory to a dealer may take several months and span thousands of miles. Pianos are rarely air-freighted, so most pianos travel in containers on the decks of ships at sea for several weeks. These containers may languish on the docks, exposed to blazing sun or freezing temperatures, before they clear customs and are delivered to dealers. Dealers may hold boxed units in their own warehouses for months at a time. Grand pianos remain on their sides when boxed, causing action parts (the key mechanism) to sag because they are not resting as they are intended. It is no wonder that when new pianos are first unboxed, they are in much turmoil due to the stresses of temperature, humidity, and travel. Therefore, they require a fair amount of preparation once they hit door of the dealer.

What Goes into a Good Prep

When considering a piano for purchase, inquire about how the dealer will prep your piano, if at all, prior to delivery to your home or institution. Several steps must be completed in proper order to fully prepare a piano. The space where the work is to be performed should be well-lit and relatively noise free for the best results. The steps needed to properly prepare a grand piano are as follows, and the process is very similar for a vertical piano.

Step 1: The piano is unboxed by movers and placed in the work area on its feet.

Step 2: A piano technician unwraps the instrument and removes packing materials from inside and underneath the piano.

Step 3: The technician undoes screws and removes certain parts in order to pull the action mechanism from the piano.

Step 4: The technician then releases the action by removing wood sticks and ties that have locked the action in place for shipping. He also brushes out any debris in the action bay left behind from the manufacturing process. It is amazing what you can find in new pianos! We have found chisels and other tools, a rude comment chalked onto the inside, and even a comic book!

Step 5: The technician then checks and tightens the cast iron plate's mounting bolts to a factory recommended setting using a torque wrench. Lifeless sounding pianos can be brought to life by screwing the plate down and consequently adding down-bearing where there was little or none. Plate bolts that are too loose cause the tone to be lifeless. If a technician makes the bolts too tight, the soundboard can be damaged or the plate can crack.

Step 6: The tech tamps down the strings on the plate pins and bridge pins. This process is known as "seating the strings." If this is not done, the tonal transfer through the bridge will be incomplete. Tapping too hard can mash the string into the top of the bridge (not a good thing), but tapping too softly won't accomplish the mission. Seating the strings also prevents erratic tuning and instability. During this process, the tech inspects the entire scale for damage, stringing deficiencies, or any other potential problems with the scale. This is a noisy process that drives nearby nontechnicians mad!

Step 7: The tech then systematically checks and tightens each and every screw in the action assembly; there are more than 250. Some may not have been secured at the factory; others may have become loose with wood shrinkage.

Step 8: Next the piano is checked for any issues that need rectifying to bring the instrument to factory specifications. The tech also checks out the touch to make it consistent from note to note. A complete regulation requires at least two dozen observations and adjustments to each of the 88 key mechanisms. The keys have to be rechecked to make sure they operate as a consistent ensemble. This process should not take as long as a full rebuild regulation, in which new parts have changed all the values. Checking the string level and rectifying inconsistencies is also completed, as well as any adjustment needed to the pedals.

Step 9: Now the technician focuses on giving the piano a good solid tuning, checking the pitch across the scale and determining if it is close enough to fine tune now or if a pitch raise must be done first. It is common for new pianos to require a pitch raise. During a pitch raise, the tech moves quickly through the scale raising the pitch and stretching each of the strings. Afterward, he can go back through and do a fine-tuning.

Step 10: With a good solid tuning on the piano, the technician will then check out the hammer voicing. This involves first checking the shape of the hammers to ensure consistency and proper shaping, adjusting where necessary by filing with a sandpaper board. Next, the technician plays each note up and down the scale, making chalk markings on the tops of the keys inside to indicate voicing needs. He then goes back and needles portions of hammers to bring the tone down to a base line. After that, he may iron hammers to bring up the tone, or apply a hardening solution. The hardening solution must be allowed to dry for several hours or sometimes overnight before the tone can be tested again.

Once the piano technician has completed all these steps, he reassembles the piano and moves on to the next instrument. The finished unit may be double-checked by a cabinet touch-up specialist before it is shipped to the customer.

This work can be mind-numbing when performed day after day by a house technician. Most top-level techs have enough private-customer income to avoid this kind of work. One dilemma for many retailers who want to embrace the "to prep" philosophy is to be able to attract and hold enough capable techs to perform this kind of work.

To Prep or Not to Prep

Now that you have seen the steps of piano preparation, can you imagine what the customer, who insists on getting a new piano delivered "in the box," is missing out on? In a customer's home, this preparation will likely never be done to the extent it should be.

Also you can now understand why impressions built on your experience with Brand X as a raw, unprepared piano may not be accurate. The only way to assess accurately the performance of a particular model is to review it in a fully prepared state.

The benefits of prepping a piano should be fairly obvious, but below are more reasons why prepping is so important.

◆ As a new owner, you'll never know what your piano could have played like if it hadn't had a good prep.

◆ Fully checked and prepared new pianos will likely last longer as parts designed to swing in a certain plane of motion are not out of alignment from day one.

◆ Fully prepared new pianos are likely to have fewer annoying service needs in their first years of ownership.

◆ Fully prepared new pianos have better tuning stability in the early years of ownership.

◆ Your shopping experience when you encounter fully prepared pianos at the dealership is enhanced because you can judge an instrument at its peak of performance, as it was intended by the manufacturer.

The controversy over piano preparation is argued in every dealer boardroom and throughout the professional piano community. Some retailers adopt a policy of not prepping because they want to streamline their merchandise-handling processes and save the hundreds of dollars that would be spent on each unit they sell. These dealers see pianos as a commodity, often sold at prices below minimum levels of profitability. These dealers frequently deliver pianos "in the box" to customers' homes. They predicate their business plans on volume selling at discount pricing, with minimum expense loads.

Key Note

Some showrooms may have more than 100 acoustic pianos on display at a time. Even at a dealership that is dedicated to well-prepared pianos, you can expect that there will be times when several pianos need tuning. This is normal and nothing to be concerned about.

For large companies with multiple locations selling hundreds of instruments, prep expenses are a line item in their budgeting considerations that can be in the hundreds of thousands of dollars annually. Nevertheless, many see it as a worthwhile expense. These retailers believe that fully prepared instruments show better to prospective buyers, so they will sell more pianos in the long run. They also believe that the preparation process heads off expensive in-home service calls after delivery. These retailers believe that offering exquisitely prepared pianos at every price point builds a positive reputation in their marketplace. Dealers in this camp delight manufacturers by presenting their brands to the public in their best condition.

The Cost of Piano Prep

A decent new piano preparation on a vertical piano takes three to four hours to complete and $150 to $200 for a technician who knows the work and works efficiently without interruption. A decent, new grand piano preparation takes from eight to twelve hours and $400 to $600. Some technicians work faster, while some charge more per hour, but any way you slice it, prep adds up to a tidy sum that dealers must spend when selling hundreds of piano per year.

Categories of Pianos

Now let's briefly explore the different types of pianos, to help frame what price categories they fall into. (For more on piano descriptions, see Chapter 8).

Vertical Pianos

The only significant physical variance among *vertical pianos* is the height, or the measurement from the floor to the top of the lid. Typically, the prices rise with each increase in size category. (By the way, manufacturers nearly always round up to the nearest whole inch. Thus, 48-inch upright pianos are rarely 48 inches when actually measured.) Various heights have different names:

- 40"–43" high are console pianos, the shortest vertical pianos built today. New consoles can still be found starting at about $2,000.

- 44"–46" high are studio or studio upright pianos. For decades, these have been the staple for institutional school use and are usually built a little heavier-duty than consoles. New studio pianos generally start at about $3,000.

def•i•ni•tion

Vertical pianos are instruments that measure about five feet wide (left to right) and about two feet deep (front to back). Their flat back is usually placed against a wall.

Console Piano.

Studio Piano.

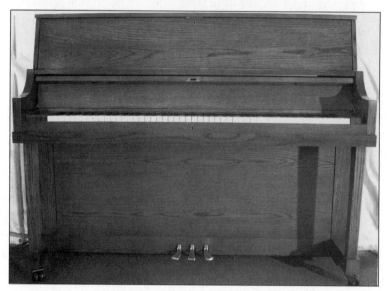

♦ 47"–52" high are the professional upright pianos. The moniker "professional" is only the descriptor for the category, not a designation of quality or performance. New pianos in this category usually start around $4,000.

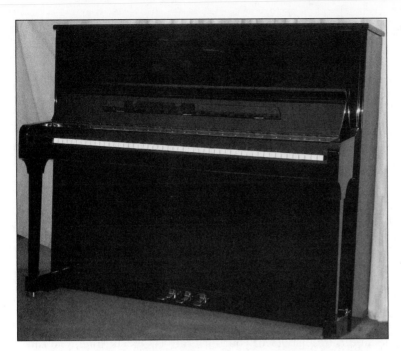

Professional upright piano.

In the 1930s, home designs departed from the formal parlor, popular in Victorian homes of earlier times. As a result, piano makers shifted away from the really tall uprights (60"+ from the turn of the century) to significantly smaller designs called spinets. These little uprights measured from 34"–39" high. Spinets were the rage through the early 1970s. As spinet production was discontinued in the late 1970s, all spinets available now are used, and their prices vary with condition, age, and sentimental value. Typically, most sell for less than $1,500.

Spinet pianos had inherent limitations in tone and a peculiar issue with the key-action design and performance. The height of the spinet limited string length and soundboard area, so consequently, the tone was thin and often tinny. For these and several other technical reasons, most teachers and professionals today do not recommend spinet pianos.

The old uprights from the 1880s to 1930s (often referred to as Victorian uprights) were designed to have a useful musical life expectancy of 40 to 50 years. All of these pianos are now long beyond their musical life. Few if any of these pianos have any true antique value today. And few of these pianos have the intrinsic value to warrant costly restoration. Most experts agree that these pianos are not suitable for anyone seriously pursuing piano lessons, especially beginners.

Spinet piano: notice that the music rack rises above the top of the piano.

Today, the console piano is the most popular size category. As such, most consoles have cabinets in traditional furniture styles. If your furniture is Queen Anne, you can probably find a console in the Queen Anne style. Likewise, if your furniture is Italian Provincial, you will likely find similar styling in a console. Studio pianos offer fewer colors and styles, and their tendency toward straighter lines makes them look boxier. A few companies, however, also offer beautiful furniture cabinetry in their taller pianos.

Grand Pianos in History

Grand pianos generally stand on three legs, but occasionally they have four or six legs. They come in a variety of lengths, but all are legitimately referred to as grand pianos. Decades ago, names were conceived for several grand length categories. Grands were identified as baby, parlor, living-room, semi-concert, cupid, or petite grands. Many of the names were attached to marketing campaigns by various manufacturers. These names have been bandied about over the years to the extent that no one really knows to what size they actually refer.

Measure your space, your acoustics, and your wallet, and then shop for grand pianos based on actual measured size and your other considerations. Grands all have the same width (left to right), just short of 60 inches. Only the length varies (front to back). There is no single standard for sizes. Each manufacturer has its own set of scale design sizes.

Grand piano.

An evolutionary dead-end branch of the grand piano began in the 1860s, called the square grand—grands which stood on four legs and were rectangular in shape, resembling coffins, some said. The strings ran left to right, parallel to the length of the keyboard. Even when new, these beasts played like trucks, had poor dynamics and volume, and lacked tuning stability. Today, most technicians will not touch them. Their cabinets were beautiful, with elegant rosewoods and mahoganies, but as instruments, they were duds. Square grands died out by the late 1880s.

From the 1920s through the late 1930s, player-grand pianos came into fashion. Most of these instruments came in six-legged cabinets and are often referred to as "gate" legged pianos. The extra legs were necessary to support the additional weight of the player mechanism. Today, many of these pianos have had the players removed. We advise caution in acquiring ex-players as instruments with which to study piano. Typically, player pianos had longer keys (inside the piano, not visible), and the leverage was "off" compared to a nonplayer action. More importantly, these pianos have long ago passed their predictable useful musical life expectancy. We do not recommend these five- and six-legged grand pianos.

Grand Pianos Today

The smallest acoustic grand piano size made today is 4'7" and is often referred to as a "petite" or "fetal" grand (i.e., smaller than a baby grand). These grands are so small that they rarely produce much overall volume and few have any decent bass response. Of course, there are a few exceptions. New grands in this category often start at about $5,000.

Most mainstream manufacturers start their line-up at between 4'11" and 5'6", known as their "baby" grand category. Some scale designs (the physics in the layout of the strings, bridges, and plates) operate more efficiently than other designs. Like a book and its cover, don't judge a piano only on length. Play it and listen to the tone, volume, and sustain throughout the breadth of the keyboard. The standard baby grand category pricing starts at about $6,000.

The medium category of grands falls into the 5'7" to 6'5" lengths. Typically, these are the most suitable for many homes. They offer more tone and volume than the small sizes, without the bulk of the larger grands. Because they are less costly than the larger sizes, they also fit many more family budgets. Pianos in this category will start from about $8,000. Remember, this is only a starting point and prices rise each year. High profile brands will cost thousands more.

> **B-Sharp**
>
> Watch out for acoustic overkill—placing a large grand piano in a room that can't handle the sound it produces. Your budget might be big enough to take on a seven to nine foot grand piano, but your room size and acoustics may not be up to the challenge of such a powerful instrument.

Professional musicians with the requisite space and wallets demand the larger sizes, from seven to nine feet in length. The longer the grand piano, the thinner the strings, which can, in turn, sound sweeter. The power of larger soundboards allows greater dynamic range and control—overall, a more professional playing experience.

So ... What's It Gonna Cost Me?

New vertical pianos can be found on the market starting at just over $2,000. New grand pianos start at just above $5,000. Entry-level pianos in these price ranges come from factories in mainland China, and some are good bargains and deliver good value.

New Japanese verticals can be found starting at just over $4,500, with grands starting at just over $10,000. Larger professional models can run three to five times these amounts.

Pianos from Indonesia and Korea are fetching prices between those of the Chinese and Japanese, primarily due to labor rates. These factories are rapidly approaching those of the Japanese in quality control and performance.

Eastern European products are in the handcrafted category by definition and heritage. Their pricing hovers just above that of the Japanese. There are decided inconsistencies in some of these instruments, and factories are all over the scale in quality.

American-made pianos are very few today. There are only five truly American brands: Steinway & Sons in New York, Mason & Hamlin in Massachusetts, Charles Walter in Indiana, Baldwin Artist grands and verticals in Arkansas, and Astin-Weight in Utah. These are limited production facilities and are in the higher price ranges. Verticals, on average, start at about $7,000 (although some brands offer an introductory model for less) while grands' average starting point is about $30,000.

Western European, primarily Austrian, German, and Italian factories, are regarded as some of the finest available. These pianos are also produced in limited quantities and are among the most expensive. These high-quality verticals start at about $11,000 with grands starting at about $35,000.

In our training and travels to piano factories, we have asked the following questions several times and never really received what we believe to be a satisfactory answer. "Why do size increments in pianos generate such huge selling-price differentials? Why does a 5'8" brand X grand sell for $20,000 and the 6'1" brand X grand sells for $30,000? How could it possibly cost another 33 percent to produce the model that is only 7.4 percent larger? Why does the 44" upright sell for $5,000, while the 48" model sells for $7,000, and the 52" model sells for $10,000?" We have asked these types of questions while on factory tours, or during training sessions, and found that we became highly unpopular with our hosts. Looking over some historical sales literature and vintage sales sheets, we found this kind of price differential has been the case going back as long as anyone can remember. It is tradition, tradition and the fact that there will always be a genuine and painful premium for larger pianos. Bigger is better in pianos, and you definitely pay dearly for bigger.

The Least You Need to Know

- Labor costs in the country of origin significantly influence the ultimate price of a piano.

- Retailing costs, such as finance charges, rents, advertising, moving, and technical expenses, add to price.

- New piano preparation is tedious and expensive but benefits the customer.

- New vertical pianos sell from just over $2,000, while new grand pianos command a price beginning just over $5,000.

- Lowest-priced pianos come from China, followed by Indonesia and Korea.

- Japanese pianos and Eastern European pianos are in the mid-tier of pricing and the most expensive are from the United States and Western Europe.

Chapter 3

Shopping Strategies

In This Chapter

- ◆ Adopting the piano shopping mindset
- ◆ Having a plan
- ◆ Communicating with the salesperson
- ◆ Typical sales styles and demos
- ◆ Tactics to watch out for

For many people, the purchase of a piano is the most expensive acquisition they will make after a home and a vehicle. While folks may know what to look for and which questions to ask about cars and houses, for many, pianos are a mystery. It is natural to fear what we don't understand. The goal of this chapter is to reduce your fears and raise your understanding level so that you can shop with confidence. Buying a piano should be fun. To help make it this way, we will help you adopt a piano shopping mindset with a proven recipe for success. We also give you shopping strategies and communication tips to guide you through the process. And we give you the inside scoop on what to expect from salespeople and sales tactics to watch out for.

Getting Your Head Around Piano Shopping

As with many pursuits, attitude is everything when it comes to shopping for a piano. Even if you're not an experienced piano player, you *can* trust your own instincts and judgment. You *can* have the confidence to stand firm in the face of a strong sales pitch and come out with a piano that fits your playing needs, budget, space, and aesthetic preferences.

> **Key Note**
>
> To help yourself remember all the information you learn about various piano makes and models after visiting dealerships—and to double-check that the salesperson's pitch was accurate—ask if brochures are available for the pianos you are considering.

During the shopping process, it's natural to feel uncomfortable at times because you feel like you're in over your head, evaluating instruments that you don't fully understand or know how to use. You might also worry that you can't trust a salesperson or dealership. We want you to feel empowered by the knowledge we share in this book and that you can supplement through additional research. In Chapter 5, we discuss how to use the Internet to verify information salespeople give you, and throughout this book we dispel myths about what makes a good piano good. By the time you finish this book, you will know more than many new salespeople know!

The key to adopting the right mindset is to educate yourself about pianos, including how they work, what they're made of, where they come from, what they should cost, and what your choices are. Then, remind yourself that this purchase is for you (or your family or an institution you work for), so you have a right to ask questions, get clear answers, see a demonstration, and be shown models that fit your selection criteria. You have this right whether you are a concert-level pianist or can't play a note. In short, be strong!

Go In with a Plan

Have clear objectives when you enter your first piano store. In Chapter 1, you identified who will play the piano you're purchasing, decided on your budget, and measured your space. Knowing your specifications for these three criteria will make your first stop much smoother.

If you're still uncertain, do some homework. Utilize manufacturers' websites to learn more information about the sizes and furniture styles that are available. Also, use these sites to locate authorized dealers in your area. Understand, though, that many instruments are greater than the sum of their technical specifications. Until you see, touch, and hear a piano, you can't fully know if it's right for you.

If you've done your homework (defining your criteria and doing some online research) before visiting dealerships, you are ready to get out there and look seriously. It may be tempting to walk into your first store and try to avoid a salesperson by saying you're "just looking," but try not to do this. Remember what we advised about having a confident mindset. You are ready to get serious! Only when you let a salesperson show you around, discuss the pianos, and do a demo, can you learn what you need to know about touch, tone, features, benefits, construction, materials, discount pricing, special financing terms, and more.

Rhythm and News

If you're a parent or other family member purchasing a piano for a child, or for the whole family, you might be tempted to bring your children along on the shopping excursions. This is okay if your kids are old enough and sufficiently mature to sit through long demonstrations or technical discussions, or if they are such accomplished players that they need to try out the instruments. But, in most cases, the shopping experience and purchase decision should be left to the adults. Present your family with a new piano, and they will be thrilled with whatever *you* have decided on.

As you shop, try to focus on pianos that are within your budget and that your home can comfortably accommodate. This might sound like obvious advice, especially if you've already worked on defining your needs and know what you can afford and fit. But, when you get in a store, it can be easy to forget all that and get swayed by the many other options available. The larger and more expensive instruments will always play better and sound better than smaller, less expensive ones. So you may become frustrated trying to find a smaller, more affordable piano that plays, sounds, and looks like the big expensive ones you've fallen in love with. But there are many choices out there, so keep looking and you will find the one that works for you.

Communicating with Piano Salespeople

The key to communication between a piano shopper and piano salesperson is to make it a two-way street. If you are both honest and straightforward with each other, and both ask and answer enough questions, you will have a win-win situation on your hands. This means both sides must be forthcoming with information and questions.

What the Salesperson Expects of You

If you are up front and honest with the sales staff, you can expect reciprocal treatment from them. When you enter the store, tell the person who greets you that you are part way through your due diligence process (fact-finding) and will likely not purchase today, but that if you see something you like and are treated well, they will be on the short list for your consideration when you are ready to buy. A real salesperson could not ask for a better introduction and opportunity. Truly professional salespeople focus on earning your long-term business and your referral business, not on just a quick, one-time sale.

If you are a player and want to play the pianos at a given dealer as part of your evaluation of options, also say this up front. Allow the sales staff to guide you to the models or sizes you are comparing. Ask them to allow you to play uninterrupted for a few minutes. Tell them you will have some questions when you are finished with your comparisons. This is a reasonable approach and should be agreeable to any salesperson.

> **Key Note**
>
> It is a common practice in the piano industry for each salesperson to have printed business cards. Ask for the card at the beginning of your visit. This will help you develop rapport since you can call the salesperson by name, and you can use the card to make notations regarding models and prices. (You can also use the shopping forms provided in Appendix B.)

As you start working together, be prepared to tell the sales staff about your space and budget requirements. Also expect to be asked other questions about who will be playing the piano, levels of experience, and room acoustics, and more so that they can begin to narrow down their field of products to the few that will best match your needs.

The more you tell a salesperson of your needs, the faster the two of you will come to the right products for you. This is what salespeople train for. Many have spent hours and hours in product training to make professional presentations to customers and to give them the tools to make an intelligent choice. So go with it and let them do their stuff.

What You Can Expect of the Salesperson

Salespeople are working to earn a living in a competitive business, so of course, they're going to present their products in the best light and encourage you to purchase. It's the nature of sales to accentuate the positives and downplay the negatives of products for sale, but the most professional of salespeople will present their products on their own merits. If the dealerships you visit are selling decent instruments, plenty of true and relevant information is available about those instruments to build a great features-and-benefits presentation.

Unfortunately, some weaker salespeople will spend more time educating a customer about all the bad things their competitor sells rather than presenting what is good about their own products. Should you find yourself in such a situation, short circuit this negative approach and ask the salesperson to let you draw your own conclusions about the other guy's products. If the salesperson persists, do yourself a favor and leave the dealership. A good sales experience doesn't involve negativity.

<table>
<tr><td>Rhythm and News</td></tr>
<tr><td>In your shopping process, decide early on if you will collect price information as a selling price or as a total price, which includes sales tax and delivery charges. It is easy to get confused by salespeople if they go back and forth between these figures. Although you may want the total price as a single figure, it may be wiser to ask your salesperson to list the selling price and all other costs involved. This way, you will have the actual selling price, plus you will discover what the store charges for delivery are and may find out charges other than sales tax are involved. It is standard in the piano industry to charge for delivery but also to include one in-home tuning post-delivery at no additional cost.</td></tr>
</table>

What you should expect from salespeople, and can insist on, is that they tell the truth about construction, countries of origin, warranty information, and other basic piano features. Factual information about these aspects can always be verified by the literature that is shipped with the instrument, manufacturers' websites, brochure information, or a call to the manufacturer's representative.

When to Give Out Your Contact Information

If you have not settled on a piano and are therefore not ready to purchase, the salesperson will ask for your contact information. As the shopper, you control which information you disclose to the salespeople you encounter.

If you visit a store and quickly determine there is nothing for you there and are absolutely certain you will not return, you are not obligated to render your information. You might even relate this in a nice way to the salesperson asking for it.

If you visit a store and find one or more instruments you believe will be on your short list for consideration, and if you feel comfortable with the service you have been given by your salesperson, give your name and number. Let your salesperson know which days and times are good to contact you by phone. If you prefer not to be called, give your e-mail address.

If you do not feel comfortable giving your contact information whether you are interested in that store's products or not, then just don't do it. But providing your name and the city you live in will protect your salesperson's interest in the event you return to the store and purchase during his or her time off.

Sales Styles and Demonstrations

Now that you have an idea of how you and piano salespeople will communicate, let's take a deeper look at what you might encounter in the selling process.

Sales presentations vary in approach, of course, since selling styles are as different as the people involved. However, two types of sales presentations are the most common: the romantic charmer type and the nuts and bolts technical type.

The Charmer

The romantic/charmer salesperson's presentation plays (literally!) to your emotions. This type of salesperson is usually an accomplished pianist who aims to win you over with his or her music. If you are not a player, having the salesperson play the various instruments will be very helpful in enabling you to hear their tone, but don't fall in love with the piano just because the song, or the salesperson, moves you.

This type of salesperson may neglect to talk about features and benefits of the products, so you will need to ask about the model, its size, where it was built, the manufacturer's suggested retail price, and any features you should know about, as well as warranty and service information. (You can use the forms in Appendix B to help guide your questions.)

If you are a player, ask the salesperson to let you do some playing yourself. You will learn more about touch and tone than you would by just listening.

The Technician

The other type of sales presentation is more like an engineering course covering the nuts and bolts of a piano. Salespeople who take this approach may bombard you with every last detail of the piano's parts and functionality and throw lots of technical jargon at you. Even with the knowledge you'll gain from the technical crash course we give you in Part 2 of this book, you are still likely to find your head spinning after one of these presentations.

While it's great to have an educated salesperson who has plenty to convey and nothing to hide about the features of an instrument, make sure that the salesperson presents the benefit of each feature. If the salesperson presents a feature, followed immediately by another feature, ask him or her to back up and explain why that feature would be important to you as a piano player or the parent of a player.

It's important that you also get a gut feel for how you like the piano. How does it sound and feel to you? If you are a player, ask to try it out so that you can get a more balanced picture. If you don't play, ask the salesperson to do so. You probably won't be charmed by the music you hear if the salesperson is not a virtuoso, but you will be able to glean an idea about the tone.

Key Note _____

As you learn about a piano's technical features and tone, make sure also to ask about information on service and warranty.

Whichever type of sales presentation you're getting, keep in mind that formal piano demonstrations are designed to include feedback from you. Don't let the salesperson go on with the demo if you have already determined that the instrument is not right for you. Also, don't ever feel put on the spot to perform if you don't want to. Demonstrations of some electronic instruments with built-in teaching systems do include asking you to push a few keys or buttons, but you won't be expected to play an acoustic piano unless you want to.

What to Watch Out For

Chances are, you will encounter honest salespeople who take a straightforward approach to presenting their products and helping you find the best one for you. As with any type of sales, however, you may have the misfortune of running up against someone who is unscrupulous or uses unfair, high-pressure tactics. In our many years in this business, we've just about seen it all, so let us warn you of what to beware of and run from.

Selling Brands Without Authorization

Some brands are directly competitive with each other. A good example of this is the two Japanese companies Yamaha and Kawai. You will likely never find both of these products, as new units, on a dealer's floor. We know of fewer than five authorized dealers for both brands in a single store across the nation.

It is important for you to know which products dealers are authorized to sell in new merchandise. Knowing this will clue you in to their predictable bias when presenting their products. This bias is natural but can also be confusing for you, as most dealers will supplement their floor stock with several used pieces of the most competitive "asked for" brands that they are not authorized to sell new. This is not deceptive as long as these units are clearly identified as used. All dealers want their showrooms to look as if they sell all brands, to make the customer feel there is no need to shop anywhere else.

The rub comes when an unscrupulous salesperson tells you he can get you a "new" brand X, when, in fact, his dealership is not an authorized dealer for brand X. We often have customers tell us that they have visited another dealership that sells a particular brand when we know that dealer is not an authorized dealer of that brand. These customers usually report that they saw a few of those pianos on hand and were told the company is a dealer. If there is any doubt in your mind about whether or not the dealer you visit is an authorized dealer for the product you want, call the distributor and ask. Or check the manufacturer's website for the authorized dealers in your area. Do *not* buy a new product from a dealer who cannot be verified as an authorized dealer from the distributor or the manufacturer! If you do, you will end up with a warranty that's worthless and be left with no recourse for future repairs if needed.

Bashing Other Dealers and Brands

A common sales tactic is to bash the brands that the dealer you're visiting doesn't carry or to speak unfavorably about other dealerships.

Comments you are likely to hear about brands a dealer isn't authorized to sell may include these, many of which are often not true:

- The new ones are simply not as good as the old ones.
- They are made in China.
- They are full of plastic (by the way, even if this is true, it's not always a bad thing, as we explain in Chapter 11).
- They have laminated soundboards.
- They sound way too bright (regardless of where they fit on the spectrum of tone).

- They are just going into bankruptcy or some insolvency issue.

- They were bought out by so-and-so.

- We carried that brand, but we dropped it because …. (In reality, the dealer was probably canceled by the manufacturer.)

- They use a lot of particle-board in their case construction.

- They are very inconsistent; some are good and some are bad. Not all are "keepers." (This kind of statement is intentionally vague and somewhat pointless, but casts doubt.)

Typical comments made about other dealers, comments that often are not true, may include:

- That dealer has a terrible reputation for service.

- That dealer is on the verge of insolvency.

- That dealer has been in business for only two years. We have been in business for 30 years and have 10 stores. (This may have relevance, may not.)

- The salespeople at dealer X are known for being untruthful.

- That dealer was run out of several cities before coming here.

Any salesperson who harps on negative aspects of the competition or competitive products should be treated with caution. Ask the salesperson to focus on the positive features of their own brands, and if they can't seem to do that, you're better off leaving.

The Nail-Down

Nail-down is the term given to an instrument that is placed on the sales floor, not to be sold, but to make the brands they do sell look better. Frequently, they will have one of these competitive instruments pulled apart to show several "bad" features. Often, the dealer will de-tune or simply not tune the instrument so it will deliberately sound bad. The instrument may also be unregulated to deliberately feel or play unevenly.

Ask your salesperson if that dealership is an authorized dealer to sell the "nail-down" instrument. If the answer is yes, be sure to verify that on the manufacturer's website. If they aren't, ask to be shown their own products that they are authorized to sell.

Pressure Tactics to Close the Deal

The part of the sales process known as *closing* comes after the demo, gaining commitments, and overcoming objections. In theory, if a salesperson overcomes a prospect's final objection, the sale is made. However, it doesn't always work that way. Professional and successful salespeople know when and how to close a sale and don't try to do it prematurely. Unfortunately, you may encounter some who try to pressure you into making a decision on the spot. This is often referred to as a *hard closing*.

def•i•ni•tion

Closing is the act of gaining a commitment to purchase. "The closing" refers to the paperwork, signatures, and payment part of the process. **Hard closing** is being pressured into buying, and is not a professional way to make a sale.

Frequently, a hard closing results in sales that unwind and cancel, customers who badmouth a dealership, or customers who are dissatisfied with their purchase. If you find yourself in a situation where you are being pressured before you are ready to buy, let your salesperson know that you are just not ready. That should be the end of it.

Some of the ploys you might hear if you're being pressured to close the deal include:

◆ *This price is only good today until 5 P.M.* Chances are that if the leadership of the company has approved selling that unit at that price, they will honor it until the unit is sold. There are rare exceptions to this with bona fide sales involving factory/distributor incentives, or other specials, but it is more likely that the salesperson is trying to make a quota or end-of-month deadline. Do not be pressured into making a decision until you are ready. However, know that you may in fact lose this "deal" if another customer buys the unit.

◆ *This is the last one of its kind.* Unless it is a used piano, it is likely that another can be ordered.

◆ *Wholesale prices are rising next month.* Prices do go up, never down. Dealers want to posture for a LIFO (last in, first out) situation, but most have existing stock on hand at the old prices for several weeks or months. If it was profitable for them to sell it last month at a certain price, and they still have some old stock on hand, it will still be profitable for them to sell it next month, in spite of the increase. You do run the risk, however, that the store might run out of the model you want at the old wholesale price.

Each one of these examples can actually be true, but most of the time, they are just attempts to inject an artificial sense of urgency to the situation. In Chapter 21 we talk more about how the closing process should go to get a fair deal you can be comfortable with.

So-Called Special Event Sales

Retailers are always on the lookout for innovative situations that lure customers in with a sense of urgency to overpower their reluctance to make a decision and purchase. When we learn of special sales events, we believe we will get a better price than at our local dealer. Examples of these types of events are:

◆ College or armory sales

◆ Hotel suite sales

◆ Stadium or convention center sales

◆ Warehouse sales

◆ Parking lot sales

◆ Discount membership store sales

Often you'll receive a letter in the mail describing a special event and how you will save lots of money. Some of these letters will also lead you to believe that your purchase will directly benefit the institution. Sometimes these events do benefit the institution by underwriting a portion of the costs of the loan program associated with them. But, contrary to popular belief, your purchase will not be tax deductible.

Unfortunately, these off-site sales foster poor decision-making and bad matches of instrument to customer. If you have done your homework or some previous shopping in regular stores and are nearly ready to buy, you may want to patronize one of these events. But be aware that outside events are not the place to be educated about pianos in general or about specific brands or models. There is little time allotted for each appointment, and the pace is accelerated. Outside events are only for serious buyers who know exactly what they want and what they should pay.

Key Note

If you can, plan your final buying excursions for the last few days of the month. You will likely strike a good deal with salespeople who are at their hungriest as their month-end closing looms.

One of the most successful sale events a retailer can mastermind is the "GOB" or going-out-of-business sale. As consumers ourselves, we understand the temptation to hit these sales for rock bottom prices, but we don't know why anyone would spend thousands of dollars with a merchant they know is going out of business immediately! What about delivery? Prep? Service? Also this is especially problematic when you go to a GOB sale hosted by an unscrupulous dealer who has found a way to conduct these sales over and over again. Often outside crews are contracted to conduct these GOB sales. These mercenaries have no loyalty to the product, the dealer, the community, or to you. They will not be around minutes after the event has closed or in the months after you bring your piano home and have a problem or question.

We are firm believers that you can find the same products at the same price, or even lower, at reputable, mainstream dealers, who are staying in business and will be there to help you with service after the sale. Buying a piano is a big purchase. Don't get duped!

The Least You Need to Know

- ◆ "Just looking" at pianos won't get you very far. Let a salesperson show you around and demonstrate some pianos.

- ◆ Open, honest communication between you and your salesperson will help narrow the field to the best pianos for you.

- ◆ Watch out for salespeople who attack competitors' brands or other dealerships and use tactics to persuade you to make a decision before you are ready.

- ◆ Beware of off-site (not at a store) special event sales as these tend to put pressure and artificial time constraints on your decision.

4

Myths and Misconceptions

In This Chapter

◆ Why you might feel ill-equipped to make a wise purchase

◆ Learning to trust your own instincts

◆ Pros and cons of involving a third-party expert

◆ The role of a piano teacher in the selection process

◆ Common myths that can steer you off track

When making a major purchase such as a car or computer, most people don't go it alone. Think about what you've done in the past before shelling out lots of money for a product. Did you ask friends and family for recommendations? Did you read about various brands and models in trusted consumer magazines? Did you get the inside scoop from more subjective sources such as blogs or other Internet forums or by chatting with your neighbors around the mailbox? If so, you're probably considering doing some of these same things before selecting a piano.

By the time you enter a showroom, your head will be filled with advice from many people and places. Your Aunt Edna told you that pianos get better with age (they don't, usually) so she wants you to buy used. Your neighbor swears by the new Chinese models, but someone else told you they're awful. An interior designer has told you that a piano with an ebony finish won't match your sofa. You think you read somewhere that the best pianos have solid ivory keys (they don't), so you're not going to accept anything less.

You might even take an expert along on the shopping expedition with you. So, between the person accompanying you and all the voices in your head, you have quite a committee put together to make this purchase! Is that a good thing or bad? In this chapter, we'll help you decide. We show you how to trust your own instincts, listening skills, touch, and judgment, even if you're not an experienced player. We point out the advantages and disadvantages of bringing along a third party. And, we debunk common myths and misconceptions about pianos to keep your shopping process in tune.

Do You Need an Expert to Accompany You?

If you are not a piano player, or at least not an experienced one, it's normal that you might feel inadequate upon entering the piano-buying process. You may be tempted to employ the talents of an expert—someone who knows more than you do about pianos and who can keep you from making an expensive mistake. This might be a teacher, technician, or accomplished player. Involving an expert is fine, but if you do so, understand the realities of the situation.

One of the harshest realities is that it's nearly impossible to find a genuinely disinterested third party to help you make your decision about a piano. They may have a financial stake in your buying decision. Teachers, piano technicians, interior designers, and others often work with piano dealers to bring in potential buyers. They frequently earn outside commissions for their efforts. Don't be shocked by this! They may actually be performing a valuable service for both you *and* the dealer. But good experts have done their homework and recommend only reputable dealers and quality products. They are sensitive to your budget, décor, and preferences in touch and tone. Unfortunately, not all experts are reputable experts. Some are not as knowledgeable or honest as you would hope. Let's take a look at how you can protect your best interests, starting with how to trust your own natural "expert" instincts.

This is *Your* Purchase

Nearly every car radio and home stereo has bass and treble controls. Some even have elaborate graphic equalizer settings. You don't employ the talents of an expert to set these for you, do you? You probably monkey around with the dials and buttons until the music sounds right to you. Some people like a heavier bass. Some like the highs.

You know what you like in sound when you hear it. Buying a piano is not all that much different. It's okay to get advice along the way, but the ultimate decisions and choices are yours, so you need to trust yourself. Trust your own eyes, ears, and fingers.

Key Note

Give yourself permission to be in charge! It will be your piano.

Why should you go with your own gut when selecting a piano and not rely solely on the advice of others?

- ◆ You are the one writing the check!

- ◆ You are the one who must deal with service problems down the road.

- ◆ You are the one who will live with the furniture styling for the next 20-plus years.

- ◆ You are the one who must enjoy the sound and feel of the piano's touch and tone.

Each acoustic piano has an inherent sound or tone of its own. Pianos brighten a little as they age but sound pretty much the same over their useful musical lives. You don't have to be a piano expert to know what tone you like. Listen to several instruments and you will begin to hear the subtle differences. This process takes a while, so be patient. It doesn't matter what your teacher, mother, child, brother-in-law, or the salesperson likes. What matters is that you settle on an instrument with a tone that pleases your ear.

Take Recommendations with a Grain of Salt

No matter what the product, people tend to recommend certain products over others for a variety of reasons. Much of the time, the recommendation has more to do with the person making it than with the needs of the person making the purchase. There are Ford guys who would not think of driving or recommending any other make of car. There are Chevy people who are just as loyal to their brand.

While we applaud brand allegiance when it is deserved, we caution you to be wary of those who always want to recommend the "best" or "top-of-the-line" piano regardless of the price. Some people let status and prestige of a brand trump performance and value. Some of these folks have a tendency to recommend what they have, or what they would like to have, without regard to your needs and budget. So when someone recommends a particular type of piano to you, ask them to tell you specifically why they prefer that brand or model.

Break Free of Old School Ties

When giving advice, people often recommend a brand that they played on in college or in a recital, or you might feel drawn to a brand you knew as a student. Nearly every college, university, recital hall, concert stage, and recording studio buys a new Steinway & Sons, Yamaha, or Kawai piano. While these are all excellent brands, they might not necessarily be the best ones for you, so don't feel you must go with these recommendations.

The reasons that institutions choose these brands may have little to do with your own needs, budget, or likes and dislikes. Instead, the institutional purchasing decisions are often tied to "free" school loan programs. Manufacturers, retailers, and school music departments partner on annual loan contracts for significant numbers of pianos worth hundreds of thousands of dollars. Schools commit to buying a small percentage of these units each year. The manufacturer gets professional exposure and eventual sales. The retailer receives entrée to institutional sales and an opportunity for an annual retail outside-sale event. The school enjoys the use of many new pianos it likely could not afford all at one time.

In addition, institutional purchases are often made by a committee of music department faculty and administrators. When a college selects a piano, it is not necessarily an endorsement of a particular brand but simply the best deal at the time.

So before rushing out for the brand you know from school, or that someone recommends from their own school days, keep in mind that the purchasing process and needs of an institution are likely to be quite different from your own.

Help from a Piano Teacher

Piano teachers are part-and-parcel of our industry and are responsible in part for the finished product of the musician, whether child or adult. No matter what the quality of the piano, you cannot get from here to there without a teacher, which is why most teachers are revered by their students and by parents of students.

For decades, we have worked in retail locations that have large recital halls. These are often utilized by the neighborhood piano teachers for their semi-annual student recitals. Through this experience, we have learned that it is possible to be an excellent teacher and know very little about pianos as an instrument. Being a strong piano teacher does not always mean being an expert on, or qualified judge of, piano makes and models. Keep in mind these potential points about a teacher when seeking their advice:

- ◆ Teachers may not have breadth and length of experience with a variety of brands and models.

- ◆ A teacher may not have updated knowledge of emergent brands from Eastern Europe or China or the evolution of Korean brands over the past 30 years.

- ◆ Some might recommend brands or models that have been discontinued or manufacturers that have gone out of business.

- ◆ Your taste in tone may not match that of the teacher.

- ◆ Teachers often have touch performance needs that differ from yours.

- ◆ A teacher may have an outdated understanding of pricing or pricing suggestions that do not match your budget.

- ◆ Some teachers may not have played on a grand piano for years and are not familiar with the various functions of the pedals. Most of their playing and teaching has been on uprights, which do not have identical functions.

We have spent hundreds of hours speaking before teachers' association meetings, hosting teacher symposia, and producing product information and educational materials for teachers, with the belief that educated and updated teachers can help their students make better piano purchase choices.

If your teacher appears knowledgeable, up-to-date, and sensitive to your needs and budget, then let him or her participate. Multiple heads are better than one, as long as they are working toward the same goal.

Teachers are best positioned to assess the current, near-term, and long-term performance needs of your student. Without their professional input, many students could end up with inferior instruments or no instruments at all, and some students could pay a price much higher than the value and performance warrant.

At many strong and reputable dealerships across the country, it definitely *is* possible for a customer to purchase a decent piano at a fair price and receive great service without the guidance of a teacher. But teachers can be valuable assets to you if you lack confidence about your ability to shop for a piano.

Also, at some dealerships, teacher-assisted purchases provide added incentive for the seller to strike a fair deal. To most sellers, a family or individual buyer represents a potential single sale. To any smart dealer, the profile of a family shopping with their teacher represents a potential for a long-term relationship with an influential member of the teaching community, which is likely to result in multiple future sales. This can get you more attention, better prices, and probably better service.

Debunking Myths About Pianos

Over the years, we have heard it all when it comes to the malarkey that surrounds pianos. Or, at least, we think we have until the next one hits us! Below are a few of the more classic recurring themes to be aware of. Knowing the truth about pianos will help keep you from making mistakes.

Brands and Models

MYTH: *This brand X piano was made by Steinway & Sons.*

REALITY: Steinway & Sons has never made any piano that didn't read "Steinway & Sons" on the front and inside. A few of their concert grand pianos read a larger "STEINWAY" on the front and sides for the cameras. It has been a common sales tactic going back to the 1800s to link lesser brands to high profile makers like Steinway & Sons.

MYTH: *This piano is an upright-grand.*

REALITY: The term upright-grand was a common marketing gimmick at the turn of the century to add the grand piano cache to a simple, but tall upright.

MYTH: *All pianos made in China are garbage and should be avoided at all costs.*

REALITY: Some Chinese pianos are genuine good values and will give good service, especially for beginners. Chinese pianos are typically not acceptable for serious students and players, however. You can learn more about Chinese pianos in Chapter 14.

Components

MYTH: *This piano has solid ivory keys.*

REALITY: Ivory keys have never been solid. Pianos have had wooden keys covered in ivory.

MYTH: *The harp in this piano is solid gold.*

REALITY: Precious metals have never been used in any parts of pianos. Plates or "harps" are always cast iron and painted a golden color. Occasionally, high-end manufacturers have electroplated some of the visible hardware in a grand piano in either a gold or silver tone, but the standard finish is nickel or brass.

MYTH: *Older pianos were made of solid rosewood.*

REALITY: Even the grandest of grand cabinets from yesteryear were actually made of more common woods like poplar and maple but were veneered with exotics. Pianos, both upright and grand, have rarely been made of solid wood that you see used as the outside layer.

MYTH: *New pianos are all particleboard and plastic.*

REALITY: Yes and no. Only Yamaha and Kawai utilize plastic in their actions as of this writing. Most technicians see this as a good thing. Nearly all pianos available today have some engineered wood products in their cabinets. Common particleboard that you might be familiar with from your local home improvement store is not used in piano construction.

MYTH: *Laminated soundboards are found only in terrible pianos.*

REALITY: Multi-layered soundboards have been around since the 1950s. If the layers are composed only of spruce, and the tone is good, then the piano has a more durable soundboard. There are many worthwhile consumer-grade and economy pianos with laminated soundboards.

MYTH: *Solid, single-layer soundboards are a sign of a good piano.*

REALITY: There are dozens of brands and models of pianos with solid boards that are marginal at best.

MYTH: *The color, finish, or wood of a piano's cabinet affects the tone.*

REALITY: The finish, color, and finish veneer are only skin deep and have no effect on tone.

MYTH: *Player piano mechanisms affect the touch of the piano when played manually.*

REALITY: Only in the old player grands from the 1920s and 1930s did the mechanism affect the touch. Modern electronic player mechanisms do not touch the keys when not in use. Some installations may affect the pedal functions, however.

Age and Provenance

MYTH: *Older pianos were built better than new pianos.*

REALITY: With the exception of art-cases, designer sketch cases, and the use of exotic veneers, this simply is not the case if comparing like products.

MYTH: *Like violins, pianos get better with age.*

REALITY: Pianos do break in and season out to become more stable. This happens in the first couple of years. After that, it is a gradual decline over time.

MYTH: *Pianos older than 100 years are worth a lot of money.*

REALITY: There are tens of thousands of pianos that are more than 100 years old. The huge majority of them are worth less than 500 dollars. They may qualify as antiques from a decorative standpoint, but they are usually worthless as working musical instruments.

MYTH: *This piano was once owned by …*

REALITY: A common sales tactic when selling used pianos is to claim a provenance (pedigree of sorts) of a previous ownership, preferably an illustrious, impressive ownership. Unless there is valid documentation to support this type of claim, do not believe it.

Care and Tuning

MYTH: *Piano keys should be cleaned and treated with milk to stop them from discoloring.*

REALITY: This recommendation derives from the era of ivory keys, which, for most pianos, came to a close in the 1940s. No matter where this idea comes from, though, it doesn't work. And, even if it did work, you would not want to catch a whiff of the spoilt dairy scent that wafts up from piano keys treated with milk. We've had the not so pleasant experience of smelling pianos saturated with milk, and believe us, we wouldn't want to wish such a fate on you!

MYTH: *This piano has not been tuned for 20 years, but it is in perfect tune.*

REALITY: The piano may sound in tune, but that's because it is "in tune" with itself. No acoustic piano stays in tune and at concert pitch for much more than 18 months.

MYTH: *Pianos should not be machine tuned, only tuned by ear.*

REALITY: Nearly all piano tuners use ETDs or electronic tuning devices. ETDs translate sound from the piano into graphic or numeric representations on a screen. The actual tuning is still done by hand, moving the tuning pin tighter or looser, using the tuning hammer or lever. It is the skill of the tuner's hammer technique that determines the quality of the tuning, not the machine. The use of an ETD enables tuners to work in noisy environments where aural (by ear) tuning would be impossible.

MYTH: *Brand X pianos stay in tune longer.*

REALITY: If we rule out the cheapest of the cheap piano category, all the rest stay in tune about the same. Pianos go out of tune because the music wire stretches and the wood expands and contracts. No brand or model is materially more stable than others.

The Straight Scoop on What to Look For

If you or your child is a beginning student, don't feel you have to invest in an expensive, high performance piano. On the other hand, you don't want to sacrifice quality by purchasing an old junk starter piano that might be poor performing, worn-out, and inconsistent and therefore could stifle learning. A piano for a beginner student should:

- ◆ be able to hold a tune at concert pitch.

- ◆ have a consistent touch all across the keyboard.

- ◆ have a touch that is in the mainstream of the spectrum—not too hard and not too easy.

- ◆ have a decent degree of *repetition sensitivity*.

def•i•ni•tion

Repetition sensitivity refers to the ability of a note or key to reset and play again in a quick fashion. Two issues are at play: How many repetitions (or times the note can be played) per minute are possible and how high the key must come up to allow the mechanism to reset and be ready to play again.

- ◆ have a pleasant tone that is in the mainstream of the spectrum of harsh to mellow.

- have mechanicals, e.g., pedals, keys, etc., that work well and are free of distracting noises.

- be serviceable for a predictable length of time to match the investment and need.

For students with intermediate to advanced levels of skill who show aptitude, talent, and promise, teachers typically want these students to have instruments that:

- have a high degree of sensitivity and repetition in the action response.

- possess a *dynamic range* that facilitates wide expression.

- have sustaining properties and tone color that facilitate advanced interpretation.

- are sufficiently durable to withstand more dedicated practice hours.

Upper-level students deserve instruments that have performance capabilities commensurate with their level of play.

def•i•ni•tion

Dynamic range refers to the number of levels of dynamics or volume (loud, medium, and soft volumes of play) achievable on a given piano. Professional performance pianos facilitate well over a dozen discernable levels of volume for expression. Entry-level pianos may offer four or five.

The Least You Need to Know

- It can be difficult to find impartial, truly disinterested third-party opinions about pianos.

- Trust your own eyes, ears, and fingers because the decision is ultimately yours alone to make.

- Piano teachers can be valuable advisors if they have up-to-date knowledge on current brands, models, or pricing.

- There are common myths and misconceptions about pianos; don't believe everything you hear.

Piano Shopping on the Internet

In This Chapter

- The risks of online piano purchases
- Using the Internet wisely to find information about pianos
- Manufacturers' websites and specifications
- Considerations for shopping digital and used pianos online

Most folks today would not think of shopping for a big-ticket item without first going to the Internet, whether just to do research or with the intention of making the actual purchase online. Having so much information at your fingertips can be very helpful, but when it comes to buying a piano, keep in mind you are considering the purchase of a musical instrument with lots of intricacies, as well as it being a large piece of furniture. On the Internet, you can't feel the keys or accurately hear the tone as you can at a dealership. It's important to shop the old-fashioned pounding-the-pavement way for this unique product.

We have nothing against online shopping in general. We simply want you to be aware that the Internet is typically not the best place to purchase a piano. That doesn't mean you shouldn't use it at all in your piano buying process. The Internet can be quite useful for some stages of the purchase, but you do need to understand the limitations.

The aim of this chapter is to point out the advantages of researching your options online and to help you be a more educated consumer, even if you do end up making the purchase on the Internet.

The Perils of Online Piano Purchases

A piano tuner of some renown recently bought a used grand piano from a man in New York City over the Internet. This colleague of ours has years in the piano business and is a Registered Piano Technician. He spent $10,000 on a high-profile brand of grand piano that was advertised on the Internet as "completely restored." When he received the piano a few weeks later it was completely original, meaning no restoration work had been done. The piano needed at least $6,000 worth of work to put it into the completely restored condition that the seller had claimed it was in.

> **B-Sharp**
>
> Don't buy a piano over the Internet unless you are willing to travel to the piano with a qualified technician to check it out in person.

The number of negative online piano purchase experiences we have been told of vastly outweighs the number of successful ones. Whether selling a new or used piano, online sellers can misrepresent brands, models, age, and conditions of their products. And frequently, sellers have inflated ideas about an instrument's worth. Because of the anonymity of the web and distances involved, buyers rarely see the merchandise before it arrives and have little recourse if what arrives differs from what they thought they had purchased.

One of the biggest problems with buying a piano online is the fact that most pianos advertised online as new are, in fact, not new. To understand why, you first need to know what makes a piano genuinely new and what makes it not new. In the piano world, the term "new" means that the instrument has moved from the manufacturer, often through a distributor, to an authorized retail dealer, who then sells the piano to you. Only an authorized dealer for a particular brand can deliver a truly new piano from that brand.

A piano is not "new" if:

◆ it comes through any other channels, such as middlemen, or a dealer who is not authorized to sell a certain brand.

◆ it is sold and delivered, the warranty is registered, and then the piano is returned to the dealer who resells it to someone else.

◆ a dealer goes out of business and sells remaining stock of a particular brand to another dealer who is not an authorized dealer.

◆ it was damaged in transit and was rejected by a customer or a dealer, and then liquidated by an insurance carrier or trucking company.

So what does all this have to do with new pianos not being on the Internet? Nearly every manufacturer that distributes pianos in the United States has prohibitions written into their authorized dealer agreements that prevent the dealer from advertising new pianos on the Internet. If they do advertise online, they must not display prices. Therefore, new pianos are almost never sold over the Internet in the United States by authorized dealers.

So if you see a so-called new piano advertised online, it is likely to be liquidated merchandise or freight-damaged goods—pianos that were "totaled out" and picked up by insurance companies after fire, flood, or hurricane claims—or from other nonmainstream dealers with product that is suspect and warranty protection that may be nonexistent. No traditional store dealers in the United States show retail prices on new, brand name pianos on the Internet.

Useful Piano Information Online

While we caution against making most piano purchases online, we don't want you to not use the Internet at all in your buying process. The web can expose you to hundreds of opportunities and choices that you might never see in weeks of physical store shopping. So use the web for research and then visit a local dealership to buy.

You may ask, "If I cannot get prices on the Internet, what information can I find?" How will it help in my research process? Good question. Product information, sizes, material specifications, cabinet styles, countries of origin, design features, testimonials, and listings of authorized dealerships organized by zip code can all be found on manufacturers' websites. (We list the major manufacturers' sites later in this chapter.)

Rhythm and News

Internet piano purchases can end on a good note. We recently talked to a man who flew from California to Minnesota to purchase a 15-year-old C. Bechstein, 9-foot, concert grand for his church, a piano he found online for a very good price. He took his piano technician with him to survey the piano. The travel expenses and payment for the tech's time were substantially offset by the huge bargain he did get on this rare instrument. At any given time, there is likely to be no more than one, if any, C. Bechstein, 9-foot, concert grands less than 20 years old for sale in the United States, let alone at a substantially below-market price, so it was an amazing find. And, for the seller, the likelihood of a buyer for this instrument was slim to none in his small town. This is a clear example of the power of the Internet to connect the right buyer with a rare and extremely narrow-market instrument.

You can also seek out the inside scoop on various piano makes and models by reading Internet forums dedicated to discussions of pianos. Piano World (www.pianoworld.com) is one site to check out for reference materials, facts and figures, photos, and discussion forums. These discussion groups, blogs, and chat rooms are frequented by teachers, technicians, musicians, academicians, and shoppers just like you. All have opinions to offer and experiences to share. While you might find that you can get useful answers to questions you have by commenting in these forums, do use some caution when participating in these sites.

B-Sharp

Watch out for the same type of comment—such as a claim that a particular brand of piano is prone to mechanical problems—posted repeatedly in different blogs or discussion groups. This could be the unethical handiwork of a salesperson or manufacturer's rep trying to drive people away from a particular brand the competitors sell.

Some people who post comments are salespeople or manufacturers' reps posing as teachers, shoppers, and other unbiased parties. Erroneous information can be posted about products and pricing in an attempt to steer customers in one direction or another.

Most blogs and discussion groups have monitors or facilitators to catch abusers, and many sites have regular industry pros who "out" offenders whenever discovered. So if you do use the Internet to gather information about the instruments that interest you, try to stick to the manufacturers' websites and those of your local authorized dealerships, and use caution if you choose to go to more subjective forums.

Information from Manufacturers

Manufacturers' websites are a wealth of information about makes, models, and specifications. They should be part of your research to understand the instrument, the brands and the market.

A List of Websites

Included here is a list of piano manufacturers' websites and some suggestions for how to interpret the information found on these sites. This list is not intended to be exhaustive. There are dozens of *stencil pianos* being produced in Chinese factories that change too quickly to include. But these sites will certainly get you started searching out product information on the major players in the industry.

- American Sejung Corporation (brand names include: Hobart M. Cable, Falcone, George Steck), www.ASCPianos.com

- Bösendorfer, www.Boesendorfer.com

- Baldwin (brand names owned include: Baldwin, Hamilton, Howard, D.H. Baldwin, Wurlitzer, Chickering & Sons. Now owned by Gibson of guitar fame), www.Gibson.com

- C. Bechstein, www.bechstein.de

- Estonia, www.EstoniaPiano.com

- Fazioli, www.Fazioli.com

- Heintzman & Co., www.hzmpiano.com

- Kawai, www.KawaiUS.com

- Pearl River (another brand name Pearl River makes is Ritmüller), www.PearlRiverUSA.com

- Schimmel (another brand name is Vogel), www.Schimmel-Piano.de

- Samick Music Corp. (brand names include: Wm. Knabe, Sohmer & Co., Samick, Kohler & Campbell, Pramberger, Remington, and Kohler digitals), www.SMCMusic.com

def•i•ni•tion

A **stencil piano** is an instrument built by a manufacturer with another brand name placed on it. Typically, these pianos are built under contract with a retailer, distributor, or another manufacturer.

- ◆ Steinway & Sons (other brands are Boston and Essex), www.Steinway.com
- ◆ Charles Walter, www.WalterPiano.com
- ◆ Wyman, www.wymanpiano.com
- ◆ Yamaha (brand names include Clavinova and Disklavier), www.Yamaha.com
- ◆ Young Chang, www.YoungChang.com

A Note on Specifications

On the manufacturers' websites, you'll find a great deal of information about the pianos' specifications—their engineering and materials. But, specifications tell only part of the story; they don't tell you about the musical properties or the precision and care that went into the assembly. What this means is that some manufacturers or dealers might tout certain specifications that, in fact, are irrelevant to performance.

Case in point, several years ago the string length of piano bass strings became a big focal point of sales presentations, even to the point of publishing such data on websites and in brochures. Thinking that this was one of the most important factors when comparing various pianos, customers began asking for the length of the #1 bass string on particular models.

The reality is that longer strings do often give a sweeter, more resonant tone, but one or two inches one way or the other will not make a discernable difference. Some scale designs operate more efficiently than others, driving more and better sound from shorter strings. Overall string length is only vaguely related to performance. The *speaking length* of the string is a more relevant measurement.

def•i•ni•tion

Speaking length is the actual length between the points at which the string frets off at both ends. Speaking length should not be confused with overall length, which is often cited in specification lists. The speaking length is the part of the string that actually produces sound. The difference between these two lengths (speaking and overall length) may vary as much as 15 percent.

Another example about specification involves the pin block or wrest plank (the wood that holds the tuning pins). Whether a tuning pin wrest plank has 11 layers of laminated birch or 6 layers of hard maple is not a compelling reason to buy one or the other, despite what you read or hear. Both pin blocks do a good job holding the tuning pin where the tuner places it. One salesperson will extol the virtues of multiple wood grain changes while another will extol the virtues of fewer but thicker layers. One company uses beech wood because that is indigenous to its factory area. The other company uses maple for the same reason. It really doesn't make any difference.

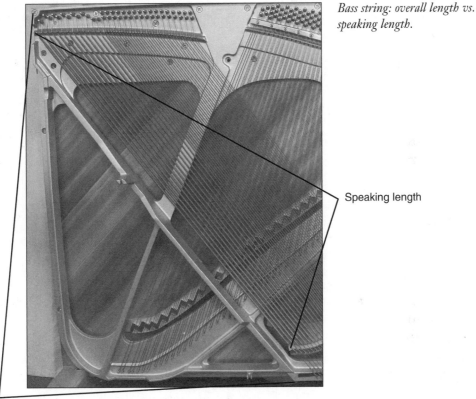

Bass string: overall length vs. speaking length.

Speaking length

Overall length

A few years ago, a famous company touted a 52-layer pin block. Because the tuning pin that actually goes into the pin block is only about 1½ inches long, each of the 52 layers would have had to have been less than 1/32 of an inch thick for the tuning pins to utilize all those layers. At that same time there was a company whose block comprised only three layers. These layers were about a half an inch thick. The arguing point was for the tuning pin to hold, it needs the grain direction changes of multiple layers to put end grain around the circumference of the round tuning pin. More layers would have more grain direction changes and, therefore, more holding power. The counter to this argument insisted that with so many wafer-thin layers, there was more glue between each layer and less wood fiber holding the tuning pin. Actually, both of these designs, and all the others between them did an adequate job of holding the tuning pin firm. Most pianos less than twenty years old go out of tune because the wire stretches as the piano expands and contracts with moisture and humidity changes, not because the tuning pins are turning in their holes.

A multiple-layer pin block.

To give all of this some context, as a consumer, you may be interested to know how many cylinders are in the engine of the new truck you are contemplating, but not likely concerned with how many bolts are used to secure the main bearings of the crank-shaft. Statistics and specifications are part of the piano shopping and presentation process, but you should be more interested in how those numbers and materials translate into performance and durability.

> ### Key Note
>
> Keep in mind that isolated Internet specifications and poorly prepared presentations often leave the consumer with a blizzard of useless and insignificant information, which confuses more than it educates.

In short, use the manufactures' websites wisely. You can glean important information from them, but remember that they are sales tools and that for a comprehensive understanding of an instrument, you will need to see and hear it in a dealer's showroom.

Buying a Used Piano Online

As you've probably realized by now, we're not big fans of buying pianos on the Internet and would prefer to see you use the web for information only. One exception, however, is that you might be able to find a good used piano online, but this should come after you've done all your research and visited some dealers. If you do decide to shop for a used piano on eBay, Craig's List, or any other online sales forum, browse around carefully to get an idea of pricing for various brands, models, and ages. You may see several instruments that fit your needs and budget. To determine which one is right for you, we encourage you to follow these recommendations:

1. Only consider pianos that are located within a distance you are willing to travel. Do not buy a piano unless you have inspected it personally.

2. Only consider traveling to see a piano if you are willing to pay a qualified piano technician (a technician that *you* select) to survey the instrument for problems or rebuilding needs.

3. Compare the price with other similar makes, models, and ages. Make sure you are not paying more than the current market value.

4. If you buy from a private party, assume that a used piano is sold as is, with no warranty expressed or implied and with no returns or credits allowed. Your lack of warranty protection should be factored into your assessment of the piano's value.

5. If you buy from an online dealer, understand that any warranty is only as good as the dealer's reputation, their time in the business, and their resources to make good on a claim.

6. If you buy from a private party, plan for a prompt pick-up by a piano mover at your expense. Moving expenses must be factored into the value.

7. Plan to have your used piano tuned in the first few weeks by a tuner of your choice and at your expense. Service expenses, too, should be factored into the value.

8. Be prepared for most private-party sellers to require payment in cash or by bank (cashier's) check.

9. Do not give the seller all of the money until the piano is being loaded onto your moving truck.

Like buying a car online, a used piano purchase can be made more convenient by shopping online, but it will only have a happy ending if you tread carefully and add an in-person element to the deal.

Shopping Digital Pianos Online

Digital and electronic instruments have none of the individual tone and touch characteristics of acoustic pianos, so it might seem okay to purchase a digital piano online. Unfortunately, we know of many disappointed online buyers. Some never received the digital piano they paid for or received the wrong model or color. Others received an instrument that was damaged or not working.

It can be tempting to consider buying a digital piano online, though. A search for many of the popular brand names and models will result in multiple dealers in Canada, the UK, and other countries willing to do business at discount prices. Prices may be lower on these sites, but the discounts do come with pitfalls:

1. United States distributors for the make and model you want will not honor the warranty if sold by a dealer outside their network. The distributor that sells to the online dealer will likely not honor the warranty either because it has been delivered out of their territory.

2. Since 1903, nearly every consumer electronic product sold in the United States has been safety tested by the Underwriter's Laboratories and rendered "safe" with their UL label. From toaster ovens to TVs, from computers to spas, all must bear this label if approved. Digital pianos purchased over the Internet from outside this country will likely not have this safety testing.

3. Digital pianos built for use in other countries have different voltage requirements and odd plug sizes and configurations. Converters are available, of course, but this is very sensitive digital equipment, as much as or even more than, computer equipment.

4. The Federal Communications Commission (FCC) requires that all products sold in the United States meet certain radio-frequency emission standards. Digital pianos have power supplies, amplifiers, and other electronic circuitry that must be certified FCC compliant to be legally sold in the United States. FCC compliance assures that your equipment is safe to operate in the presence of other compliant equipment. We would hate for you to make your neighbor's garage door opener engage or stop Grandpa's pacemaker! Bootlegged electronic equipment sold from outside the United States rarely has this important FCC inspection and certification.

5. Different designations or languages can appear on the dashboard controls of digital pianos from outside the United States. We know of an English-speaking

customer who purchased a digital piano over the Internet but was not planning on his dashboard controls being identified in Japanese symbols! His owner's manual was no help in that it, too, was printed in Japanese.

6. Digital pianos built for use in other countries may not have the same peripheral equipment you would get with U.S. products, such as disk drives, benches, owner's manuals, and software.

7. Foreign-made digital pianos may not have the American song styles or voices you want and expect.

8. Local distributors or dealers will not support units they did not sell, and keep in mind large digital pianos are fairly complicated units.

We are not saying that you could never find a good, safe deal for a digital piano online. The Internet is a vast place, so anything's possible! But, we do want you to be aware of the potential complications and costs, so tread very carefully.

Purchase Online Or Go Local?

While the Internet can lure a buyer in with competitive pricing and endless selection, keep in mind that a well-run, honestly-operated piano store can bring many things to a local community that the Internet does not. A selection of new and used instruments to see and play; music lessons and referrals to piano teachers; accessories and sheet music; hosting or sponsoring of student recitals; music scholarship donations; and support for local athletic teams are examples of how a local dealer can enhance a community. Stores also support the local community in the form of local property and sales tax revenues, something to consider for where you want your dollars to go. Plus the risk of making a bad purchase can be lower when you're in the hands of a reputable local retailer.

Rhythm and News

Local dealers aren't always perfect. Some in remote areas have such a monopoly in the region that they may price their pianos measurably higher than in other more competitive areas. Don't feel you have to hop in the car and drive hundreds miles to get a deal, however. Give your local dealer a shot at your business and try to negotiate with the salesperson or the owner or manager. Express that you prefer to buy locally, and hope to come to an agreement. Have a figure in mind that you have researched and give the local dealer the opportunity to meet your price.

The Least You Need to Know

- ◆ Buying a piano over the Internet has its risks.

- ◆ In blogs, discussion groups, and chat rooms, watch out for unscrupulous sales-people posing as customers to taint unsuspecting shoppers' opinions.

- ◆ No authorized U.S. acoustic piano dealer is allowed to quote new piano prices on the Internet.

- ◆ Utilize manufacturers' websites to glean information, but keep in mind that the specifications listed don't tell the whole story.

- ◆ When considering a used piano online, see it firsthand and have a registered piano technician inspect it.

6

Psst ... Wanna Buy a Used Piano?

In This Chapter

◆ Determining the value of used pianos

◆ What age does to a piano

◆ How to shop used pianos at a dealer

◆ Proper inspection of a used piano

One major decision you'll need to make as you embark on the piano buying process is whether to purchase a new or used model. Many families decide that they will seek out a used piano because it will undoubtedly be cheaper. Industry statistics indicate that for every new piano sold, four used pianos change hands. It may turn out that a used piano is the right way to go based on your needs and budget, but we recommend doing so only after careful consideration of all your options, both new and used. In this chapter, you'll learn how to understand the value of a used piano and what to look for in one so that you make a wise decision.

Pianos Are Not Like Wine

One of the most common misconceptions surrounding pianos is that age supposedly brings value to a piano. Pianos do not improve with age, nor are older pianos necessarily built better or better performers than new pianos.

Predictable useful musical life expectancies exist for certain genres of pianos. A piano may have been of excellent quality during its prime, but it may have outlived its musical life by the time it hits the used market. A big part of what makes up the predictable life expectancy for an acoustic piano is the materials and engineering that go into the major components, including finishes, hammers and dampers, bass strings, tenor and treble strings, action parts, bridges and soundboards, and more. (These parts of a piano are defined and described in Chapter 7.)

Another common misconception is that a used piano is a good buy if its current condition is good—that is, it doesn't appear to have reached the end of its musical life yet. The value of a used piano must be based, however, not only on its current condition, but also on its remaining useful musical years, balanced against its selling price. This is akin to buying a car that is running great right now but has 200,000 miles on it. How much longer will it run? If the selling price is rock bottom, it might be worth it to you to buy the car to get you by for a short while until you can buy a better one, but if the price is not so low, then it's probably not worth it.

The situation is the same with pianos. If a 30-year-old brand X upright is selling for half the price of a new one, at first blush this might seem to be a good deal. But, if brand X pianos typically have a useful musical life of 35 to 40 years, the deal might not be so good.

> **B-Sharp**
>
> When considering a used piano, try to find out if it was used in an institutional setting. This can shorten the useful musical life of a piano's components by half or more.

What to Look for in a Used Piano

Time takes its toll on pianos. The pressure from the strings, gravity, dust, and aging all tend to worsen a piano's tone, *sustain*, and tunability. Customers often tell us that their 20-year-old piano is just like new because it was hardly played at all. In reality, a little play is better for a piano than to have it just sit for 20 years. And regular tuning is a must to keep the proper tension. If a piano you are considering is privately owned, ask the owner when the piano was last tuned and how often over the years it was tuned. Ask to see receipts of the work that was done so you have documentation of the instrument's service history.

A good used piano must be able to be tuned to concert pitch and hold the tuning. It must have keys that do not stick and stutter (stuttering is when a key comes back up too slowly or jerkily after you press it) and that are consistent. When you employ a tuner to inspect a potential piano for any such problems, you might be told that the piano needs a *pitch raise*. Get an estimate of the costs involved so you can factor them in before making a commitment.

def•i•ni•tion

Sustain is the length of time a note produces a sound.

A **pitch raise** involves tuning the piano in increments because the pitch is so low that it can't be brought up in one tuning.

When shopping for a used piano, we recommend that you rule out the following:

- ◆ Pianos that have seen more than five years of hard institutional service.

- ◆ All but highly recognizable brand names.

- ◆ Asian pianos older than 25 years.

- ◆ Vertical pianos less than 40" tall, or more than 52" tall. This rules out spinets, consolettes, and old uprights.

- ◆ Pianos that have come from an insurance claim loss situation, such as flood, fire, or other disaster.

- ◆ Pianos that have lived most of their lives in climates far more humid than your own (for example, you live in the desert, but the piano has resided in the southeastern United States).

- ◆ Pianos from private parties, teachers, technicians, or rebuilders, unless, you pay to have it surveyed by an *independent* technician.

- ◆ Pianos shown to you in an uninsulated and unheated garage or storage facility if evidence suggests they have been there longer than a few days.

It's best not to buy any used piano until you have shopped the new market and seen your options. Doing this will give you a better idea of value and performance when you look at used instruments. For instance, a new, decent Chinese piano will likely be

Key Note

Please see the Glossary of Terms in Appendix A for *rebuilt, reconditioned, refurbished,* and *restored.* These terms are frequently misused when describing used goods to potential customers, so they are good for you to be familiar with.

superior in every respect to a 50-year-old American console or spinet that might sell for the same price.

Buying a Used Piano from a Dealer

Most dealers sell used pianos. These pianos have come to the dealer as trade-ins or have been purchased from private parties for re-sale in the store. Often, a dealer or the dealer's representative inspects pianos before purchasing them. Then, once in the store, warehouse, or shop, the dealer cleans up the piano to make it look newer. Typically, the piano is then tuned and some *regulating* done.

def•i•ni•tion

Regulating is the process of adjusting the key mechanism to make all the keys play consistently.

When you come in to shop for one of these used pianos, the salesperson should be able to tell you the age of the piano and what work has been done to it, if any. Buying used from a dealer, the piano will usually come with some kind of warranty, wholesale or free delivery, and, typically, one in-home tuning.

Rebuilt or Refurbished Pianos

Some dealers will rebuild a piano to help it command a higher resale price. Rebuilding is very expensive and rarely done on uprights. Even on grands, rebuilding is usually limited to brands with a high intrinsic value, such as Steinway & Sons and Mason & Hamlin. Occasionally, one will see rebuilt Knabes, Chickerings, and Baldwins, but fewer and fewer of these are being rebuilt today. Reconditioning, on the other hand, is not as involved as rebuilding and can consist of as little as polishing and tuning, or as much as the replacement of action parts and restringing.

> ### Rhythm and News
>
> You might hear a dealer or private seller describe a piano as refurbished. While it sounds good, technically it doesn't mean all that much. A refurbished piano has likely been cleaned, tuned, and had the cabinet polished, but nothing more. Another term you might hear is restored. This should mean that it has been brought to a condition similar to when it was new, more like being rebuilt. The term is used very loosely in the piano industry, however, and can mean almost anything. So if you hear these terms being used, ask for documentation of the work done or employ an unbiased piano technician to check the instrument out for you.

If you believe you are paying a premium for a used piano because it is represented as rebuilt or reconditioned, ask for documentation of what was done, by whom, and when. If the seller did not have the work done or cannot document it, then you are looking simply at a used piano, in as is condition. If you're unsure, employ an independent technician to check the piano. The technician should be able to verify most of what the salesperson has told you. However, without documentation, it can be hard to determine how recently some work was performed.

Warranties on Used Pianos

A warranty on a used piano is a good thing to have, and some dealers do offer them. The warranty is only as good, however, as that dealer's reputation for service and satisfaction and the projected longevity of the business in your market area. Dealer used piano warranties should be in writing and specify exactly what is covered. It is common for dealers to include a parts warranty on used pianos but to have no labor warranty, or only a very short one. Parts are much less expensive than the labor to install those parts. If you can get a warranty and a positive report from a full inspection by a qualified piano technician, then you're in good shape with your used piano purchase.

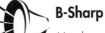

B-Sharp _____

Used piano warranties offered from private parties are rare. Private party sales are typically a one-time thing with no further expectation. If a private seller does claim to offer a warranty, tread carefully so you don't lose any money on an empty claim.

Antique Pianos

Just because a piano is more than 100 years old, it's not necessarily valuable as a musical instrument. Antique pianos (pianos more than 100 years old) are rarely well-playing or tunable if in their original condition. It might have value as an antique, either as a decorative piece of furniture or as an object of historical significance, but it may not have value as a musical instrument.

A particular category of antique instruments to avoid is the Square Grand. These rectangular-shaped pianos sit on four legs. They are often made from exotic woods,

Key Note _____

Most antique pianos are not suitable for a beginner to learn on.

typically Brazilian rosewood. So they can be appealing as a decorative object if your tastes go in that direction and if you have the space, but if you want an instrument you can play, we recommend you run, not walk, away from these beasts!

Testing a Used Piano Before Purchasing

If you are serious about purchasing a used piano, there are some simple tests you can perform even if you know little or nothing about pianos. Here's a step-by-step process to follow:

Step 1: Play each and every key on the piano. Feel how each key goes down. If you are unsure how it should feel, ask to try a new piano of the same category (e.g., vertical or grand). Does each key feel like the rest of the keys? Does each note play (make a sound)? Make sure the answers are yes for all 88 notes.

Step 2: Go back and play eight or ten keys, one at a time, along the keyboard and hold each down until the sound stops. This tests the sustain along the scale. Sustain times will be somewhat shorter at the treble end (right side) and longer in the bass end. If there are areas where the sustain is inconsistent with the rest of the piano, this might indicate hidden problems.

Step 3: Play the keys in the lower end (left-hand side) of the scale (those with the copper-looking strings). Do the notes have some degree of tone, or do they just kind of thunk? Bass strings have a shorter life expectancy than the other strings and tend to be one of the earlier component failures.

Don't be shy about taking your time to go through these steps; this is an important test. If you hear odd sounds or the feel doesn't seem right, have it investigated by a technician.

Catastrophic or significant component failures, such as cracked plates, cracked bridges, cracked soundboards, loose bridge pins, and failing pin blocks frequently manifest as tone, sustain, or tuning problems. Sometimes these problems will not be observable if the piano is a step or two below pitch. A technician will need to check for these problems. In your simple test, you are just checking to see if a piano is horribly out of tune. You're looking for notes or groups of notes that are grossly out of tune and/or have significantly less sustain. You're also looking for buzzing and rattling sounds. If an older piano has been tuned in the last two years and is now largely out of tune, this is not a good sign. Most pianos require fine tuning about twice a year to remain at pitch and retain good sound. However, unless there is something materially wrong, a piano that's tuned every two years should not sound horribly out of tune to the average ear.

Step 4: It is nearly impossible to assess the performance of a piano unless it is at pitch and in tune. Concert pitch (currently) is 440 cycles per second for the A key (five white keys above middle C). You likely don't carry a tuning fork to measure this, and 440 cycles per second for the A key gets pretty technical to understand, so we have come up with an alternative. The dial tone on most phones is a somewhat universal pitch. It should match the F key (four white keys below middle C). If the tone of that key closely matches the dial tone, and the rest of the scale sounds in tune with that key, then the piano should be at, or close to, concert pitch.

Step 5: This step is important but potentially unpleasant. Pull off the top and bottom doors of the upright, or if the owners prefer, have them do it. Inspect the insides of the piano for any evidence of rodent droppings or urine and hope that you don't find any! Depending on where the piano has been stored makes this definitely something to check out.

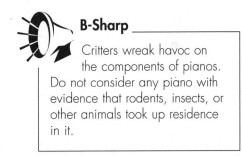

B-Sharp

Critters wreak havoc on the components of pianos. Do not consider any piano with evidence that rodents, insects, or other animals took up residence in it.

Step 6: Inspect metal parts for evidence of corrosion and/or rust. Light rust is present on most exposed steel strings in every piano beyond the age of five. Heavy, crusted rust on strings and tuning pins signals an imminent, expensive restringing job.

Step 7: Look for discoloration on casters and ends of legs and bottoms of vertical pianos. This can indicate flood situations that the instrument has endured. Pass on these pianos. A brown water-mark on the wall behind the piano, 10 inches from the floor, is also a dead giveaway.

Step 8: Look at the hammers. The hammers on older pianos with significant use will become deeply grooved from the strings. Expect some string marking on even brand new pianos just out of the box. Excessive wear will be evidenced by grooves deeper than the diameter of the strings themselves. Hammers may be worn to where the strike point is a flat broad surface.

Don't worry if any of these eight steps are difficult for you or if you're not sure you're doing them correctly or thoroughly enough. While you won't find what a trained piano technician will, these steps do empower you with some things you can do to begin to rule in or rule out a piano. If you find major, obvious problems during any of these tests, then you can probably rule out the piano with confidence and save yourself the expense of hiring a technician to do further testing.

If a piano does seem okay based on your simple tests, don't assume that the piano completely passes muster. These are just a few of the many details that trained and experienced technicians can recognize instantly. But frequently there are hidden problem areas only a tech will find, as in loose bridges or bridge pins, cracked cast-iron plates, actions that need to be entirely re-pinned, hammers that have been over voiced and over shaped, tuning pin torque below minimum to hold a tune, key bushings that are worn beyond adjustment, and the list goes on and on. The older the instrument, the more likely one or more of these maladies has invaded its sanctity. So before assuming that a piano sounds, looks, and feels okay, have a qualified technician take a look.

Bridge with bridge pins.

This is the way bridge pins look when they are sound and securely fastened. Failing bridges will have stress cracks around the pins and loose pins you can pull out with your finger.

Vertically laminated bridge.

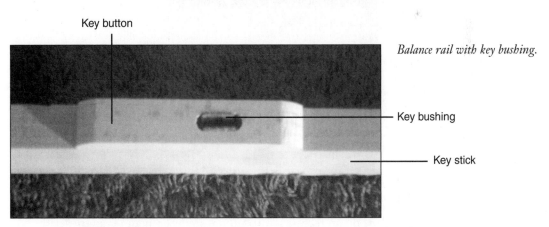

Balance rail with key bushing.

This is the way key bushings should look when new. Worn bushings will be missing or worn through to the point that the balance rail pins or the front rail pins will be rubbing on the wood.

Right Place at the Right Time

Most every retailer has at least one buyer working for them who combs the want ads and online postings for used pianos and fields calls coming in from private sellers. Chances are that by the time you get out to see a piano at a private sale, one or more of these buyers has been there and left. They've left and the piano is still there because either the seller was asking too much or there was something fundamentally wrong with it. Dealers do need to buy it a little cheaper than you do because they plan to re-sell it, but they have the experience and skills to negotiate with the seller to get the price they need. Plus they know what to look for in a piano. So if a piano is still on the market, you should wonder why the dealers passed it over. But keep in mind it could be a perfectly good piano and they have their own reasons for passing it over—they may already have enough or too many of that particular kind, they prefer to only carry certain brands, etc.

Since used pianos that are truly a good buy sell so quickly, you as an individual buyer are usually at a handicap. You'll need time to bring in a tech to survey the instrument and time to arrange for pick up and delivery. Private sellers rarely take deposits to hold the piano, but you should still try and see what time line they are willing to extend you so you can do your inspection. Sellers run ads and are motivated to sell when they receive an acceptable price, but you shouldn't be pressured into a purchase if you're not ready. Once you've done your research and some shopping around, purchasing the right used piano can be very much a case of being in the right place at the right time.

The Least You Need to Know

- All pianos have a musical life expectancy, so even if the current condition of a used piano is good, you have to factor in how long you will be able to play it.

- The value of a piano derives from its useful musical life remaining, plus the current condition, plus the price.

- Do not commit to any used piano until you've shopped the new piano market and can compare your options.

- Pay an independent piano technician to survey any used piano you are seriously considering.

- Dealer warranties for used piano typically cover parts but not labor. Private-party warranties are usually worthless.

Part 2

Acoustic Pianos—Features and Benefits

In these chapters, we go under the lid and behind the keyboard to show you what pianos are made of and how they work. We explain why pianos don't get better with age and how to tell if a new one has staying power. We discuss which parts produce tone and touch and which parts are there for support. And we take a look at some of the more recent innovations in piano-making that can help you get more bang for your buck.

Why do you need to know the mechanics and technicalities of pianos? You don't have to become an expert, but you do need enough knowledge to understand what salespeople are talking about when they tout certain features of the pianos you're considering. The information offered in this section will help you distinguish sales hype from reality so that you can find the best piano for your needs and playing level.

Chapter 7

The Modern Acoustic Piano: Fine Art Meets Physics

In This Chapter

- How pianos work—the interplay of components and parts
- Becoming a smarter consumer by knowing piano mechanics
- Differences between vertical pianos and grand pianos
- How room size and acoustics affect a piano's sound

In the year 2000, the piano celebrated its three hundredth birthday. The acoustic pianos we play today are, therefore, the culmination of more than three centuries of the instrument's development. The modern acoustic piano is an extraordinary example of applied physics and mechanical engineering. It exemplifies not only a refinement of designs over the years but also an evolution of materials and construction processes as well.

We provide a considerable amount of technical information in this chapter to help you be a more informed consumer. We realize that some of you are the types who love to know how things work, who enjoy taking objects apart to see the guts of the mechanical workings. Others of you could probably care less how the sound gets from fingers on keys to the airwaves and into your ears. That's okay. We're not asking anyone to become an expert in the engineering of pianos. We just want to make sure you know enough about the inner workings of a piano to be able to understand the terminology that technicians and salespeople might use when describing the features and condition of a new or used piano.

How Piano Scales Work

The scale of a piano, or scale design, refers to the shape and thickness of the cast-iron plate (the major support structure of a piano, also called the harp); the lengths and thicknesses of the strings; the shape and placement of the bridges; and the weight, size, and density of the hammers.

Keyboard instruments prior to the piano had no dynamics. That is to say, the strings were plucked and the volume was the same, no matter how you attacked or played the keys. Scale designers strove to incorporate dynamic control (the ability to play louds and softs) in pianos. Some of these earliest pianos from about 1700 through the 1780s were called Fortepiano; the name itself called out the instrument's capabilities. In musical lexicon, the word piano is a volume descriptor for soft play. The word forte is a volume descriptor for loud play. Therefore, loud Soft = Forte Piano. However, the dynamic range of these pianos was still too limited for the evolving musical demands of composers and performers.

The modern piano incorporates a full cast-iron plate as a critical component in its scale design. This facilitates more projection, and *dynamic range*. The piano is often called the "voice of the orchestra" because the scope of its pitch range and the span of its dynamics (from soft to loud) make it very versatile, much like the human voice. These features also make the modern piano a complicated instrument.

def•i•ni•tion

Dynamic range is how loud or soft the piano can be played and how well the player can control these volume differences and the volumes in between.

With more than 10,000 parts, today's piano is an intricate amalgamation of wood, cast iron, steel, wool felt, copper, buckskin leather, and, sometimes, advanced plastics. In the following sections, we'll walk you through the process of how these materials and parts interact to create the sounds you hear. This is where fine art meets physics.

Hammers and Strings

Picture a violin lying on its back. Instead of dragging a bow across the strings, picture yourself striking the strings from below with a piece of wood covered in felt. This is the hammer of the piano. This is what happens when you play the keys on a piano. The hammers come up from below the strings on a grand piano or from the front of the strings on an upright piano.

The strings of a piano are bound at both ends and pass over a high point, known as a bridge. As a string is brought to tension, it creates a downward pressure on the bridge. This is called down bearing. The tone is carried from the string through the bridge into the amplifier. On a piano, the soundboard (more details on this in Chapter 9) serves as the amplifier. The board vibrates and amplifies the sound you hear.

Bridges and Scale Design

Let's now focus on the bridges of the piano. The bass bridge is one of two, or in rare cases, three bridges that the strings travel over in an acoustic piano. It sits higher than the other bridge(s), which are known as the tenor/treble bridge(s). The bass bridge's job is to transmit the music energy or vibrations of the strings down into the soundboard of the piano.

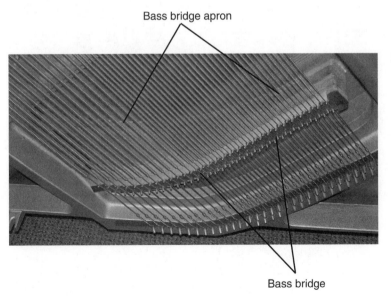

Bass bridge apron

Bass bridge.

Bass bridge

Bridge placement on the soundboard is part of the careful formula of the scale design process. One technique of scale design is to place the bridge as close to the tail of the piano as possible. This facilitates the longest string length. The problem with this method, though, is that way out by the edge of the soundboard, the tonal transmission is not optimized.

An overstrung scale occurs when the bass strings ride over the tenor (middle section) strings and cross over a separate or higher bridge. It provides for longer bass strings and better bridge placement. This idea was patented first by Jonas Chickering in the early 1800s. Prior to that, pianos had bass strings that paralleled the tenor and treble strings. The overstrung scale was first applied to a grand piano by Steinway in 1859, and within a few short years, every piano was using this design strategy.

Bass strings cross over other strings in the modern overstrung scale.

Mounting the bridge closer to the center of the soundboard optimizes tonal transmission but diminishes string length. To compromise, many designers call for a cantilever of the bass bridge. A cantilever is an apron or shelf of wood. One side of the shelf is mounted to the soundboard, and the bridge is mounted on the other side. The shelf hangs over the soundboard and allows for several more inches of string length. Often a cantilevered bridge is presented as a big selling feature, but the reality is that most pianos have this feature. So this is not a reason to buy or not to buy. It is simply a design feature. The tone is what is important, not how it got there.

Strings, Tension, and Unison

The pitch (frequency) of a note or string unison (group of strings sounding the same) is a function of the mass of the string and the tension it is under. Now allow us to explain that …. The mass of a piano string can be described in two ways—length and thickness. A longer, thinner string at a certain level of tension can have the same pitch as a shorter, thicker string at that same tension.

String unisons are strings that work together to produce the sound of a single note, one of 88 notes on a piano. Some notes in the bass section, located on the far left of the keyboard, have only one string per note. These are typically the lowest 8 to 12 notes. These strings are always wound or wrapped with copper.

As we move up the scale to the right, we encounter two strings per note. Each group of strings that produces a single note is called a unison. The strings must be tuned exactly together to form the sound of one note. Typically, pianos have 11 to 15 2-string unisons. These two-note unison strings are always wound with copper.

Finally, somewhere in the middle of the second octave, at about note (or key) number 30 from the left, unisons are comprised of 3 strings. Three-string unisons use steel wire without copper wrappings.

As the strings are brought up to proper tension, a downward force (down bearing) is exerted on the bridge and consequently down onto the soundboard. The thin soundboard is convex from the top, or bowed up slightly toward the center. The pressure of the down-bearing of the strings on the bridges tries to make the soundboard flat. Because a piano has more than 200 strings, ranging through 7¼ octaves, the struggle is dramatic. Eventually, the down bearing force always wins, and the soundboard becomes flatter, thus losing its ability to amplify properly. Fortunately, this process takes decades in most quality pianos. (Another reason why older does not mean better!)

The three strings of the unison must sound together at the same pitch and volume.

Overall, the strings exert about 40,000 pounds of pressure in a modern piano. This comprises the collective pull of all the strings. Tension in the strings creates the proper pitch for each note, while tension in the soundboard gives the tone vitality and projection.

Strings can either be single-tied or looped. Single-tied strings begin at a tuning pin and end at the opposite plate hitch pin. This stringing method was more common in older pianos but remains in some classic, new European models. A more common and modern method is for a string to begin at a tuning pin, go around the plate pin, and back to another tuning pin. This stringing practice is more expedient and used in mass production environments. It facilitates about 40 percent fewer plate pins to be installed and does not require individual loops to be turned into the end of each string.

B-Sharp

Some of the most poorly crafted pianos have single-tied strings, yet some of the finest pianos in the world have them as well. For mid- to low-priced pianos, single-tied strings are more of a sales tool than a real benefit. Don't base your decision to buy or not buy a piano based on this one design feature.

Proponents of single-tied stringing argue that the tone of each string is purer and uninfluenced by its neighbor. They also present the fact that if a string breaks, the other two in the unison can still play a decent tone and the music goes on.

Proponents of the more modern method propound the theory that single-tying adds no benefits to tone and is more labor intensive and expensive to produce.

Strings tied individually at the plate/hitch pins are known as single-tied strings.

The tension of the string is directly proportionate to the amount of down-bearing on the bridge that it generates. Too much down-bearing will inhibit the movement of the soundboard and stifle tone production. Too little down-bearing will result in too little energy transmission to the soundboard, resulting in a lifeless tone. Therefore, tension is a variable that must be considered in scale-design.

The volume or amplitude of the sound of a note is affected by the mass of the string. Higher notes have thinner strings and need two or three strings pitched together as a unison to equal the volume of the lower notes, which have longer and heavier strings. Mass is added to the lower strings to allow them to be short enough to be practical, by wrapping them with copper. The number of three-string, two-string, and single-string unisons, and the thickness of the wrappings are additional variables in piano scale-design. Without copper windings, a piano would have to be over 20 feet long!

Plates and Pins

You know now that tension of the string is one of the variables affecting pitch. As you move from left to right across the piano, the tensions of the strings need to be similar so as not to unduly stress the cast iron plate in one area over the other. The spread or distribution of the tension across the scale is another variable in piano scale design.

Several features are often presented by salespeople as exclusive to making his or her piano the best. Two of these are agraffes and pins. Agraffes are precision-ground solid brass fittings that screw into the cast iron plate. They have holes drilled into them from the front and back to the place where the holes meet in a very narrow point in the middle. This gives a precise fretting-off point and exact spacing for the strings as they pass through on their way to the tuning pins.

Most grand pianos utilize agraffes in the bottom two-thirds of their design. Some uprights use agraffes in their designs as well. While all grands use them, few uprights do. When seen in uprights, the agraffes are not a sign of quality or desirability, just a design and materials choice of the builder and a talking point for the salesperson. They are not a reason to buy or not buy a given upright.

Agraffes.

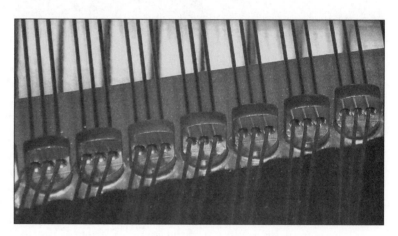

Plate pins and bridge pins are features that the string zigzags or turns around in its path from the tuning pin to the plate. Hardened steel pins about the thickness of a pencil lead and about an inch long are driven into the hardwood bridges in a staggered pattern. The strings are zigzagged through these pins. As the string is brought to tension, there is a sideways force or bearing on the string as it passes over the bridge. There is also a downward force or down-bearing as the string goes from the lower tuning pin level, up over the higher bridge, and down again to its termination at the plate pin. The plate pin is driven into a precise hole drilled into the cast iron plate. These are deliberately angled toward the rear of the piano to prevent the strings from slipping off when brought to tension.

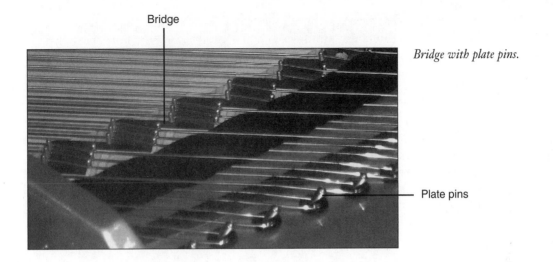

Bridge

Plate pins

Bridge with plate pins.

Dampers and Backchecks

Other parts you might hear about in a salesperson's presentation include dampers and backchecks. When one pushes down a piano key about three-eighths of an inch, the hammer travels about two inches to the string. It rebounds and is captured by a part called a backcheck so it won't "blubber" or strike the string multiple times. While the key is depressed, another assembly, called the dampers, lifts off the strings to allow them to sound. The key must be released to permit the hammer to begin another cycle. As the key is released, the damper comes back down on the string and stops the sound. All this "action" can take place in a fraction of a second, or may linger as long as the player allows it.

A backcheck is found for each key on every piano. On a grand piano, it is mounted to a stiff wire on the far end of the key. On uprights, it is mounted on a stiff wire on the end of the action assembly (all the linkage between the key you touch and the hammer that strikes the string; discussed in Chapter 9). The backcheck has a wooden core that is felted then covered in buckskin (yes, from real deer). On cheaper pianos, this buckskin is replaced with synthetic materials that never work as well or last as long.

Grand piano dampers ride on top of the strings, whereas vertical dampers are pressed against the strings by spring tension. Grand piano dampers may be up to 4.5" long in some larger grands. They have the luxury to be designed to the length necessary to stop and dampen the mass of the string they are assigned to. Vertical dampers are rarely larger than 1.5" and are hampered from being larger by hammer interference at the strike-point. This is one reason that 52" vertical pianos can have damper leakage on some bass notes.

Grand Backcheck.

Backcheck

Grand piano dampers.

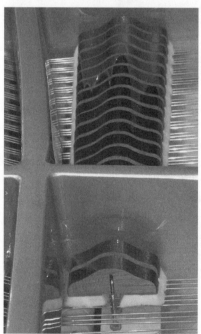

A piano in institutional use will withstand hundreds of thousands of keystrokes in its lifetime. If you were to view slow motion, time-lapse photography of this process, you'd probably be amazed to see how, when close up and in slow motion, it looks somewhat violent. Considerable force and vibration travel back through the hammer and its shank into the mechanism. It is a testimony to design, materials, and construction that pianos last longer than a few weeks!

Gaps and Struts

A designer must place several open areas in the plate casting to accommodate the bridges. To bridge these gaps there must be vertical and horizontal struts cast into the iron plate to support the tension. How many, where, and how big the gaps should be are significant variables in piano scale design.

Grand plate showing windows for tone escapement and struts.

Tone holes

Struts

Decisions must be made on thicknesses of the castings, where to leave windows for tone escapement, and precisely where to locate fasteners, stringing appliances, etc. Too much iron can dampen the sound. Too little iron can be unstable and even dangerous.

> ### Rhythm and News
>
> In our examination of piano scale design, we've identified nearly two dozen variables at work. Change one variable and the result ripples throughout the entire project. A minute change here or there can create a huge change somewhere else. Frequently, salesmen point to plate structures and tout them as an exclusive feature. In our experience, nearly all modern piano plates are more than adequate for the job.

How Key-Action Mechanisms Work

When we look at the key-action mechanism, also called key-action assembly, more physics come into play. The key-action mechanism is the linkage that connects the key and the hammer.

In a typical grand piano key-action mechanism, thousands of parts must be engineered and constructed to within thousandths of an inch tolerance. For instance, the power of a keystroke can be lost if the key frame is not bedded or flush on the key bed. A hammer will blubber or strike a string multiple times if it is not checked by the backcheck. A hammer will block against a string if it is not released by the let-off button. A key will not repeat if the repetition lever spring does not impart enough tension. A note will not cut off cleanly and predictably if a damper felt does not seat firmly and evenly on the string. As you can see, each of these tiny little parts has a function to perform with a specific timing and movement within the keystroke; too soon or late, too little or too much, and the performance fails.

The key-action assembly also incorporates a diversity of materials: wood, aluminum, steel, iron, brass, lead, and several kinds of wool felt. These 10 or so divergent materials may expand and contract with moisture and temperature at different proportions and rates. They must withstand hundreds of thousands, even millions of keystrokes over the life of the piano. Each of the 88 keys may have as many as 50 individual parts. Each of these parts must be fitted to work in conjunction with the others to allow the key to work as specified. In addition, all of the 88 key assemblies must work in consort with the rest to provide an even and consistent touch across the keyboard.

Vertical Pianos vs. Grand Pianos

Vertical pianos and grand pianos have many similarities, but they also have some significant differences that affect the way they perform.

Why the Touch of Grand Pianos Is Better

The strings of a vertical piano are perpendicular to the floor. The key action sits in front of the strings. The hammers rest at about a 45-degree angle to the floor. In a grand piano, the strings are parallel with the floor, and the action sits below the strings. The hammers rest at about a 45-degree angle below that of the floor. Over the lifetime of the piano, this fundamental 90-degree orientation difference is significant in the performance and consistency of the two styles of instruments. The grand piano hammer is controlled by gravity, and the vertical hammer is bound by springs and levers. As a result, a grand piano key can be played faster and more sensitively.

Vertical piano mechanisms depend more on springs and levers to control the motion of the hammers and dampers to and from the strings. Grand pianos possess the luxury of using a free and constant force known as gravity. So, springs wear out and change value, whereas gravity never changes. Therefore, grand pianos always have a repetition sensitivity advantage over upright pianos. The upright piano mechanism becomes noticeable and somewhat of a hindrance beyond the upper intermediate levels of play and instruction.

There is nothing wrong with learning to play on an upright piano. Hundreds of thousands of students have. Your teacher will tell you that after about year four or five, there will be a progress advantage to practicing each day on a grand piano.

Bigger Is Usually Better

All else being equal, which is rarely the case, bigger is better in grand pianos. Longer strings generally have a sweeter, more resonant tone. More square inches of soundboard area usually develop more volume and sustain. Bigger pianos may accommodate longer keys—piano keys extend well beyond the fallboard, and the unseen part of the key is longer than its visible component—that should offer better leverage.

We have encountered a few prospective customers who have drawn the conclusion that 52" pianos are of better quality than their 48" and 44" little brothers and sisters. Rarely are there qualitative differences from one model to another within a brand name line-up. The difference in the 52" piano is quantitative, that is, it will have a bigger sound, not a better quality sound or more responsive touch.

Yet bigger pianos have a number of downsides. They are bulkier and take up more space. The taller pianos usually have fewer cabinet designs and finish options. Plus bigger sound is not always desirable when beginners are practicing scales. Sometimes less is more. Regrettably, the tallest of new uprights, at 52", exhibit a few endemic damper problems in stopping the sound cleanly and fully. These biggest of uprights are also in the upper range of pricing, whereas lower profile grands can be bought for the same money, or less. For big pianos, we believe that grand pianos are preferable to verticals for touch reasons. This advice comes from our 44+ years of experience in the piano business. Our advice may run contrary to what your teacher recommends, or what the piano tuner prefers, but it comes from the heart.

Key Note

A lower profile grand piano is often preferable to a higher profile upright piano.

We have heard salespeople and others say, "If you can't buy at least a 6-foot grand, don't bother with a grand. Get the 52-inch upright instead. It will have better tone." Or, "If you must get an upright, consider only the 52-inch model." This, of course, may be because either of these categories will produce a nice commission for the salesperson, or it may honestly be their opinion.

But there are several considerations attached to these recommendations:

◆ Six-foot-size grand pianos in the most popular brands fall in the $25,000 price range and higher—rarely within a beginner's budget.

◆ Fifty-two-inch upright pianos in the most popular brands often cost nearly $10,000 or higher. Yet many wonderful new grands fall into this price range or less.

◆ A repetition limitation is inherent in *every* upright piano ever made. One must let the key return nearly all the way up before the mechanism resets and is ready to play another note. *Every* grand piano mechanism contains advantageous geometry and components that allow only the pressure to be relieved on the key for the mechanism to reset and be ready to play. This allows faster play, more expressive play, greater dynamic control, etc.

◆ The shape of a grand piano allows for optimum bridge placement and sound transmission and projection. Every upright piano made is a compromise because of its upright nature and its rectangular shape.

◆ Overall string length may be longer in a 52" upright, but the critical speaking length of a string is likely shorter than its counterpart in a small grand. Overall soundboard square inches may be greater on a 52" upright, but much of it is blocked off, as dead area, by design. (Sound energy travels with the grain of the wood in a soundboard. In a vertical piano, the grain runs diagonally. The top left and bottom right corners of the soundboard are relatively useless tonally and are blocked off to recycle sound energy back into the board.)

We believe the only reason a customer should consider a 52" upright is when he or she absolutely does not have room for any kind of grand piano, absolutely wants the best tone and most volume available in an upright, and has a budget that will accommodate a decent quality 52" instrument.

Room Acoustics and Your New Piano

The size and shape of your room have a definite effect on the tone and volume of your piano. It can be painful to listen to a big instrument in a room that's too small for it. Large pianos possess projection characteristics that cannot actualize in cramped quarters.

The height and shape of your ceiling are also significant acoustic factors. Sound bounces and returns differently from pitched, vaulted, beamed, cathedral, and flat ceilings. Wood, plaster, acoustic tile, acoustic sprayed (cottage cheese or popcorn type) all produce a different acoustic signature.

Windows and wall treatments affect sound significantly as well. Lots of glass and shutters bring a very reflective element into the equation. Hanging tapestries and draperies produces a softening effect. Even the ratio of hard wood furniture to soft, stuffed furniture can affect acoustics.

Floors also represent a critical element in the mix. Thick pile carpet with premium thick padding; short, dense glue-down carpets; wood floors; ceramic tile or marble floors—all of these variations in flooring can produce a spectrum of sound from soft and deadening to harsh and reflective. Often a thick area rug placed under the piano can make a huge difference in tone and volume when the piano sits on a hard surface.

Seasoned professionals can help advise you on placement and acoustics. The more detail you give them about your room, the better they can guide you to the right instrument.

The Least You Need to Know

◆ Pianos are complex instruments with more than 10,000 mechanical parts.

◆ The strings exert tremendous pressure at about 40,000 pounds on the piano.

◆ The scale design of a piano is a complex matrix of variables where no one element is more important than another.

◆ Grand pianos play faster and more fluidly than vertical pianos, and are therefore preferable for more advanced players.

◆ Room size, acoustics, and even furnishings can affect the tone and volume of a piano.

Chapter 8

What Makes a Quality Acoustic Piano

In This Chapter

◆ Materials pianos are made of

◆ Mass production versus handcrafting

◆ The geographic origins and composition of tone

◆ The difference string thickness makes

So you'd like to buy a good piano and get a good value for the price you pay. You'd like a piano with a sound that pleases you and that will last for many years. In other words you want a quality piano. So what makes a piano high quality? The greatest sales presentation in the world can't put quality into a product. No stamp, seal, or association assures quality. Quality must come from a mindset of leadership and commitment from the manufacturers who make the product. Dedication to quality must run from the chairman of the board to the worker who boxes up the finished product. Every link in the chain must connect with the concept of quality, or the pursuit of it is lost. All this holds undeniably true with pianos.

In this chapter, we help you understand how the various types of materials used in making pianos, as well as different styles of craftsmanship, affect the quality of the finished product, and ultimately, your satisfaction with your purchase. We also help you evaluate the type of tone you prefer, and we look at some of the physics about strings and the sounds they produce. Not a physics whiz? Don't worry. We tell you just the bare minimum you need to know to be dangerous on your quest for a good piano.

Design Is the Cornerstone of Quality

Usually, a piano designer does not start out to build a 6-foot grand piano or a 48-inch upright. He starts with a physics problem, and the scale evolves as he works toward a solution. Piano designs are perfected over decades, and when perfected, they are rarely altered. Some of the most famous brands and models go back to the 1920s and 1930s or earlier.

Consider some of the concerns of a piano designer: overall string length, speaking length of the string, thickness or gauge of the string wire, bridge placement, cast iron plate thickness and configuration, uniformity of stress over the plate, single or double copper-wound strings, and triple/double/single string notes (unisons). Does it make your head spin? This is all in a day's work for a piano designer. Many factories have adopted design technologies to enhance and speed up the process of design evolution. This approach, however, will never replace the mind, hand, or ear in the conception of fine quality pianos. Without a top-notch design, no amount of craftsmanship or quality materials will make a good piano.

> **Key Note**
>
> Good pianos are combinations of good designs, good materials, skilled artisans with attention to detail, and the time necessary to hold crafting to the highest standards of excellence.

Piano Materials

All pianos today have materials in common—cast-iron plates, plastic key covers, steel strings (some with copper winding covers), steel tuning pins, and wool-felt hammers and dampers. Many of these components are purchased from vendors who supply these same parts to many different piano manufacturers. This produces a situation similar to a Ford, Volvo, and Jaguar being mechanical cousins—while they may look different and have vastly different prices, they share some identical parts. The same holds true with certain mechanical parts of a piano.

At each step in the process, choices must be made as to parts' specifications. To save a nickel on each hammer felt is to save $4.40 on each piano. When you make 50,000 pianos, this equals nearly a quarter of a million dollars per year!

With large companies, cost analysis has become an art form in piano building. Many dollars are at stake; but if saving that nickel on hammers causes the ultimate performance of the instrument to slide below the public's needs and expectations, then all is lost. Clearly top-tier pianos in the $50,000+ category have few or no compromises in materials selection. As the price decreases, the number of compromises increases. Entry-level pianos are in fact built to a price point supported by marketing analysis more than a certain level of musical performance.

Piano Craftsmanship

A fork in the road in piano-building methods appeared in the past century, primarily due to the introduction of assembly lines and interchangeable parts. This created a divide between mass production and handcrafting. Both theories and practices of manufacturing have merit—both can produce good pianos, and both have some weaknesses.

High-Volume Mass Production

A factory utilizing high-volume mass production techniques can build more pianos at a faster rate. Mass production uses an assembly line in which the workers are trained to perform one simple function in the fabrication of the piano. Training is often quick and simple, and the worker skill level can be limited to one or two simple and repetitive functions. It is rare that a worker is trained to perform other functions on the line. Even rarer is the worker who understands how his or her function relates to the whole.

By definition, the parts for any mass-produced product, not just pianos, are generic in nature and not specific to an individual unit. For pianos, so much of their make-up is wood, and wood density and

Key Note

More expensive pianos offer better and more finely crafted parts and components. The differences are incremental in nature and are rarely things that the consumer can see. However, an experienced player can certainly feel and hear the results in design and material differences. Also, design and material compromises frequently translate into compromised longevity and durability.

dimension vary. So in mass-production situations, the wood parts must be fashioned to permit a certain give or take so they can fit many or all models.

Mass production makes extreme use of automation wherever possible. The high-volume style of production is less dependent on workers and more dependent on machinery and supply lines, or raw materials and pre-made sub-assemblies. Some companies, including Yamaha and Kawai, have achieved extraordinary levels of precision in the manufacture of their parts and the assembly process.

Low-Volume Handcrafting

The philosophy of handcrafting is based on producing a limited number of units built to high levels of fit, finish, performance, and durability. In this type of manufacturing, the workers are typically cross-trained and have a skill level for performing many or all of the building functions. Training for these workers often requires years of apprenticeship, thereby making them much more valuable to their company than workers in mass-production factories.

While the product moves throughout the production process in a somewhat similar fashion to that of mass production, the worker in a handcrafting environment has control over a unit until he or she is satisfied that it meets the high standard of a master craftsman. Workers perform quality control at each function or stage, and must personally sign off on any unit to which they have contributed.

With more time to spend on each unit and fewer units to produce, materials selection can encompass a wider variety of processes and seasoning. For example, designers can employ more expensive hard woods, which tend to reflect sound energy back into the soundboard better than softer woods, whereas in a high-volume setting, designers tend to rely on softer woods or plywoods. Casting processes for plates can follow the more traditional wet-sand techniques as opposed to the vacuum process expediencies of mass production (see Chapter 10 for more on the casting process).

def•i•ni•tion

Intarsia is the technique of creating a wood mosaic inlay.

Because of the extra time permitted and the craftsmanship available, parts for handcrafted pianos can be fit more carefully and closely to each individual unit. Finishing can encompass more stages, resulting in more beautiful or intricate finishes with *intarsia* inlays and marquetry.

Which Type of Craftsmanship Is Better?

As always in the piano world, the proof is in the touch, tone, sustain, cabinetry, and durability. Brands make their mark over decades, and the features in any musical instrument are only as good as the original design, materials used, and quality and care in construction and assembly. Mechanical products, such as cars, lend themselves well to mass-production, as Henry Ford proved. Pianos are combinations of a great deal of mechanical detail and a variety of materials, yet they are also encased in furniture that must perform musically and achieve superior sound.

We have seen bad and good examples of instruments born from both manufacturing processes. Both can produce high quality pianos. The nature of the build process should be only one consideration to factor into your decision-making process. As always, the real proof is how the piano plays and how it sounds.

> **Rhythm and News**
>
> The romantic vision of gray-haired old men wielding mallets and chisels to handcraft a piano represents only a small part of today's handcrafting process. Even in a low-volume, handcrafting environment, we have been surprised to see a Computer Numeric Control (CNC) machine, which is a remarkable robotic cutting and milling device, right next to that old craftsman!

An Introduction to Sound and Tone

Each piano has an inherent voice—its distinct tone and sound—that is a product of its scale design, hammer configuration, and build quality. This inherent voice is amplified and projected by the soundboard. The soundboard itself is not usually a participant in the tone character, which is what makes scale designing the very top of the craft of piano building.

Since each piano comes with a certain sound, we encourage you to do some homework and listen to several brands and sizes to discover what sound you like before you decide on one for the next 50 years. It is true that a top-level piano technician can "voice" the hammers to influence the tone of a piano a few percentage points one way or the other, but the basic tonal character is built into the instrument at the factory—in other words it's hard-wired—making its materials and scale design, key compositions of its inherent sound.

There are three basic sound camps in the piano world today: the European sound, the Asian sound, and the domestic American sound. Let's examine each of these categories to give you a sense of what you can expect to hear out of each of them.

The European Sound

Into the late 1700s in Europe, the modern piano was still evolving from harpsichords and clavichords. The pianos at that time had a thin sound and the instruments were fragile, often not surviving lengthy performances. Their fragile construction resulted in lower volume, less sustain, thinner tone, and less tuning stability. Although the earliest pianos did not have the dynamic range of modern pianos, they did begin to develop a somewhat universal tone with a great clarity that was somewhat heavy in the *fundamental* and weaker in the *partial tones*.

Today, European pianos usually have a heavier bass in their sound, mainly because of the way European music has developed over the past 125 years. With the rise of nationalism, composers were inspired to stir men's souls with rhythmic movement in the lower tones, such as with marching music. European builders used—and continue to use—indigenous woods of beech or birch to form their cases (grand rims and vertical cabinets) and bracing (support members under the grand piano and back supports on verticals), and they found that cold-growth spruce from the Alps worked best for their soundboards. The results of these characteristics deliver a clear, bell-like tone to most ears.

def•i•ni•tion

Partial tones, sometimes simply called partials, are basically overtones or sympathetic vibrations of other higher pitched strings.

Fundamental tones are the main tones for each note on the piano, the strongest sounds you hear.

The Asian Sound

At the turn of the twentieth century, Japanese manufacturers were known as great imitators rather than great innovators, yet this attitude has changed dramatically over the past 60 years. Today, Japanese manufacturers represent the forefront of the most recent developments in piano designs and material evolutions.

In those early days, the Japanese emulated more accessible European pianos as the basis for their piano beginnings. Without the philosophical underpinnings of the original scale-design engineering, they ended up with the clarity of European sound, but with even fewer of the partials in tone. This made piano tuners happy, as the partials are simply noise to them. Partly because of their own design tweaks and their materials selections, they also developed a certain subtle metallic quality to the tone as well. As the Korean, and later the Chinese, designers came along, they copied these early Japanese designs, materials, and production techniques. The tone of Asian pianos is often described as clear, bright, with a little edge to it.

Most of Asia lacks great stands of hardwoods. What they do have are indigenous woods that are faster growing but softer woods such as mahogany, teak, and large stands of pine. Today, cases and bracing in most Asian pianos are constructed of native mahogany with soundboards made of spruce from Alaska.

The American Sound

In the mid to late 1800s, American piano makers, many of whom had recently emigrated from Europe, latched onto local materials including maple and spruce from the local mountains of the eastern United States, and later those from Alaska and Canada. The goal was to build pianos stronger than their European counterparts, so American pianos quickly became recognized for their durability.

American music in the past 100 years has had a more lyrical development, and piano designers have catered to more balanced designs across the scale. Many American designs offer remarkable projection for their size. Their sound spectrum includes more of the partials at greater amplitudes, offering additional color and breadth to the tone. American manufacturers produced a warm, round, hollow, and woody sound.

In looking at all three sounds, nearly a generation and a half of music students have had their only significant exposure to piano sound from Asian pianos. (Yamaha and Kawai have done a phenomenal job in garnering endorsements from teachers and technicians and now dominate the institutional market.) Rarely have even American graduate-level piano students been exposed to European grands due to their rarity and price. Steinway & Sons is represented in many college-level environments as the sole American representative. In the past, mid-priced American models from Knabe, Chickering, Baldwin, and Sohmer were popular and kept the American sound present in the ears of students and performers, with lower-end Wurlitzers and Kimballs dominating home-use instruments. Today, many music students hear the domestic sound of American piano as tubby, muddy, dark, thick, and heavy because they have grown up to a sound from overseas.

Making Sense of the Sound

As much as sound is a personal matter—something you and only you can know if you like or don't like—it is also a piano feature that can be analyzed and described scientifically. We can examine the various sound camps graphically with the use of a decent microphone and a reasonably good *oscilloscope*. If you take a 6-foot grand piano representative of each of an average American, Asian and European brand, you would see clear differences under the scope. What we would see on the scope is: when you play concert A, which is 440 cycles per second (this is what today is considered concert pitch), on each of the instruments, you will see a typical bell-shaped curve on the screen. This curve comprises pinpoints of partial tones that register audibly on the scope with just one note played, and there will be three distinct signatures to the composition of that *sine wave*.

def•i•ni•tion

An **oscilloscope** is an instrument that can visually display sound waves.

A **sine wave** is a graphic representation of a wave form.

Asian Tone Signature

European Tone Signature

American Tone Signature

Concert A played on Asian, European, and American pianos.

On the Asian piano, you'll see the greatest amplitude on the fundamental pitch of 440 cycles and nearly an absence of partial peaks to the left and right of that fundamental. On the European example, you'll see a lower amplitude on the middle spike and some degree of amplitude on the partials on either side. On the American sample, you see a greater distribution of amplitude to a wider range of harmonics (little spikes to the left and right of the main tone). All of this speaks to the tonal color and its impact on the ear of the listener. None of the three is better than the other, each is just different, and one may be more pleasing to your ear than another.

Another aspect of tone is the brightness scale into which each genre, brand, and model falls. If you were to envision a spectrum of tone that on the left end is very mellow and on the right end is extremely bright, the sound of each piano will fit somewhere along that scale of brightness when played at the same volume level and with the same attack (or touch of the key). To give you the extremes of this scale in examples, imagine the sound coming from a medium-size portable radio wrapped in six layers of your grandmother's thick quilt—this would be on the mellow end of the scale. Now imagine the sound of a hammer banging on a metal trashcan lid—this would fall on the bright end of the scale.

Over the years, we have actually heard several pianos that fit both descriptions, and everything in between. Luckily, pianos you are likely to consider will fall somewhere closer to the middle of this spectrum. Again, different scales of brightness are not better or worse, just different and a matter of personal preference.

B-Sharp

Don't let a salesperson tell you what sound or tone is best. Listen with your own ears to determine what you prefer.

The degree of sustain that the piano enables is another important component of tone. Plunk a key on a piano and hold it down until you can no longer hear or feel the note—this is its sustain. You can quantify sustain by clocking this amount of time. To be fair, you must only compare pianos of the same length or height, as these have an impact on sustain. Longer sustain is better (it is also very hard to fake in poorer quality designs).

Tone is also characterized by the relative projection qualities of grand pianos. Typically, manufacturers understand that pianos 6 feet long and larger are used more in institutional or recital settings, where the intent is to fill a room with music for listeners to enjoy and critique. As a result, designers typically engineer more projection into these larger instruments and the sound is more ambient, reflecting back to the player from the walls, floor, and ceiling. The mid-sizes, around 5'8", offer a more personal listening experience for the player, with sound collecting more just behind the music rack for the player to hear. If you plan to play for your own personal enjoyment most of the time, you might consider this aspect of tone more carefully and listen for it when you're shopping.

String Thickness—What Difference Does It Make?

To accomplish changes in pitch, scale designers must add and subtract mass to the strings. Designers do this by changing the length and thickness of the wire. For example, the thickness of the wire necessary to achieve lower notes would be too thick to work around the pins in the piano or too long to fit in the cabinet (or your house for that matter). So designers add mass by wrapping the wire with one or two layers of copper windings, and this allows the sounds of those lower bass notes.

For the same scale to be played at the same pitch, 5-foot long baby grands must have thicker strings than 9-foot long concert grands. The same is true for uprights. The shorter uprights have thicker strings than the taller professional uprights.

Thicker strings do not flex as easily and therefore do not have the singing, lyrical qualities of the taller/longer pianos with thinner, more flexible strings. For this reason, when customers ask for a more lyrical, or song-like, piano, salespeople steer them to bigger pianos. Customers often think that the salesperson is just trying to sell something bigger and more expensive, but bigger pianos usually do sound sweeter and more pleasing and have more dynamic range in the fine gradients of volume. Unfortunately, they also cost more!

Hopefully now you understand some of the technical, musical, and performance considerations in selecting a piano. These aspects are much more important to the quality than whether the piano has German strings or 40 widgets rather than 20. In the final analysis, it always comes down to touch and tone, and the quality found in the eye and ear of the beholder.

The Least You Need to Know

◆ Design, materials, and craftsmanship all play a part in the quality of a piano.

◆ Handcrafted pianos from low-volume production facilities are often touted as better than high-volume, mass-produced pianos, but that's not always the case.

◆ Assess the aspects of tone including brightness, sustain, and relative projection.

◆ People hear tone differently. There is no one "right" sound for a piano.

Chapter 9

The Composition of Touch and Tone

In This Chapter

- ◆ What to look for in a soundboard
- ◆ Why hammers are a critical element
- ◆ The role of the strings
- ◆ Unlocking the key to a good key-action
- ◆ What you should feel in the touch of a piano
- ◆ Pushing the pedals

In Chapter 7, you learned about the inner workings of a piano—how the many parts and components work together to produce sound. Now, in this chapter, we build on that knowledge by offering the straight scoop on how certain major components affect touch and tone. The more you know about this, the better you will recognize a sales presentation that's on the right track, providing you with correct and useful information.

The Soundboard—A Critical Component

The speaker and amplifier of an acoustic piano is the soundboard, a thin ($^{1}/_{4}$" to $^{3}/_{8}$") layer of wood under or behind the cast iron plate. It is the soundboard that actually produces the sound of the piano that you hear, since strings by themselves lack the necessary mass to push enough air to be heard. The tone is transmitted from the strings through the bridges that press against the soundboard.

All Spruced Up

Nearly all soundboards are made of spruce wood (tone wood). Companies have experimented with many different kinds of materials for soundboards, but none works as well as spruce wood.

The goal is to find wood that has grown in a very cold environment. Excessive cold encourages slow growth, resulting in closely joined growth rings that are more regularly spaced and more linear in direction when the tree is sawn into quarters to make a soundboard. All of these characteristics affect the transmission and amplification of the tone.

The wood itself has a unique cell structure that acts like little tone chambers that transmit and amplify the sound energy imparted by the strings. There is probably more controversy over soundboards and their construction than over any other component in the piano, since they are so critical to the sound, and very expensive to replace.

Companies often get really nit picky about their sources for spruce. Their specifications for grains per inch, uniformity of color, and linear nature of the wood grain are pretty stringent. European spruce tends to be a little whiter and finer grained than Alaskan or Canadian. This is simply a characteristic of the wood, not necessarily an indication of quality differences. What we look for in a good board is fine, closely aligned grain running straight and true, with uniform color, no wavy, darker color spots (often mineral content), and no irregular patterns.

Key Note

Soundboards do not create or modify (or should not modify) the sound of a piano. They only amplify it.

Life Expectancy

The soundboard must be as flexible as possible to amplify sensitively even the softest of sounds. Yet it must be sturdy enough to withstand great tension for the musical life of the piano. To accomplish both flexibility and strength, *most* companies taper or thin the edges of the boards before fastening them into the piano. This tapering allows the soundboard to be more flexible, thereby enhancing performance. Also the industry standard is that the soundboard be made from a single layer of quarter-sawn spruce boards glued edge to edge.

The useful musical life expectancy of a soundboard depends on many variables in the construction and materials of the other parts of the piano. Most soundboards will show cracks and reduced crown (a convex bowed shape) at anywhere between 30 and 60 years. It's one of the most expensive components to rebuild or to replace, as it requires the piano to be unstrung and the plate to be hauled out. Some quality rebuilders feel an obsession about replacing soundboards and do it on nearly every rebuild, while others prefer to *shim* and preserve the original soundboard and almost never replace an original board. We are minimalists on this issue. Unless the original board has failed, with substantial loss of crown and multiple unrepairable cracks, we vote to preserve the originals whenever possible.

def•i•ni•tion

A **shim** is a thin tapered piece of wood used to fill a gap in the soundboard.

Soundboard Controversies

Some of the soundboard controversy over the years has developed over the source of the spruce, i.e., Alaskan vs. Adirondack vs. Alpine from various sides of the Alps mountain range. Most of the controversy, however, has arisen over a practice by some companies to create soundboards using a laminated technique that uses multiple thinner layers of spruce, rather than a single layer of wood. These laminated boards are invariably stronger, resist cracking more effectively, and frequently lead to extended warranties. Top-end manufacturers have resisted using laminated soundboards for a variety of reasons, and as a result, many experts relegate pianos with laminated boards to the lower echelons of quality and performance. While laminated boards are not the standard, the practice is growing.

As always, the verdict comes down to the question, "How does it sound?" We've heard pianos with solid spruce soundboards that sound dreadful and ones with laminated boards that sound beautiful. One thing we do know for sure: laminated soundboards are more durable.

A grand piano soundboard.

In this picture you can see what a grand piano soundboard looks like without the strings and the cast iron plate. This is a complete grand piano soundboard with the bridges attached.

Hammer Time

Next to the scale design, as described in Chapter 7, the hammers—the felted parts that strike the stings—contribute most significantly to the tone of a piano. The size, weight, shape, density, tension, core wood, under-felting, stapling, and gluing of the hammers can all affect tone production.

Hammer Construction

Hammers are made starting with a hardwood core, and are traditionally made in 2-foot-long strips from which individual hammers are cut or sawed apart. Hammer felt (more on this in a minute) is cut from large sheets into triangular-shape strips and is fastened to the wood hammer core under tremendous pressure. It is this pressure that gives hammers the resiliency to strike the strings and rebound thousands of times over the life of the hammer.

Many kinds of wire staple fasteners have been devised over the years to augment the holding power of the glue in the construction. (Your salesperson may make the type of fastener an important selling point.) Three types of fasteners are common staples, used from the top and bottom relying on the holding power of the wood against the staple, and t-wire and compression-wire staples that rely on the physical properties of the wire going completely through the hammer head and are crimped or twisted and crimped on the other side.

 B-Sharp

If the glue degrades or the felt swells because of the pressure, the hammer felt may become detached from the core. This condition renders the hammers worthless, and they must be replaced.

Common Stapled Hammers
Driven through felt and into the wood core
from both sides.

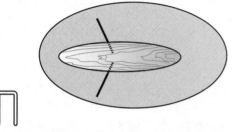

T-Wire Stapled Hammers
One hole is drilled through felt and wood.
T-wire is forced in and ends are crimped back.

Compression-Wire Stapled Hammers
Two holes are drilled through felt and wood. Staple is
forced in and ends are twisted and crimped back.

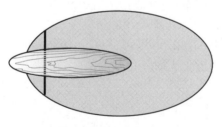

The hammer size and weight must be matched to the string gauge and speaking length as they relate to the scale design. Too small or light, a hammer leaves power untapped. Too large or heavy, a hammer overpowers the scale and actually diminishes the tone. Designers and manufacturers play with the variables a great deal to find just the right match of hammer to piano string for the model.

The bass hammer is larger than the treble hammer.

The mass-production larger factories, such as Yamaha, Kawai, Samick Music Corp., and Pearl River, use their own proprietary hammers. These larger factories control the raw materials, designs, and manufacture of these critical components, and they have tweaked their variables to come up with the best performance in the most cost-effective manner.

Hammer-making is an exacting and expensive process. Unless a company is producing 20,000 or more pianos per year, it would likely buy hammers from a variety of vendors that specialize in this component. (Steinway & Sons in New York is an exception; they make their own hammers.)

Since most European manufacturers are relatively low-volume piano builders, producing just a few hundred or thousand units per year, it is not cost effective for them to make their own hammers and key-action assemblies (the linkage between the key and the hammer that strikes the string). The bulk of European manufacturers subcontract these components to a specialist company called Renner. (The Renner action is much touted and is considered by some to be the international performance standard. Typically, Renner actions are installed with Renner hammers.)

The Felt

The best hammer felts are made from virgin wool—the very first shearing of sheep. Virtually baby hair, virgin wool has the longest fiber and greatest lanolin content. It can be removed from each sheep only once. That is why it is so rare and expensive. With each successive shearing, the wool fiber becomes drier and more brittle (like human hair) and has less lanolin content.

Hammer felt is graded by weight in pounds, which is measured by weighing a square yard of the prepared felt. So when you hear or read specifications about 18-pound hammers, for instance, you'll know it does not refer to the weight of each individual hammer, but to the weight of the whole square yard it was made from.

Hammer felts are mounted, under great pressure, to the wooden core of the hammer. Tension must be in the hammer felt to offer a resilient bounce off the string after it is struck, sort of like that bounce a new tennis ball has right out of the can, as opposed to an old one that's been in an open can left in the trunk of your car for a couple of years. Too much tension and not enough tension are not good; either can stifle tone production.

Under-felting is a term you will want to be familiar with. Frequently, manufacturers use a thin layer of colored felt attached to the wooden hammerhead core under the final white felt that plays the string. This is often pointed out by salespeople as a supreme selling feature, yet we are not convinced. If everything else is right with the hammer, under-felting is probably not necessary.

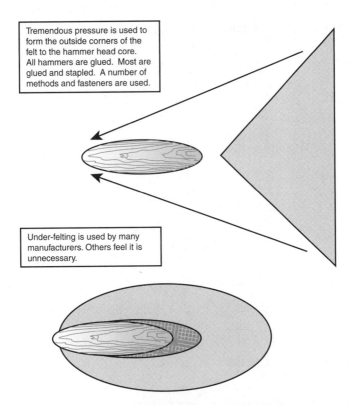

Tremendous pressure is used to form the outside corners of the felt to the hammer head core. All hammers are glued. Most are glued and stapled. A number of methods and fasteners are used.

Under-felting is used by many manufacturers. Others feel it is unnecessary.

Hammer head with under-felting.

Hammer head with no under-felting.

Tone Regulating Hammers

Even the best quality hammers must be tone regulated (often this is called voicing) after they are installed. Factories and dealerships give more of this time-consuming treatment to more expensive pianos than less expensive ones. Tone regulating consists of altering the shape of the hammer and changing the consistency of it by softening or hardening it.

Shaping takes place by filing the hammer with proper grit sand paper mounted on a stick. The hammer should be somewhat diamond shaped so that the surface striking the string is not too broad.

Softening hammers to tone down the sound typically consists of puncturing (sticking) the felt with needles, a process which breaks down the fibers and loosens them up. Too many needle sticks, sticks too deep, or punctures in the wrong part of hammers can make them worthless such that they must be replaced.

Hardening hammers to bring out more sound typically occurs by ironing the felt with hot irons. (Not too hot or the hammers can be scorched and ruined.) Another method is to introduce a hardening agent into the felt by dissolving the hardening agent in a solvent and dripping the right amount onto the hammer felt in just the right place. Prudent techs do this slowly, a little at a time. One must wait at each step for the solvent to dry completely before trying the sound.

All these processes sound rather dramatic, even somewhat barbaric, considering they are frequently perpetrated on brand new, expensive instruments. The more expensive the instrument, the more likely it will have been treated to put it at that 110 percent level of performance that discriminating customers desire. We have heard customers announce, "I don't want any piano that has had the hammers doped or lacquered." But nearly every factory and field technician uses this process to build tone. It is perfectly okay.

The useful musical life for a set of decent hammers, on a piano played regularly, is about 25 to 35 years, with regular shaping and voicing along the way. It's not a huge process, given that replacement runs about $500 to $1,500.

Especially when looking at used and rebuilt pianos, a salesperson may point to new hammers. Be advised that most rebuilders simply install raw hammers and expect the owner to provide shaping and voicing in the home, at the owner's expense, which can involve two or three days of expensive tech time.

In recent years, manufacturers' brand names of hammers have been given greater profile. Great discussions are generated among enthusiasts about what brand and even model of hammer is better, discussions usually related to rebuilding an old piano where there is a choice of materials involved. Hammer choices are not options when it comes to new pianos. You may hear brand names like Renner Blue, Imadegawa, Abel, Ronsen, Wurzen felt, and others mentioned in sales presentations. A piano is a musical instrument. It should be more than the sum of its parts. Quality components are important, but the proof is in the performance.

So what is the best hammer for your new piano? More than likely, it's the one the manufacturer specified. The real proof for this is, you guessed it, how the piano sounds to your ear. If you like the sound compared to other pianos in that size and price range, then it does not really matter what hammer they used. If you don't like the sound, it certainly does not matter!

Strings and Copper

The silver-looking strings in the top two-thirds of the piano scale are simply steel music wire, of the proper thickness gauge, tied at one end or looped around a hitch pin and then fastened to the tuning pin at the other. The silver strings are known as the tenor and treble strings. Tenor strings are located near the center of the piano while the treble strings make the higher pitches toward the right end of the piano (when facing the keys). Tenor and treble strings are grouped into threes; thus one hammer strikes three strings per key.

While one might think that the strings create the tone, they actually affect it very little. Even if we restring the piano with another brand, the change in tone will be imperceptible, just as changing strings on a Stradivarius violin does not change the beautiful sound of that instrument.

Copper windings on the bass strings in the lower third of the keyboard give needed mass to the wire string, thereby allowing strings to vibrate at a pitch lower than their lengths. Without the copper windings, the strings would have to be 20 feet long or longer to attain these lower pitches. Hardly practical! Cheaper pianos of the past contained strings wrapped with steel plated or painted copper. These steel-wound strings never sounded as rich and warm as the genuine solid copper-wound strings.

> **Rhythm and News**
>
> During the war years, when factories needed copper to make brass for shell casings, most pianos produced had steel-wrapped strings.

Copper-wound bass strings.

Some of the best wire for strings comes from a German company named Roslau. You will undoubtedly hear that name as many manufacturers and rebuilders use Roslau wire. Rebuilders will favor one brand of wire over another because of its handling properties, price, availability, or durability.

If installed properly, a decent set of tenor and treble strings (the silver looking ones) should have a useful musical life of 40 to 60 years. Copper-wound strings in the bass section will likely last 25 to 40 years. To restring an entire medium-size grand piano, the cost will run between $1,500 and $2,000, including the several requisite tunings needed to stabilize the piano. Because the price of new vertical pianos starts at about $2,000, vertical pianos are rarely restrung unless for sentimental reasons.

The Key to Good Key-Action

The key-action assembly, or "key-action" for short, consists of all the linkage between the key that you press and the hammer that strikes the string. The second assembly is the underlever/damper assembly which comprises all the linkage that activates the damper system, which stops the tone when the key is released.

Dampers in a grand piano sit on top of the strings.

Grand piano key-action.

Underlever/damper assembly.

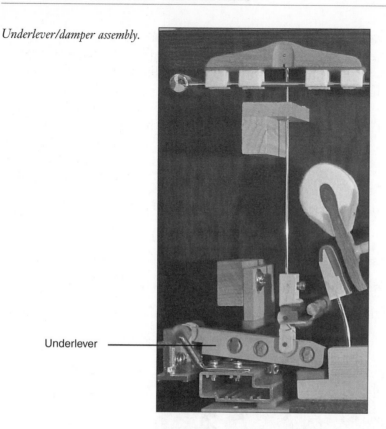

Underlever

The grand piano key-assembly consists of the key-stick with its front- and balance-rail bushings, plastic/ivory/ebony key covering, the hardwood key-button, the lead key-weights, the capstan, the backcheck wire and the backcheck. The vertical piano key-subassembly would be the same, only shorter and without the backcheck.

Backcheck   Key-stick   Key leads

Capstan   Key-button   Balance-rail bushing   Front-rail bushing

Grand piano key assembly.

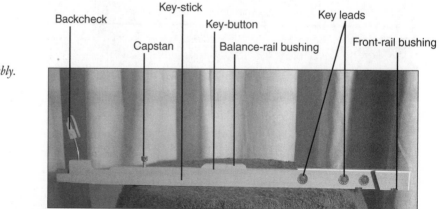

It is in these three assemblies that the bulk of the 10,000 parts of the modern piano reside. Traditionally, parts are made of hard woods, like maple or hornbeam. These woods are used because of their strength to weight ratio and their resistance to warping, as well as to their ability to be machined. Beginning as early as 1967, Yamaha and Kawai, two of the largest and highest profile mass-production houses, began to substitute advanced plastics and later, carbon fiber parts in this critical area. They have taken a lot of heat from the conservative piano community, yet, they are steadfast in their belief that their materials and designs are stronger, lighter, and more stable than wood. They even have studies to back them up. We have no quarrel with these types of parts, and you should not let any salesperson sway you one way or the other because of them. They can only be an advantage in durability and performance. They do not, however, constitute a reason to buy or not to buy a piano.

Many of the European companies embrace key-actions from the Renner Company in Germany. While these actions are top quality, they are only as good as the care and craft taken to install them. In addition, how much time a factory spends in the final regulation adjustments also affects the touch. Just because a piano has a Renner action does not make it a good piano. Again, test how it feels and plays to you.

Plastic action parts.

Reach Out and Touch It

The touch of a piano is a very personal thing. Some teachers want their students to play pianos that have a hard touch, to build muscle tone and control. Some players want the lightest touch they can control. With pianos, how different is touch?

The touch of a piano is 50 percent reality and 50 percent impression. Let's talk about the reality part first. The international standard for grand pianos is regulated to a down weight of between 52 and 55 grams to press the key down. We assure you that unless you are a most accomplished pianist, you will not feel the difference between these amounts. The key dip, or the distance the key travels downward, is another international standard measurement.

If everything is standardized, how can so many pianos feel and play so differently? This is where the other half of the touch equation comes in. The impression part comes from the voice of the piano. If a piano speaks more boldly, with an edge to the sound or is brighter, the impression is that it is easier to play. You are getting more bang for your buck at the keyboard. If a piano has a thicker, warmer, more mellow sound, the impression is that it is harder to play. While it is true that the geometry in some actions allows them to be slightly more responsive, these differences hardly account for the noticeable differences in touch.

By voicing the hammers slightly brighter, technicians commonly satisfy a customer complaining about hard touch. Magically, the touch is "lightened."

With respect to the tone, in Chapter 8 we identified the three distinct genres of pianos, and they all impact the impressions of touch. European scale designs typically deliver a very clear, bell-like tone, sometimes crystalline without being metallic. As a consequence, such pianos are often criticized for having too light a touch. Domestic, American scale designs typically deliver a round, hollow, woody, mellow, "darker" sound. They are criticized for having too heavy a touch. The Asian pianos are somewhere in the middle. The Asian sound is frequently criticized for having a slightly metallic edge to its tone.

What the Pedals Do

Modern vertical and grand pianos have three pedals. Depending on the manufacturers' specs, the left and middle pedals may have different functions, but the right pedal sustains the tone on both verticals and grands.

The pedal on the left is called the *soft pedal* on both vertical and grand pianos. Formally on a grand piano, it is called the *una corda pedal*. Inside vertical pianos, the left pedal activates levers that move the hammers half the distance to the strings. This movement limits the blow of the hammers and causes softer play.

On grand pianos, the left pedal activates levers that move the entire key action slightly to the right. You can actually see the keys move. The result inside the piano is that the hammers now strike two strings instead of three in the unisons, thus making a slightly softer tone.

Pedal lyre assembly.

The middle pedal on most new vertical pianos is called a *practice pedal* because it activates levers that drop a felt mute strip between the hammers and the strings. The drop in volume is significant, affecting touch only slightly.

On some older verticals and inexpensive grands, the middle pedal is a *bass sustain pedal*. (However, we know of no music written for this function.) When this type of pedal is depressed, the dampers on the bass strings are lifted, thus sustaining the sound of these strings. The middle pedal on most better-quality grand pianos is called a *sostenuto pedal*. The function of this pedal has been described as "having a third hand on the keyboard." To work the pedal properly, a key or a group of keys is played, and while the keys are held down, the pedal is depressed. This function captures the dampers of the notes played and sustains them as long as the pedal is held down. It does not sustain any other notes. A true sostenuto function is rarely found on vertical pianos; typically it is available only on the highest-end 52" models.

The right pedal is the one most commonly used in everyday playing. It works the same on uprights as it does on grand pianos. Called the *sustain pedal*, it is sometimes mistakenly referred to as the loud pedal. This pedal works levers that lift all the dampers away from the strings, allowing the notes to sustain as long as the pedal is depressed. When depressed, this pedal also allows the rest of the strings to vibrate sympathetically, adding a fullness to the music.

> **Rhythm and News**
>
> Through the 1970s, many European and Japanese pianos had only two pedals. For many foreign manufacturers, a sostenuto middle pedal seemed like a Western affectation with little demand. Although few composers have ever written for this pedal function, it is our opinion that a grand piano should perform the functions intended for a performance piano.

Part of learning how to play the piano is learning when and how to utilize the pedals for a desired effect. Advanced players even learn to master the techniques of partial pedaling to achieve nuances of tone and sustain beyond the typical on and off of most beginners.

Pedals need to be adjusted periodically to take up slack as they wear. They should be adjusted to have very little lash, or lost-motion, when the pedal is depressed. Pedals should function smoothly with a minimum of mechanical noise. Squeaks coming from pedals are a common malady. They can be difficult to diagnose and to treat permanently because the noise can come from a dozen different places along the linkage.

Now you are familiar with the parts of a piano that affect touch and tone. Good performance comes from quality designs, quality materials, and attention to detail in the build. All are critically important.

The Least You Need to Know

- The soundboard is almost always made of a single layer of spruce, but some laminated boards are desirable as well.

- Virgin wool hammers strike the strings and contribute to the tone of the piano.

- Strings are made of steel music wire and usually have copper windings to produce the lower notes in the bass section.

- The key-action is the linkage between the key that you press and the hammer that strikes the string.

- Touch is 50 percent reality and 50 percent impression.

Chapter 10

Finding an Acoustic Piano with Stability and Longevity

In This Chapter

◆ Piano support features

◆ Different cast iron plate methods

◆ Woods used to build pianos

◆ Veneer and cabinet construction

◆ Moisture issues

As you make the rounds of your local piano retailers, you will undoubtedly encounter a salesperson who focuses on the technicalities of piano support features such as cast-iron plates, back posts, and wood construction. The terminology can be confusing, so one of our goals in this chapter is to help you understand what these parts and processes are so that you can separate hype from reality as you evaluate your options.

These sales presentations often miscast piano support components as critical to tone production. The reality is that support parts instead play a significant role in the overall stability of the instrument for touch, tone, and longevity. You're making an expensive purchase that you want to live with happily for as long as possible, so understanding these features will enable you to identify the pianos that are likely to be the most stable and long-lived.

Cast Iron Plates: Vital to the Life of a Piano

The cast iron plate, also called a harp, performs a vital role in the life of a piano by supporting most of the 20 tons of pressure the piano endures. These plates are heavy structures, weighing several hundred pounds even in small uprights. They should be designed and crafted so as not to affect the sound of the piano.

A cast iron grand plate that has been removed from the piano.

Iron Plate Casting Methods

Two processes for casting the iron plates have evolved over the years: wet-sand casting and V-Pro casting. Salespeople typically sing the praises of one method over another.

The truth is that there are pros and cons to each type. We want you to understand the differences so you can make an informed decision.

The traditional wet-sand casting process involves pressing a positive form (or die) into damp sand and then carefully removing it. Then, hot molten iron is poured into the sand mold. The mold is allowed to cool and then broken apart, and the plate is removed. Then, the plate is air cured outdoors for several weeks, months, or even years. The curing process allows the grain in the metal to align and harden with seasonal weather changes. At the end of its curing process, the plate is sandblasted smooth, ground to specifications, filled, finished, and installed into the piano.

In 1977, Yamaha designed and patented a revolutionary process for casting the iron plates in pianos. This process is called V-Pro casting, for Vacuum Shield Mold Process. The V-Pro method involves a sophisticated mold lined with a membrane that enables a very precise end result. The molten iron is sucked into the mold by a vacuum, a faster and more precise process that allows not only more plates to be made faster, but less machining after the foundry work.

The refinement of this casting process allowed Yamaha to use less metal than the traditional wet-sand method. The V-Pro method offers such manufacturing expediencies that it has been licensed by Yamaha to nearly every Asian manufacturer of pianos today.

Controversy rages back and forth between the adherents of the two manufacturing processes, with advantages to each.

> ### Rhythm and News
>
> If you are considering a piano manufactured in Japan, Korea, Indonesia, or China, it probably has a cast iron plate fashioned by the V-Pro process.

Sales personnel selling pianos with wet-sand cast plates may tell you that V-Pro plates produce metallic overtones. Those selling a product with V-Pro plates may tell you that vacuum-cast plates are more precise and consistent. Yet, in a comparison of a particular model of piano that has had both types of plates installed, we have not been able to tell the difference. We have heard brands that use the wet-sand cast method exclusively but sound somewhat metallic, but we've also heard instruments with vacuum-cast plates that don't. We recommend listening to the tone of the pianos you are comparing and coming to your own conclusions.

Plate Size, Shape, and Design

Salespeople will also likely point out the size and style of the cast-iron plates in vertical pianos.

Some upright pianos feature a full-perimeter plate, which extends to all four corners of the piano and around the entire perimeter. Full perimeter plates add strength and stability to the piano. Additional mass and support inside means that the manufacturer can make smaller back posts in the frame, or none at all. The traditional vertical plate, however, is not a full-perimeter plate. Its design spans the top and is somewhat X shaped, then narrows at the bottom. See the accompanying illustration of a partial plate.

If the piano plays well and sounds good, and the brand and model have a strong reputation, the design of the plate should not determine your purchase.

Full-Perimeter Plate.

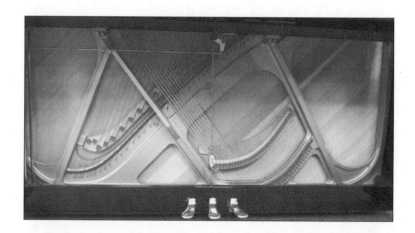

Partial Plate.

Before the turn of the twentieth century, American grand pianos often had plates that did not extend all the way to the front, through the tuning pin area. They were called three-quarter plates. Piano designs evolved toward a full plate design for greater stability and to allow higher tensions to support the upward creeping concert pitch tensions. Some older designs called for a full plate, but featured open windows or rectangular cut-outs where the tuning pins were inserted. In these pianos you can see the wood of the pin block or wrest plank surrounding the area where the tuning pins are driven in. Some high-end European grands still maintain this open design today.

Rhythm and News

The plate in the piano should last throughout the instrument's life span. If it cracks, the plate must be removed from the piano and sent to a foundry, where it can be heated and welded properly. The cost of refurbishing a plate is so expensive that people rarely go to the trouble of doing it unless the piano has a very high intrinsic value or is a family heirloom headed for restoration at any cost. Plates are never replaced with new ones; the cost would be prohibitive.

The open plate design is not without its detractors. Those in favor of it say it promotes finer tuning and better tuning stability, because the coil of the string around the tuning pin is closer to the tuning pin wrest plank (pin block). This allows for less flex in the tuning pin itself and enhances bearing angles. People who prefer a full plate design say that more cast iron in the plate creates greater mass and rigidity and thus greater tuning stability.

Ultimately, the controversy is usually moot, because unless you're on the market for a very expensive European instrument, you will rarely encounter open-plate designs. These instruments have many more compelling reasons to be considered than the design of the plate.

Furthermore, we believe that all of the cast iron plates in present-day verticals and grands are over-engineered and more than adequate for the scales they support, back-posts or not, open style or not, V-Pro or sand cast.

Plate Bushings

Another feature a salesperson might talk about is whether or not a piano has *plate bushings*. Plate bushings are designed to help support the tuning pin. They are tubes of hardwood, such as maple, or occasionally synthetic nylon, that are driven into the tuning pin holes in the cast iron plate. They are about $3/8$" in diameter and about $1/2$" in length. The tuning pin is driven in and turned through the plate bushing. The bushing isolates the tuning pin from the plate and decreases the flag-poling, or flex, of the tuning pin between where the tuning hammer (lever) contacts the top of the pin and where the pin actually goes into the wood of the pin-block (wrest plank). Some really expensive pianos do not use plate bushings, and some really cheap pianos do use them. This is not a reason to buy or not buy a given piano; it is just a design element.

Plate bushings.

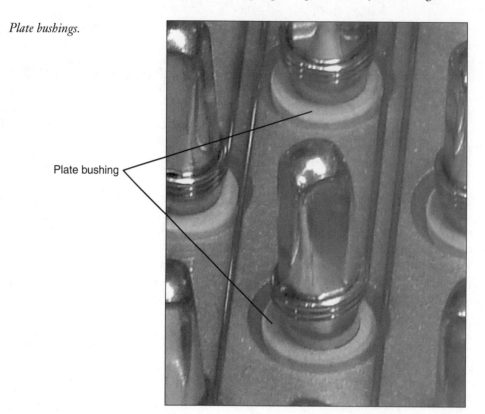

Plate bushing

Agraffes vs. Pressure Bars

Some salespeople will point to agraffes as if they were a life or death feature. Agraffes keep strings aligned and evenly spaced. Most vertical pianos, however, use a pressure bar to do this. A pressure bar is the heavy chrome piece just below the tuning pins in the top two-thirds of the vertical piano scale. It sits just above the v-bar cast into the plate and serves as the final fretting off point for the strings before they wrap around the tuning pin. The pressure bar is screwed into the cast iron plate.

Some manufacturers use agraffes instead of a pressure bar in their vertical pianos, although agraffes are more commonly seen in grand piano designs. Because agraffes keep the strings more evenly aligned than pressure bars, they can prevent string unisons from having slight twanging sounds that arise if one string sits higher than another.

We have seen good and not-so-good pianos with pressure bars and agraffes. The presence of agraffes is not a reason to buy or not to buy any given piano, though you might put agraffes as a small mark on the positive side of the scorecard.

Pressure bar.

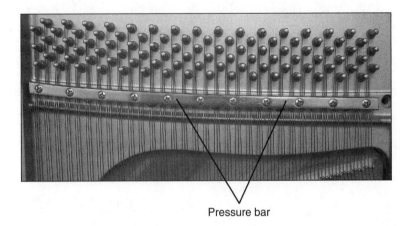

Pressure bar

Everybody, Even Pianos, Needs a Strong Back

Over the years, the backs of upright pianos have been a great source of sales presentation hype. The fact is, most of the pianos built today have adequate back construction to do the job. The wooden frame back of an upright works with the cast iron plate to support the extreme string tension of the piano throughout its life. As this is a shared responsibility, the heftier the plate, the lighter the back construction can be.

A few pianos on the market have no back posts at all. These pianos typically have beefier plates to support the stress.

Some makes and models follow a process in which the soundboard, posts, ribs, and filler blocks (between the posts) are all constructed of the same wood (spruce). This is called homogeneous construction. The theory is that the entire structure will expand and contract at the same rate with fluctuations in temperature and humidity. Sounds pretty logical, right? It is, though it's not a reason for buying a particular model; it's just a feature to put on the positive side of the scorecard.

> ### Rhythm and News
>
> Institutional pianos designed for school use usually have massive posts in their backs. Why? Someone wrote a school-bid specification 70 years ago, and institutional pianos have been built to this specification ever since, whether or not it is needed.

Vertical back with back posts.

Vertical back without back posts.

Would You Look at That Wood!

The modern piano is a wonderful amalgam of materials, including cast iron, steel, copper, plastic, wool felt, buckskin or synthetic leathers, adhesives and fillers, synthetic and organic finishes, and of course wood. The major weight of a piano comes from its cast-iron plate. The major bulk of a piano comes from the wood in the cabinet and back. Sales folks will often rattle off cabinet part names and materials, such as cross-banding and lumber core, as if you should know or understand them. Our focus in this section is the wood used in the visible cabinet of the upright piano and, to some degree, of grand pianos, so that you will know what they're talking about.

Although the cabinet of a piano has very little impact on the sound of the instrument, and, in most cases, is merely a wrapper, the cabinet is readily visible. As a result, salespeople will frequently point to cabinet parts and relay their competitor's "failings" in these areas. Therefore, we want you to know the truth before you fall victim to these common deceptions.

> **B-Sharp**
>
> Be sure to look inside and on the back of an upright piano and underneath a grand piano to check for matching of materials, flaws in the wood, poor or sloppy gluing, or other flaws a manufacturer thinks you're not likely to spot.

Piano cabinets consist of a core made of processed wood covered in thin layers of fine cabinet wood called veneer. Quality cabinets are veneered on their insides and edges as well as on the outside. Don't worry, veneering is neither a sign of shoddy construction nor cheating. It is a common woodworking technique. As a matter of fact, veneering is often necessary because of the type of construction.

A great deal of time is spent in grain matching finish veneers on wood-look cabinets. Therefore, wood-look pianos usually cost more than black or white ones.

In the 1960s, new woodworking technologies developed in the realm of engineered "sheet stock." This "particle board" or "chip-board" is used under high-pressure laminates for counter tops and kitchen cabinets. Today, the evolution of this material is called MDF, or medium density fiberboard. Many vertical piano cabinet cores are made of MDF today. It is very strong, very flat, and nearly warp free. Cabinets have become better looking because joints have stopped showing through the veneers due to the fact that sheet stock doesn't expand and contract as much as previous cabinet materials.

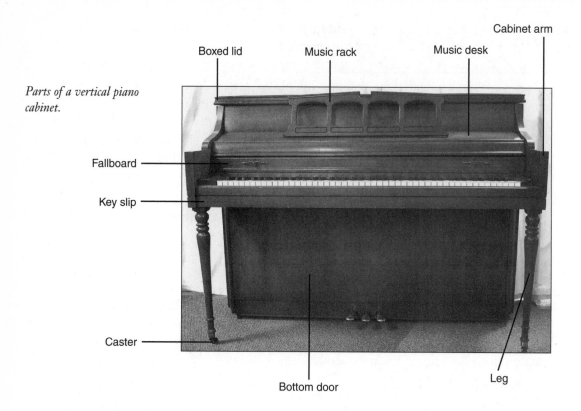

Parts of a vertical piano cabinet.

Cabinet arm

Boxed lid   Music rack   Music desk

Fallboard

Key slip

Caster

Bottom door   Leg

Nearly all of the core material in a piano is hidden. It only comes to light when presented by a salesperson about a competitor's product in order to denigrate it. Yet nearly all piano cabinets on the market today, in all price ranges, have some kind of engineered wood product somewhere in the cabinet. We believe the finesse and quality of the fits of the cabinet parts and the final finishing of the cabinet are more important than what lurks beneath the veneer.

Key Note

Salespeople often say, "You don't want Brand X, it has particle board in it." Most pianos, however, use some sort of engineered wood product effectively.

However, we do not know of any manufacturer that is using particle board or MDF in the rim construction of grand pianos. Rims are constructed with a variety of plywoods that are bent into shape. Particleboard and MDF are too brittle to bend in this manner. In addition, we do not know of any manufacturer using engineered wood materials in legs. Grand piano legs are usually hardwoods laminated for strength, much like a baseball bat.

Some companies have begun to substitute plastic and even metal parts for the wood in their piano cabinets. We believe this practice is suspect and are, therefore, not fans of this development. Some companies have also experimented with foam materials beneath veneers and finishes on small cabinet parts. We are not fans of this technique either, because metal and plastic parts tend to make noise when they vibrate, while wood in these same areas absorbs vibration from the strings.

Most consumers find out about construction practices on a particular piano not from the manufacturer but from the manufacturer's competition. In other words, a sales rep for brand X might tell you that brand Y has an MDF core or uses foam materials. Although the manufacturer might have experimented with these practices at one time, they very well might have stopped years ago. The only way to know is to ask the authorized dealer of the piano you are considering buying to show you the same part on a current model.

How Wood Cutting Affects Price

Let's talk for a bit about how wood is cut. You might wonder why you need to know how the wood for your piano was cut. Does it really matter? Our goal is to keep you from being overwhelmed by an overzealous nuts and bolts salesman. Pianos are an amalgam of a variety of materials. Seventy-five percent of a piano by volume is wood. The species of wood, where it was grown, and how it was milled is critical to the performance and durability of the instrument. If manufacturers cut costs by using cheaper kinds of wood or even cheaper cuts of wood, the quality of the piano will suffer.

Most veneer is rotary cut, a technique in which a tree trunk is fastened to a huge spindle and turned or spun at a high speed. A large knife blade is then brought down onto the rotating edge of the trunk. After the trunk is "trued" during the first few turns into the outer layers, whole sheets of thinly sliced wood veneer are cut off and set aside to cure. The veneer from a single tree trunk is called a "flitch." Flitches are identified and kept together to match exactly.

Tree trunks that are destined to be cut for lumber are ripped lengthwise, with the timbers cut to the desired thickness. These timbers or planks incorporate both sapwood and heartwood. Each piece shows the grain configuration of a lengthwise slice through the tree. Plain-sawn wood will have a repeating curved pattern to the grain as the plank is cut from the round tree. This cut pattern may be good for building houses, but it is not the best method for building piano cabinets. Plain-sawn wood planks have a tendency to cup or warp with the curved grain pattern.

Rotary wood cutting.

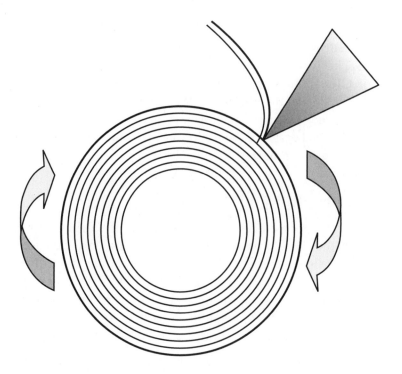

Rotary cutting spins the log and shears off sheets of thin wood for ply-stock or veneers.

Furniture-making calls for the use of quarter-sawn wood. This method is one in which a tree trunk is cut in half lengthwise. Then that half is cut in half lengthwise again. This leaves a long, pie- or wedge-shaped hunk of wood. Boards are now cut off one of the flat sides of the wedge shape. This process gives us wood that has a straight grain running the length of the board, with less tendency to cup or warp as the wood cures. Quarter-sawn wood is more expensive, but it is best for piano cabinet making. Quarter-sawn soundboards, especially, are definitely a positive mark on your scorecard.

The construction of grand piano cabinets comes with special needs and fixes. Manufacturers have struggled for 300 years with the lids of grand pianos. Grand lids can run as long as 9 feet; and with the exception of the fly piece that folds back, they are completely unsupported across their length and width. They typically range from only ³/₄" to 1" thick. Grand lids spend most of their lives propped up at a 45-degree angle and supported by the prop-stick at only one point, near the front corner. Some grand lids do, in fact, begin to sag a little over the years. Grands with stretcher bars (reinforcing wood strip) on the edge of the fly (that's the part of the lid that folds back) are a little more resistant to the sag factor. Grands over 7 feet often have reinforcing wood strips cross-wise under the lid.

Plain sawn lumber is cut straight through the tree trunk from side to side. Grain pattern in the boards will show evidence of the circular growth rings. Boards cut like this are more likely to cup or warp across the grain.

Plain sawn vs. quarter sawn lumber.

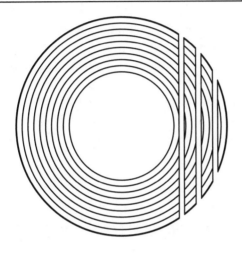

Quarter sawn lumber shows a linear grain pattern and is more stable across the grain

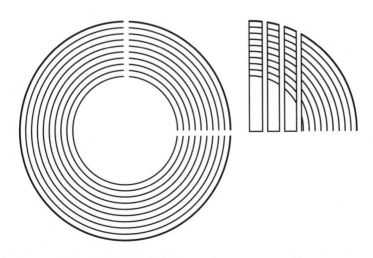

Another problem that has been accentuated over the past 40 years with the advent and popularity of the "high polish" or "high gloss" finish is the telegraphing of any irregularity from the core stock, cross-banding, or finish veneers through this large expanse of shine. The shiny finish exposes and accentuates every little flaw. Several manufacturers have solved this problem by adding a final layer or veneer of a very thin high-density hardboard or Masonite-type material. This material, which is very flat and very hard, takes the new finishes very well and stops any telegraphing of irregularities from underneath.

The quality of high-gloss cabinet panel finishes, especially grand lids, depends on the skill of the manufacturer, the materials used, and the amount of time spent on the process. If you look down the lid of a 6-foot or larger grand and get the light just right, you can see differences between expensive German pianos, when compared to Japanese, Korean/Indonesian, and Chinese pianos. The difference is subtle, but you can see it if you look closely. Again, not a reason to buy one model or brand over another, but one of the differences that is supposed to go with price.

Don't Get Caught High and Dry with Wet Wood

If you are considering buying a piano that was built in Asia, you will undoubtedly hear about how the wood has been dried or cured for its final destination. Let's look at the process and how it benefits you.

The moisture content of wood is critical to woodworking. When a tree is first cut down, there is a great deal of water within the cell structure of the wood, often more than 50 percent by weight. Such a high percentage of water makes it useless to build with when "green." The water must be cured or dried out of the wood to make it dimensionally stable enough to work with.

In the old days and with some companies today, the wood is sorted and stacked outside and left to air dry for several months, even years. Experts disagree about the value of the lengthy process of air drying wood versus the modern methods of computer-controlled drying rooms or kilns, where wood is artificially dried in a carefully controlled environment over a matter of weeks.

Most piano manufacturers dry their wood prior to construction. The problem is that for pianos made outside of the United States, they must often sit in a climate that is considerably higher in moisture for perhaps several months. The finished product will absorb moisture until a stasis is reached. When the piano is finally shipped and reaches its final destination, it will likely give off moisture to reach another stasis with the new environment.

When you are crafting a complex mechanical and musical instrument with engineered tolerances to thousandths of an inch, even a 1 percent movement in a 12-inch expanse of wood can cause an ⅛-inch shift. Wood moving under brittle gloss finishes can wreak havoc. Wood moving through glue joints can force apart critical pieces.

Key Note

Salespeople will often talk at length about the wood of a particular brand and how it is dried. This is okay because wood drying is an important factor in piano construction.

In the late 1960s, problems became evident in the pianos imported from Asia. We saw it again with the Korean pianos in the early 1980s. Now we are seeing problems with the early pianos from young Chinese factories exporting to the United States

The problems resulted mainly from dimension shifting of the wood as it acclimates to another climate. In addition to cabinet panels and backs changing dimension, delaminating, and so on, other wood-related issues involve critical tone-producing and amplifying components, like bridges and soundboards. Yamaha and Kawai conquered these problems in a relatively short time. The two Korean giants Samick and Young Chang had data from the Japanese experience to help guide them through these evolutions, and the Chinese today have a wealth of experience and science to help them through even more quickly.

European pianos were rare in the United States until the 1970s. By numbers, they still are. Several manufacturers that began to distribute pianos here had moisture problems with rim delaminations and soundboard cracks. We don't hear about any of these problems today. With a few exceptions of fledgling factories in China, and some Eastern European start-ups, new pianos have few wood-moisture problems, and the pianos are getting better all the time.

Key Note

To avoid moisture absorption, Asian pianos are often sealed into vacuum bags containing moisture-absorbent silica gel desiccate inside their crates or boxes, often inside the piano as well. These should be removed from inside your piano prior to delivery.

The past 50 years have seen a dramatic change in the technology of handling and preparing wood for manufacturing. The harvesting and transportation of trees for lumber has become a virtual science. To avoid wood-shifting problems after export, worldwide exporters of instruments can now cure batches of materials down to a moisture content that is destination specific.

Occasionally, a piano in transit will be exposed to extreme weather conditions that damage it. Pianos are often shipped from the Far East and Europe in steel containers. If these containers are exposed to salt air, rain, or intense heat, the piano might suffer.

We have also seen pianos that were shipped from the Eastern part of the United States during the winter in heated trucks. If a truck broke down and the doors were opened, the crated pianos were subjected to a blast of arctic air.

Although factory warranties cover these types of problems, your dealer should inspect your piano before he delivers it to you. And, this is why you should never have a piano delivered to your home in the box. All these problems are rare, but they do happen.

The Least You Need to Know

- A cast iron plate or harp is the support system that fights the 40,000 pounds of pressure exerted by the strings.

- Both vacuum-cast and traditional wet-sand-cast plates have advantages and disadvantages, but the proof is in the tone.

- Back construction in vertical pianos varies, depending on plate design.

- The wood finish you see on the outside is always a veneer.

- Nearly all vertical pianos employ plywood or other engineered wood in their cabinet parts.

- Wood must be "cured" or dried before it is used in cabinet parts so that it does not crack or change dramatically in dimension.

Chapter 11

Innovations in Modern Acoustic Pianos

In This Chapter

◆ How modern technology has improved piano quality

◆ Advances in glues, plates, pins, and more

◆ New finish materials that make piano upkeep easier

◆ Computer-assisted technology

◆ Debunking myths about the Golden Era of pianos

As you shop for a piano, you might find salespeople touting the latest and greatest innovations in the models you are considering. You might hear, "This piano has asymmetrical soundboard tapering." "That grand has a wider tail." "The action rails of this one use seamless aluminum extrusions." You might have a hard time understanding what they're talking about, much less determining whether these features really do make a difference.

In this chapter, we help you make sense of these and many other statements so that you can see how they factor into your decision.

A Brief History of Piano Innovation

Three hundred years of piano making has brought us to where we are with the modern musical instruments available today. Most of the major design changes came before the turn of the twentieth century. These included: the over-strung scale, continuous bent rim, full grand and vertical plate castings, full escapement actions, and the full 7¼ octave (88 note) keyboard. Each of these innovations was fundamental to increased tone production, sustain, durability, stability, playability, and versatility.

Since about 1900, finer adjustments and tweakings have been made to increase performance and nuance.

New Materials for Better Performance and Price

Much of what has happened in the past 50 years in piano making has come in the form of new and improved materials. The materials that hold your piano's parts together, that make it work, and that encase it all, have been improved to enhance the piano's tonal qualities and staying power.

New Glues Hold It Together Better

Organic hide glues (from animal renderings) have been replaced in piano making by a variety of modern adhesives that offer longer "open" working time before they set, stronger holding power, continued flexibility with age, and no attraction to insects (termites and other wood borers). Aliphatic-resin glues, urea resin, urea-formaldehyde glues, and high-frequency-setting glues represent some of the modern glues that have taken over as the basis for cabinet and back construction.

Advances in Rails

Another structural innovation comes with the main rails or action rails, to which many of the hundreds of little wooden or plastic action parts are mounted. Rails are a critical part in every piano. Most upright pianos have one rail. In most grands, however, three rails support the action and damper parts. Traditionally, these have consisted of wood. Long expanses of wood, which are susceptible to warping, twisting, shrinking, and swelling, can cause the mechanism to move out of critical alignment and fastening screws to become loose. To solve this problem, Steinway patented its "tubular metallic-action frame" way back in 1878, but it wasn't until the late 1960s that most companies began to use seamless *aluminum extrusions* for action rails. Older used pianos as well as some of the cheapest pianos on the market still use wood. Aluminum extrusions are definitely a positive on the balance scale of your decision making.

def•i•ni•tion

Aluminum extrusions are pieces of bar stock that are squeezed through a die to form its resulting shapes. In pianos, these extrusions are typically used for action rails.

Plastics Are the Answer

Other developments include the introduction of plastic into the action mechanism. No other single development has engendered more angst among a very traditional and slow-to-evolve industry. Manufacturers and dealers fling brick bats daily about the use of plastic in piano actions. In the late 1940s through the early 1950s, some low-end American manufacturers used early plastics in their actions. These plastics were used primarily in spinet pianos with drop or indirect action mechanisms. One critical part in particular, the elbow, was made of this early plastic. As these pianos aged, this early plastic became brittle and frequently shattered under the stress of playing. From this point on, the use of plastics in piano actions was tainted with memories of this negative experience.

Plastics have come a long way since then. Both Yamaha and Kawai have had prestigious labs empirically confirm the benefits of their "space-age" plastic materials. They are stronger and less prone to breakage, and they are impervious to moisture and temperature fluctuations that cause wooden parts to warp, twist, shrink, and swell with the seasons or quirky weather. Most technicians line up on the side of these modern materials, which have been well tested in institutional use for more than three decades now.

With all the wailing about plastic, it is interesting to note that the two highest profile Japanese manufacturers use it. Contrary to competitive rhetoric, both companies restrict their use to only those mechanical parts between the wooden key and the wooden hammer shank. Plastics play no role in support functions or tonal functions in these pianos.

Key Note

Yamaha introduced the first plastic parts into their vertical piano actions as early as the 1960s. Kawai followed suit by adopting the use of ABS styran plastic parts in their uprights and grands as well.

Duplexing: Not a Type of Housing!

Another action mechanism innovation is duplexing. Prior to the 1960s, few pianos had duplexing to enhance the upper parts of their scale designs, though Steinway and some others adopted this tweaking of their scale designs as early as the late 1800s. Duplex scales have small steel aliquot bars (steel bearing pieces that fret off treble strings in some grands) inserted beneath the strings behind the bridge and just before the string ends at the plate pin. The idea is to encourage and to tune the un-struck, sympathetic tone of these short lengths of string. By the late 1980s, most grand piano scale designs incorporated this selling feature whether they needed it or not. If not engineered and executed perfectly, duplexing can add false beats, ringing, and other undesirable noises to an otherwise decent scale design. If well-executed, duplexing should be a plus on your score card.

Duplex scale with aliquot bars.

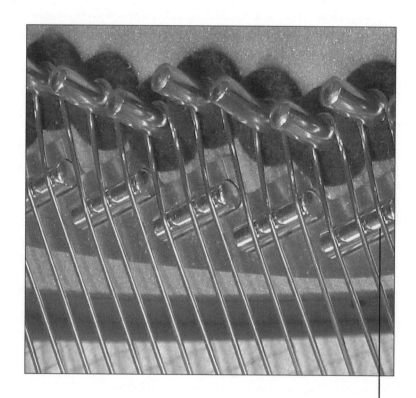

Aliquot Bar

Under the Hood

Piano tuning pins have also seen innovations in the past 30 years. The raw steel of traditional piano tuning pins was protected by bluing, as with a gun barrel. Frequently tuning pins rusted and transmitted this condition to the string coils around them. Cosmetically these rusty pins look anything but attractive! But, more importantly, rusty strings often became so corroded that the strings actually broke under their tension. By the mid-1970s, most new pianos came with nickel-plated tuning pins that wouldn't rust. Like so many aspects surrounding pianos, there is even controversy about this one. The counterpoint to nickel-plated tuning pins is that the plating allows the tuning pin to slip in the hole. To counter this theory, some pins have the plating removed from the part that goes into the wood. We believe nickel-plated pins will increase longevity and would put that down as a positive for pianos that have them.

One of the great destroyers of pianos in years past was the common household moth. They would munch on the felt hammers, dampers, and other cloth action parts and render many pianos useless. With modern moth-proofing treatments, and many more moth-free houses today, we seldom see this kind of damage in recent used pianos.

The science of metallurgy not only has blessed the piano world with better casting processes and plating materials but has enhanced the consistency and content of the drawing of music wire for the strings and the copper-wound bass strings. We are finding that strings are retaining their musical properties longer than in years past. It is our impression that, aside from placement near an ocean or lake, new strings are slightly more rust resistant than they used to be.

On the Outside

Traditional finishes in the piano world were lacquer and varnish. Finishes were hand rubbed to a satin sheen at the factory. In the 1960s, the Asian manufacturers Yamaha and Kawai began to experiment with synthetic urethanes to achieve a high luster or high polish wet-look finish. This evolved into the modern polyester finishes that are used today on nearly 90 percent of all new grands and about 70 percent of all new upright pianos. Because polyester is harder and more scratch resistant, the finish can be repaired and buffed back to "new" several times during the life of the piano. Also polyester finishes can be cleaned with a damp cloth.

> **Key Note**
>
> Polyester finishes require no regular waxing or polishing, for the wood is sealed at the factory. These finishes are ten or more times thicker than traditional natural lacquers and synthetic urethanes.

While exotic woods, such as rosewood, were common in cabinets of the 1800s through the decline of the Victorian uprights, the early 1930s piano cabinets in the United States were primarily relegated to walnut, mahogany, oak, and "ebonized" black. The late 1940s through the 1950s saw a rash of maple and limed oak (white-washed) uprights. Ultra high-end Europeans still displayed some exotics; and during the 1990s, we saw a return of exotic woods in some American pianos, with the Steinway & Sons "Crown Jewel" limited edition grands leading the way.

Today, even moderately priced, mass-produced pianos can be obtained in such exotic veneers as African Bubinga and highly figured mahoganies. Many companies have reintroduced Victorian leg and music rack styles and are including some inlay work as well. French Provincial-styled cabinets have been around for decades.

Natural keys were covered in ivory on most quality pianos through the 1940s. The embargo on elephant ivory at last prohibited the use of ivory piano keys. Manufacturers first used celluloid, then early plastics, instead of ivory. Ivory keys actually crack, chip, discolor, peal, and flake. Modern snow white plastic will look perfect 50 years from now. In spite of this, many piano enthusiasts still desire the esthetics of ivory. Some new materials are quite similar to ivory in that they are porous, slightly off-white, and cool to the touch. They have an enhanced, tractive touch somewhat like ivory.

Key Note

Yamaha (Ivorite) and Kawai (Neotex) use patented synthetic ivory plastics in their top-line grand pianos.

Packaging, Shipping, and Set-Up

Even packaging materials have evolved. Many pianos are vacuum-sealed in foil bags inside their crates or boxes at the factory.

Key Note

Many factories employ playing machines, Vorsetzers as they are called (sometimes called pounders), to play as many as 10,000 keystrokes on their new pianos before the final tuning, regulation, and voicing at the factory.

New pianos go through an awkward stage with inconsistent voicing and unstable tuning after being unboxed. Only after a piano has been played for several weeks and has been tuned a few times will it be "broken-in." Some factories have machines that play the keys repeatedly for a period of time. The result is a more stable instrument that can be more properly evaluated by a potential buyer because he can tell how it will play and sound for years down the road.

The Computer Age in Piano Construction

All budding piano students learn about the three Bs: Bach, Beethoven, and Brahms. Today, much of the piano manufacturing world employs the three Cs: CAD—computer-aided design; CAE—computer-aided engineering; and CNC—computer numerical control. In this section we explain these technologies and point out the potential benefits to you.

Salespeople often make comments about competitive brands that "used to be hand-crafted" but today are machine built. When at the authorized dealer for the brand, ask about the specifics. You may find that the company is now using some of the following technology.

CAD, or computer-aided design, allows parts, sub-assemblies, and even entire pianos to be designed and drawn on a computer. Before any product can be manufactured, it must first be conceived, designed, drafted, and blue printed, besides having materials specified. This process could take years of trial and error to produce the first working prototype. With the use of computer-aided design, design studios that once needed 50 draftsmen have been reduced to 1 skilled designer with a powerful computer and software program.

Today, nearly all manufacturers have translated their scale designs into CADD, Computer Aided Drafting and Design, programs. Once the data is in the program, technicians can perform sophisticated analyses of plate stress, soundboard performance, and bridge placement. Some of this computer work has led to small tweaks in scale designs or entirely new designs.

CAE, or computer-aided engineering, allows for computer-testing of CAD designs and materials specifications for intricate stress factors and material suitability. This short-circuits the laborious and repetitive process of building prototype after prototype to perfect the final version. CAE programs can speed and confirm the process of scale designing by selecting string gauges and speaking lengths, optimum bridge placements, optimum soundboard tapering, optimum plate stressing, hammer weights, strike-points, and dozens of variables in a piano design.

CNC, or computer numerical control, machines take the output from the CAD and CAE files and translate it into an intricate manufacturing code that directs cutting, planing, milling, shaping, drilling, and other cutter machinery. CNC machinery can take lumber and turn it into ultra precise component parts with little human guidance. Some machines utilize laser technology with accuracy similar to the lasers used in surgical procedures. Imagine a bridge cut the exact same way down to thousandths-of-an-inch tolerances, time after time after time.

Sophisticated and very expensive, CNC milling machines are being employed by more and more piano manufacturers. Greater precision in manufacturing creates more consistent, better performing, and longer lasting products. Today it is not necessary to play five of the same model to find a "good one." Many mass-production factories have developed amazing consistency. Line up 20, prep them, and, for the most part, they will play and sound the same.

> **Key Note**
>
> The use of CNC in piano manufacturing allows for closer tolerances and tighter fits. It allows for greater consistency from one instrument to another and facilitates far greater quality control. Also, it allows factory workers to spend more time on tuning, regulation, and voicing.

We have stated that good pianos arise from three major areas: good design, good execution of design, and good materials. The use of CNC in piano manufacturing only speaks to part of one of these three pillars. CNC does not design the piano. CNC does not make the piano, only some of the parts. So just because a manufacturer has acquired CNC capabilities is not a reason to buy a certain piano. Only under the right set of circumstances can the use of CNC result in better pianos.

While prices of powerful desktop computers and CAD and CAE programs have come down to where most small businesses can afford them, CNC machinery costs millions of dollars. Only the larger and more progressive piano manufacturers use CNC technology at this time. Manufacturers that we know of include Yamaha, Kawai, Samick, and high-end, hand-crafted pianos such as Schimmel, Bechstein, and surprisingly enough, Bösendorfer. (And Bösendorfer makes only 350 pianos per year!)

One of the developments we mentioned as a result of computer modeling technology is asymmetrical soundboard tapering. In previous eras, the soundboard of pianos was a consistent thickness. As piano designs evolved, builders found if they tapered the thickness to be thinner near the edges, the soundboard could be more flexible and thereby more responsive. Most soundboards today are tapered symmetrically; that is to say, thicker in the center then thinning evenly to the edges radially in all directions. However, recent computer modeling of soundboard frequency amplification has shown it is beneficial to shape the taper around the bridges asymmetrically. A few manufacturers have adopted this innovation in their designs. Our feeling is that judgments on a piano should be based on tonal performance, not on how the tone is developed.

The Most Recent Innovations in Pianos

The past 10 years have seen an increase in the width of grand piano wheels or casters. This trend started with some of the European imports sporting very large landing gear wheel-sets and has trickled down to even the budget-priced grands. Gone are the days of the carpet-cutting, $3/4$"-wide, brass-plated steel wheel. Today, the standard is a solid brass $1^1/2$" ball-bearing caster, with many ranging up to 3" in width. The flagship Bösendorfer Imperial sports double brass casters measuring a full 5" wide and $3^1/2$" inches in diameter!

Standard caster.

Another development in the evolution of grand pianos is in the increased width of the tail (back-end or pointy end of a grand piano). Many recent scale designs are touting the benefits of broader tails, including better bridge placement, longer string length, and more soundboard area. The benefits are somewhat debatable. The real proof will always be in the tone of the piano. Look for more tail width creep in the future. One example of a company going in the other direction is Steinway and Sons, scrapping their broader-tailed model "L" for the pointier and older scale design of their model "O."

For vertical pianos, a recent innovation is a way to make them play quietly. This feature is called a practice mute or muffler rail, which is a felt strip lowered between the hammers and the strings to create a soft-play type sound. It can be activated by moving a lever under the keyboard, or more commonly by depressing the middle pedal. This feature is rarely found in American pianos built before the 1970s. It became popular as a standard equipment feature on the early Japanese verticals, and most manufacturers followed suit after that.

Concert-grand caster.

A felt strip that can be lowered to reduce the volume is known as a practice mute or muffler rail.

The most recent development in piano design has been the advent of the "slow close" fallboard, or key cover. Springs, levers, counter-weights, and viscous couplings have all been used to create a fallboard that closes slowly and won't crash down on fingers. The slow close phenomenon started with a few grands and now has blossomed to many uprights as well. Eventually, all grands and most upright styles will probably have this feature as standard equipment.

Does All This Innovation Make a Difference?

In our professional opinions, pianos today are better than those of by-gone eras. Discussions of the "Golden Era" of this brand and that brand are more sales hype from someone selling a used piano than they are meaningful reality. You already know that pianos don't get better with age. Rebuilt pianos are rarely, if ever, better than the same new model from the same company; they're just cheaper (or should be!).

The worst pianos on the market today are better than the lower end of those 30 years ago. The mainstream, middle-price-point instruments are significantly better playing, sounding, and longer-lasting than their counterparts of yesteryear. Clearly, it is the low and middle ends of the spectrum that have benefited most from the manufacturing and materials evolutions of the past 50 years or so. Top-tier instruments may be only marginally better than those of the same category a few decades ago, but they *are* better.

So as salespeople tout the innovative features of new pianos and the benefits these bring to you, you can rest assured that, in many cases, they are speaking the truth.

The Least You Need to Know

◆ Modern technology has improved the quality of pianos.

◆ Advanced methods for making tuning pins and metallurgy have resulted in better strings holding their tune and tone longer.

◆ Advances in computer technology and computer-aided machinery have resulted in better designs and better execution of those designs.

◆ Technology has improved modern pianos, further building the case that a new piano is often better than a used one.

Part 3

Acoustic Piano Buyer's Guide

Here it is … your consumer's guide to piano brand names, models, and countries of origin. You'll find information about pianos from the United States, Europe, and Asia, their history, evolution, and characteristics, as well as a thorough listing of the most popular manufacturers from those areas. We also address the topic of lower-end or entry-level pianos that can save you money. But what's the trade-off in quality for getting a bargain? We cover that here and also help you judge a piano by its cover, discussing cabinet styles, covers, and finishes so you can find the right look to blend with or complement your décor.

Chapter 12

American and European Brand Names, Models, and Origins

In This Chapter

- ◆ American pianos
- ◆ European pianos
- ◆ Current manufacturers and models

American and European pianos share many characteristics in building techniques and materials. Both American and European instruments are produced as limited editions, have a high degree of hand crafting, and boast grand piano rims made of hard woods. (Baldwin vertical pianos are the only remaining high-volume production pianos in the United States.) The two categories do have divergent tone characteristics, however, as you learned in Chapter 8.

To help you explore your options for American- or European-made pianos, we identify in this chapter the five remaining American manufacturers and nearly two dozen manufacturers building pianos in Europe and the United Kingdom. There are more piano builders in Europe and the UK than the ones we include in this chapter, but these are the manufacturers that distribute pianos in the United States and that you're most likely to encounter. Of the ones you'll read about here, several companies are quite small, selling fewer than 500 pianos per year in the United States.

Two Hundred Years of American Pianos

American piano manufacturers set up shop in the mid-1800s, selling pianos along the Eastern seaboard. Only the wealthier families of the time could enjoy a piano of their own. However, by the end of the Victorian era, nearly every respectable home had a piano in its parlor. The industrial revolution played a large part in bringing piano prices down to the point that the average family could afford one.

From the turn of the twentieth century through the 1930s, nearly 400 piano manufacturers produced acoustic pianos in the United States. The 1907 depression, World War I wartime production limitations, the Great Depression of the 1930s, and World War II wartime production limitations led to the demise of most of these manufacturers. By the 1940s there was much consolidation; brands and factories were bought, sold, and relocated.

The piano business fell into somewhat of a stasis through the 1960s. Steinway, Baldwin, and Aeolian (with its Mason & Hamlin, Chickering, and Knabe brands) led the way in performance pianos, while Kimball and Wurlitzer dominated the landscape of lesser labels. In all but the highest price ranges, a certain mediocrity fell over American pianos during this period.

Key Note

Over the past several decades, the list of truly American piano factories has dwindled to five: Steinway, Baldwin, Charles Walter, Mason & Hamlin, and Astin-Weight.

By the early 1970s, about two dozen American piano manufacturers produced approximately three dozen brand names. Today, only five of those manufacturers remain. In the *Current Manufacturers, Models, and Origins* section of this chapter, you'll find each of these manufacturers' products listed for your reference.

Western Europe: Where It All Began

Europe was the birthplace of the piano more than 300 years ago. Piano factories began to spring up throughout Western Europe in the late 1700s, and some of those have survived to present day.

Although Western European pianos have been available in the United States since before American independence, these pianos were enjoyed only by the wealthiest families. Not until the 1960s did European piano manufacturers begin regularly exporting their pianos to dealers in the United States. Western European pianos are still among the most expensive pianos available in America.

Currently, pianos from Western European countries such as Austria, France, Germany, Italy, and the United Kingdom are available for sale in the United States. These pianos have set the standard for quality, performance, and longevity.

Eastern European Pianos Come to the States

On November 9, 1989, the Soviet era in Eastern Europe came to an end when the Berlin Wall crumbled without a shot. Economies in Eastern European countries changed quickly as businesses and entire industries began to privatize. In less than two decades, several piano factories in Eastern Europe have brought to the United States' marketplace instruments of performance, style, beauty, and durability, nearly comparable to their revered Western European counterparts. These pianos often sell for 25 to 50 percent less than Western European pianos.

The lines between Eastern and Western Europe are becoming increasingly blurred when it comes to piano manufacturing. Companies on both sides are sourcing raw materials and subassemblies from each other and from common suppliers.

Key Note

Now that so many manufacturers are sourcing materials and sub-assemblies from the same suppliers, it is becoming increasingly difficult to use country of origin as a major distinction between brands, particularly in Europe and the U.K.

Current Manufacturers, Models, and Origins

The remainder of this chapter is devoted to a list of most of the popular selling American and European pianos in the United States at the time of this writing. We have made every effort to be accurate, but the landscape changes continually, so you should always double-check the latest availability of models and product specifications directly with the manufacturer or through an authorized dealer. Note that models often have a letter, letters, or word after the model number; this usually indicates a distinct furniture style or finish color.

Top Picks Among American and European Pianos

You'll see that we have marked some piano models with an asterisk. This denotes specific models we regard as top picks. These selections were made on the following criteria:

- ◆ Personal experience with the model in numbers significant enough for us to make an informed judgment.

- ◆ The model represents great performance and value in its size and price category.

Many top-tier models are not included in this identification as most or all would qualify at the high performance and high pricing levels.

American and European Listings

Each of the following tables lists the manufacturer's name, followed by model numbers/names, and size specifications. Sizes listed for verticals are the height of the piano from the floor to the top of the lid and for grands are the length from keyboard to tail.

Astin-Weight

Made by Astin-Weight in their factory in Utah, USA

Verticals	
Model	*Size*
UG375	41"
UG500	50"

Baldwin

Owned by Gibson (the guitar company), Baldwin brand pianos and Howard grands are made in the Baldwin factory in Truman, Arkansas, USA. Some vertical models may bear the names Acrosonic or Hamilton.

Grands		Verticals	
Model	*Size*	*Model*	*Size*
M1	5'2"	660	43$\frac{1}{2}$"
225	5'2"	2000	43$\frac{1}{2}$"
R1*	5'8"	5000	45"
226	5'8"	243*	45"
227	5'8"	248	48"
L1	6'3"	6000*	52$\frac{1}{2}$"
SF10*	7'0"		
SD10	9'0"		

C. Bechstein

Made in the Bechstein factory in Seifhennersdorf, Germany (formerly East Germany, recently moved from Berlin). The company headquarters remains in Berlin. They make two Bechstein lines; one is the more affordable Academy lineup and the other is their high-end line. Additional lines produced by Bechstein include W. Hoffman, Zimmerman, and Euterpe.

Grands		Verticals	
Model	*Size*	*Model*	*Size*
A160	5'3"	A116	45$\frac{1}{2}$"
A190	6'2$\frac{3}{4}$"	A124	48$\frac{3}{4}$"
A208	6'10"	116	45$\frac{5}{8}$"
A228	7'5$\frac{3}{4}$"	118	46$\frac{1}{2}$"
L167	5'5$\frac{3}{4}$"	124	48$\frac{7}{8}$"
M/P192	6'3$\frac{5}{8}$"		
B210	6'10$\frac{5}{8}$"		
C234	7'8$\frac{1}{8}$"		
D280	9'2$\frac{1}{4}$"		

Bohemia

In February 2007, Bohemia was bought by Bechstein. To date, Bohemia-branded pianos are made in a former Petrof factory in Hradec Kralov, Czech Republic.

Grands		Verticals	
Model	*Size*	*Model*	*Size*
150	4'11"	111	43³/₄"
156	5'2"	113	45"
170	5'7"	118	46¹/₂"
173	5'8"	121	48"
185	6'1"	122	48"
225	7'4"	123	48"
272	8'11"	125	49"
		132	52"

Blüthner

Made in the Blüthner factory in Leipzig, Germany (formerly East Germany).

Grands		Verticals	
Model	*Size*	*Model*	*Size*
11	5'1"	I	46"
10	5'5"	A	49"
6	6'3"	B	52"
4	6'10"		
2	7'8"		
1	9'2"		

Haessler

Made by Blüthner in their factory in Leipzig, Germany.

Grands		Verticals	
Model	*Size*	*Model*	*Size*
H175	5'8"	K115	45"
H186	6'1"	K118	47"
		K124	49"
		K132	52"

Irmler-Europe

Made by Blüthner in a factory in Poland.

Grands		Verticals	
Model	*Size*	*Model*	*Size*
F16E	5'5"	M113E	44$^1/_2$"
F18E	5'11"	M122E	48"
F22E	7'3"		

Borgato

Made by Borgato in their factory in Lonigo, Italy.

Grands	
Model	*Size*
L282	9'3"

Bösendorfer

Crafted in the Bösendorfer factory in Vienna, Austria.

Grands		Verticals	
Model	*Size*	*Model*	*Size*
170	5'8"	130	52"
185	6'1"		
200	6'7"		
214	7'0"		
225	7'4"		
280	9'2"		
290	9'6"		

Estonia

Made by the Laul Estonia factory in Tallinn, Republic of Estonia.

Grands	
Model	*Size*
168*	5'6"
190*	6'3"
274	9'0"

Fazioli

Made by Fazioli in their factory in Sacile, Italy.

Grands	
Model	*Size*
F156	5'1½"
F183	6'0"
F212	6'1½"

Grands	
F228	6'5³/₄"
F278	9'1¹/₂"
F308	10'1¹/₄"

Feurich

Made by Feurich in their factory in Gunzenhausen, Germany (formerly East Germany).

Grands		Verticals	
Model	*Size*	*Model*	*Size*
F172	5'8"	F116	45⁵/₈"
F197	6'5"	F118	46¹/₂"
F227	7'7"	F123	48¹/₂"

August Förster

Made in the Förster factory in Löbau, Germany (formerly East Germany).

Grands		Verticals	
Model	*Size*	*Model*	*Size*
170	5'7"	116	45⁵/₈"
190	6'2³/₄"	125	49¹/₄"
225	7'4¹/₂"		
275	9'0"		

Grotrian

Made by Grotrian in their factory in Braunschweig, Germany.

Grands		Verticals	
Model	*Size*	*Model*	*Size*
165	5'5"	112	44"
192	6'3$\frac{1}{2}$"	116	45$\frac{5}{8}$"
208	6'9$\frac{7}{8}$"	122	48"
225	7'4$\frac{1}{2}$"	124	48$\frac{7}{8}$"
277	9'1"	132	52"

Kemble

Made in the United Kingdom by Kemble, with some association with Yamaha.

Grands		Verticals	
Model	*Size*	*Model*	*Size*
KC173	5'8"	110	43$\frac{1}{4}$"
		112	44"
		114	44$\frac{7}{8}$"
		116	45$\frac{5}{8}$"
		118	46$\frac{1}{2}$"
		121	47$\frac{5}{8}$"
		124	48$\frac{3}{4}$"
		131	51$\frac{1}{2}$"

Mason & Hamlin

Made by Mason & Hamlin in their factory in Haverhill, Massachusetts.

Grands		Verticals	
Model	*Size*	*Model*	*Size*
B	5'4"	50*	50"
A	5'8½"		
AA	6'4"		
BB*	6'11½"		
CC-94	9'4"		

Petrof

Petrof branded pianos are made by Petrof in their factory in Hradec Kralov, Czech Republic. They have been distributed in the United States by Geneva International. In June 2007, a rift between the factory and Geneva was announced. As of January 2008, Petrof is distributed in the United States by Petrof U.S.A., LLC., headquartered in Lilburn, Georgia.

Grands		Verticals	
Model	*Size*	*Model*	*Size*
VI	4'10"	P116	46"
V	5'3"	P118	46"
IV*	5'8"	P125*	50"
III	6'4"	P131*	52"
Pasat B	6'10"	P135	53"
II	7'9"		
I	9'0"		

Pleyel

Built by Manufacture Française de Pianos, in their factory in Alès, France.

Grands		Verticals	
Model	*Size*	*Model*	*Size*
170	5'7"	118	46$^{1}/_{2}$"
190	6'2$^{3}/_{4}$"	124	48$^{3}/_{4}$"
280	9'2$^{1}/_{4}$"	131	51$^{1}/_{2}$"

Sauter

Made in the Sauter factory in Spaichingen, Germany (formerly East Germany).

Grands		Verticals	
Model	*Size*	*Model*	*Size*
160	5'3"	112	44"
185	6'$^{3}/_{4}$"	116	45$^{1}/_{2}$"
210	5'10$^{3}/_{4}$"	118	46$^{1}/_{2}$"
220	7'2$^{1}/_{2}$"	122	48"
230	7'6$^{1}/_{2}$"	123.5	48$^{1}/_{2}$"
275	9'1$^{1}/_{4}$"	125	49$^{1}/_{4}$"
		130	51"
		134	52$^{3}/_{4}$"
		157	61$^{3}/_{4}$"

Schulze Pollmann

Made by Schulze Pollmann in their factory in Bolzano, Italy.

Grands		Verticals	
Model	*Size*	*Model*	*Size*
160	5'3"	113	45$\frac{1}{4}$"
190	6'3"	118	46$\frac{1}{2}$"
197	6'5$\frac{1}{2}$"	126	49$\frac{1}{2}$"

Schimmel

Schimmels are crafted in their factory in Braunschweig, Germany.

Grands		Verticals	
Model	*Size*	*Model*	*Size*
K169	5'7"	C112	45"
C182	6'0"	C116	46"
K189*	6'3"	C120	48"
K213*	7'0"	K122	48"
K230	7'6"	C124	49"
K256	8'4"	K125	49"
K280	9'2"	C130	51"
		K132	52"

Vogel

Vogels are owned and built in Schimmel's factory in Kalisz, Poland.

Grands		Verticals	
Model	*Size*	*Model*	*Size*
V160*	5'4"	V115	45"
V177*	5'10"		

Ed. Seiler

Made in the Seiler factory in Kitzingen, Germany.

Grands		Verticals	
Model	*Size*	*Model*	*Size*
168	5'6"	116	45³/₄"
186	6'1¹/₄"	122	48"
208	6'10"	132	52"
242	7'11¹/₄"		
278	9'1¹/₂"		

Steingraeber & Söhne

Crafted by Steingraeber & Söhne in their factory in Bayreuth, Germany.

Grands		Verticals	
Model	*Size*	*Model*	*Size*
168	5'6"	110	43¹/₄"
205	6'8³/₄"	116	45⁵/₈"
E272	8'11"	117	46"
		122	48"
		130	51¹/₈"
		138	54³/₈"

Steinway & Sons

The bulk of the Steinways seen in the United States are made in Steinway's New York factory in Astoria, Queens. Pianos from their factory in Hamburg, Germany are extremely rare in the United States. Often, fallboard and soundboard decals as well as plate castings, have identified "New York & Hamburg." Only certain cabinet details, model years, and action specs can determine factory of origin. Of course, Steinway itself keeps detailed records of serial numbers and factory of manufacture information. In our collective 44 years in the business, we have seen fewer than two dozen authentic Hamburg-built Steinways here in the United States.

Grands		Verticals	
Model	*Size*	*Model*	*Size*
S	5'1"	4510	45"
M	5'7"	1098	46$\frac{1}{2}$"
O*	5'10$\frac{3}{4}$"	V125	49"
A	6'2"	K52*	52"
B*	6'10$\frac{1}{2}$"		
C	7'5$\frac{1}{2}$"		
D	8'11$\frac{3}{4}$"		

Charles Walter

Made in the Walter factory in Elkhart, Indiana, USA.

Grands		Verticals	
Model	*Size*	*Model*	*Size*
W190*	6'4"	1520	43$\frac{3}{8}$"
		1500*	45"

The Least You Need to Know

◆ American and European pianos have many building techniques and materials in common.

◆ It's difficult to keep up with brand names and where they are made, so always consult the manufacturers' websites and authorized dealers for the latest information.

◆ Since the early 1990s, Eastern European pianos have altered the landscape by offering excellent pianos at good prices.

◆ The lines between countries of origin are becoming blurred, and only time will tell if country of origin will remain a marker of performance value.

Chapter 13

Asian Brand Names, Models, and Origins

In This Chapter

- ◆ The Evolution of Asian pianos
- ◆ Where they are made
- ◆ Current Asian piano manufacturers and models

In the late 1960s, high-quality Japanese products began to flow into the United States. These products eclipsed the earlier stigma of cheap Japanese transistor radios and represented exceptional value over their American-made counterparts. First consumer electronics, then motorcycles, cars, and trucks, began to give American manufacturers a run for their money. Pianos were no exception.

With good or bad timing, depending on your perspective, Japanese pianos hit the U.S. market at the height of the domestic piano mediocrity malaise. The import pianos had a fresh look and clearer (brighter) tone, and came apart more easily for servicing. Best of all, they were nearly half the price of the comparable American pianos. In this chapter, we'll take a look at Asian brand names, where they are built today, and current models and sizes available.

Asian Pianos Enter the American Scene

The first Asian pianos to enter the American market were Yamaha and Kawai from Japan, appearing in the 1960s. The second Asian wave took place in the form of a wealth of private label *stencil pianos* from Korea in the 1970s. Then Samick and Young Chang (the two largest of the Korean factories) began focusing on their companies' brand names in the 1980s. Also, in the early 1980s, private label stencil pianos arrived through Macao from mainland China. A trickle at first, pianos from China have now become a huge part of the marketplace. Korea had been the new Japan in the piano world. Now China is the new Korea.

def•i•ni•tion

Stencil pianos are pianos where the brand name on the front of the piano is not the same as that on the front of the factory. You can learn much more about stencil pianos in Chapter 14.

Yamaha bought the Everett piano factory in South Haven, Michigan, in 1973 and built some Yamaha vertical pianos there until 1986. Yamaha also built a sizable upright factory in Thomaston, Georgia, in 1979, which closed in March of 2007. Kawai recently shut down its Lincolnton, North Carolina, factory, where it had been since 1988, to move production of those uprights to Indonesia, where labor is cheaper. Not all production is moving offshore, however; Samick Music Corporation recently built a sizable factory and distribution center in Gallatin, Tennessee.

Why Asian Pianos Caught On So Well

The early Asian pianos, primarily Yamaha and Kawai, did not become famous because they were the best pianos in the world. Rather, they got the piano world's attention because they were great bargains. In the beginning, one could buy a new Yamaha or Kawai for one-half to two-thirds the price of a comparable American piano.

In addition, Asian pianos tuned more easily than domestic pianos and were richer in the fundamental tones, with less of the partials and harmonics. They also came apart much more easily for service than their domestic counterparts (2 wing nuts to remove the action in a grand versus 8 to 10 screws in 3 sizes on most domestic pianos). Tuners quickly came to love and recommend these instruments.

Yamaha and Kawai courted colleges and universities by offering free pianos and pianos at below-market prices to high-profile schools. They developed innovative school loan programs to fill music departments with a single brand. Yamaha and Kawai regularly beat out American and European competitors in school bids due to their price advantages, decent specifications, and performance.

Japanese manufacturers also attracted piano teachers by sponsoring symposia, donating scholarships, and selling pianos to teachers at below-market prices.

With the exception of some early problems with learning to cure the wood for the United States' climates (see Chapter 10) and some odd ideas about cabinet styles Americans would like, the early Japanese pianos played better than most of the domestic pianos of the day. Their landed quality (the condition they're in right out of the box), fits, and finishes were superior, all the way from Japan, to many domestic pianos coming from the Midwest or East Coast. The most important difference, however, was that they had a different sound. American pianos have a round, thick, woody, hollow, mellow sound; whereas Japanese pianos sound brighter, clearer, and more present. The sound was recognizably different and appealed to the market almost overnight.

Today, however, Japanese pianos are not the bargain they were in the early days. They have improved to the point that they compete in the world-class category. They are regularly selected by finalists in many international classical competitions and in all genres of music recordings.

To fill the need for medium and low-priced instruments, the Koreans, Indonesians, and now the Chinese have stepped into the arena. These entities have the Japanese playbook in their hands plus 40 years of data collected from the Japanese experience. The Chinese have greatly impacted the American market and are accelerating far beyond their predecessors.

What's In a Name?

Though country of origin may fade as a marker of quality and/or performance in the decades to come, we know there is some degree of misrepresentation today on this issue. It is common for Chinese pianos with European-sounding names to be passed off as German and sold at premium prices. Many Chinese and Indonesian factories now own the rights to once-popular American brand names. Often, these pianos are sold to unsuspecting buyers at premium pricing. As a customer, it's important for you to be able to judge and compare price, construction, materials, and performance and to come up with your own "value quotient."

Key Note

When offered as an alternative to a 25-plus year-old Japanese or Korean used piano, some new Chinese pianos can be a much better investment in touch, tone, durability, serviceability, and warranty protection.

We believe accurate information regarding the country and factory of origin is part of this data mix to which you as a prospective buyer are entitled.

Current Asian Manufacturers, Models, and Origins

Almost by definition, pianos made anywhere in Asia are mass-produced. The only exceptions are the Shigeru Kawai series and the Yamaha models S4B, S6B, and CFIII series made in separate facilities by a cadre of craftsmen. High-end pianos made by Samick Music Corporation's Korean factory are also considered an exception to the mass-production rule.

Remember, with the considerable flux and change in the piano world, it has become increasingly difficult to tell what is what in the piano business. Following is a partial list of most of the popular selling Asian pianos in the United States at the time of this writing. We have made every effort at accuracy, but the "straight scoop" information is often hard to come by, even for industry veterans like ourselves.

We have included the basic models, but you may come across additional model designations that have a letter, letters, or word after the model number, which usually indicates a distinct furniture style or finish color.

Also in this section, as with the American and European models covered in the previous chapter, we have identified our top picks with an asterisk based on performance and value and our experience with them.

American Sejung Corporation (ASC)

ASC pianos were shown first in the United States in 2003. They are produced in a modern factory in Qingdao, China. In addition to private labels, ASC makes Falcone, Geo. Steck, Hobart M. Cable, whose models are listed below.

Falcone

Made by ASC in their factory in Qingdao, China.

Grands		Verticals	
Model	*Size*	*Model*	*Size*
GF42	4'8"	UF09	43"
GF52	5'0"	CF/UF12	44"

Grands		Verticals	
GF62	5'4"	CF13	44$\frac{1}{2}$"
GF72	5'8"	CF16	45$\frac{1}{2}$"
GF87	6'2"	CF/UF19	46$\frac{3}{4}$"
GF208	6'10"	UF19	46$\frac{3}{4}$"
GF278	9'2"	UF20	46$\frac{3}{4}$"
		UF21	48"
		UF23*	48"
		UF26	48"
		UF32	51$\frac{3}{4}$"

Hobart M. Cable

Made by ASC in their factory in Qingdao, China.

Grands		Verticals	
Model	*Size*	*Model*	*Size*
GH42	4'8"	UH09	43"
GH52	5'0"	CH/UH12	44"
GH62	5'4"	CH13	44$\frac{1}{2}$"
GH72	5'8"	CH/UH16	45$\frac{1}{2}$"
GH87	6'2"	CH/UH19	46$\frac{3}{4}$"
		UH18	47"
		UH20	47"
		UH21	47"
		UH22	48"

Geo. Steck

Made by ASC in their factory in Qingdao, China.

Grands		Verticals	
Model	*Size*	*Model*	*Size*
GS42	4'8"	CS/US09	43"
GS52	5'0"	US09	43"
GS62	5'4"	CS/US12	44"
GS72	5'8"	CS/US16	45$\frac{1}{2}$"
GS87	6'2"	US18	46$\frac{3}{4}$"
GS208	6'10"	CS/US19	46$\frac{3}{4}$"
GS228	7'6"	US21	48"
GS278	9'2"	US22	48"
		US23	48"
		US25	48"
		US28	51$\frac{3}{4}$"
		US32	51$\frac{3}{4}$"

Hamilton

Currently produced for Baldwin by American Sejung Corporation. Production will likely shift to Gibson's (Baldwin's) new acquisition, Dongbei.

Grands		Verticals	
Model	*Size*	*Model*	*Size*
H391	4'7"	H350	43"
H396	5'1"	H310	44"
H398	5'4"	H360	47"
H399	5'8"	H370	47"
H401	6'2"		

Wurlitzer

Currently produced for Baldwin by American Sejung, ASC. Production will likely shift to Gibson's (Baldwin's) new acquisition, Dongbei.

Grands

Model	Size
C143	4' 7"
C153	5' 1"
C173	5' 8"
C203	6' 8"
C223	7' 5"
C273	9' 0"

Boston

A line of pianos commissioned and specified by Steinway and built by Kawai, to be sold through the Steinway dealer network. Verticals are coming from Kawai factories in Japan and Indonesia. Grands are coming from a Kawai factory in Japan.

Grands		Verticals	
Model	Size	Model	Size
GP156	5'1"	UP118	46$\frac{1}{2}$"
GP163	5'4"	UP126	49$\frac{1}{2}$"
GP178	5'10"	UP132	52"
GP193	6'4"		
GP215	7'1"		

Breitmann

Made for Blüthner by the Yohahy factory in Quing Pu, China.

Grands		Verticals	
Model	*Size*	*Model*	*Size*
B16	5'2"	B110	44"
B17	5'8"	B120	47$\frac{1}{4}$"
		B122	48"
		B130	52"

Dongbei Piano Company

Bought by Gibson (Baldwin) in 2006, Dongbei manufactures pianos in their Dongbei, China, factory for export to the United States, as well as for domestic consumption in China. Brand names include Hallet, Davis & Co., Nordiska, as well as others.

Hallet, Davis & Co.

Made by Dongbei in their factory in China.

Grands		Verticals	
Model	*Size*	*Model*	*Size*
Petite Condo	4'9"	Heritage	43"
Classic	5'0"	Continental	44"
Victorian	5'0"	Chippendale	45"
Parlor	5'5"	Classic	46"
Artist	6'1"	Traditional	48"
Semi-Concert	7'1"	Conservatory	50"
		Concert	52"

Nordiska

Made by Dongbei in their factory in China and distributed by Geneva International, a United States distributor of several brands.

Grands		Verticals	
Model	*Size*	*Model*	*Size*
B	4'8"	109	43"
D	5'0"	114	46"
G	5'5"	116	46"
K	6'1"	118	47"
O	7'0"	120	47"
Y	9'0"	126	50"
		131	52"

Story & Clark

Made by Dongbei in their factory in China.

Grands		Verticals	
Model	*Size*	*Model*	*Size*
Baby	4'9"	Various Names	45"
Prelude	5'0"	Cosmopolitan	47"
Conservatory	5'5"	Professional	55"
Professional	6'1"		
Concert	7'0"		

Suzuki

Made by Dongbei in their factory in China and sold through a warehouse club and direct via the Internet.

Grands		Verticals	
Model	*Size*	*Model*	*Size*
F-410	4'10"	T-43	43"
F-52	5'2"	T-45	45"
F-58	5'8"	T-48	48"
F-62	6'2"		
F-70	7'0"		

Weinbach

Made by Dongbei in their factory in China. Formerly made by Petrof. They are distributed by Geneva International.

Grands	
Model	*Size*
50	5'0"
55	5'5"
60	6'0"

Rhythm and News

Additional Dongbei brand names include Prince, Princess, Ekstrom, and August Hoffman.

Essex

A line of pianos commissioned and specified by Steinway and built by Pearl River in Guangzhou, China, and Young Chang in China and Korea.

Grands		Verticals	
Model	*Size*	*Model*	*Size*
EGP155	5'1"	EUP108	43"
EGP161	5'3$^1/_2$"	EUP111	44"
EGP173	5'8"	EUP116	45$^1/_2$"
EGP183	6'0"	EUP123	48$^1/_2$"

Hailun

Made by Ningbo Hailun Musical Instrument Co., Ningbo, China.

Grands		Verticals	
Model	*Size*	*Model*	*Size*
HG151	4'11$^1/_2$"	HU121	47$^5/_8$"
HG161	5'4"	HU123	48$^1/_2$"
HG178	5'10"	HU125	49$^1/_4$"

Steigerman

Made by Ningbo Hailun Musical Instrument Co., Ningbo, China.

Grands		Verticals	
Model	*Size*	*Model*	*Size*
SG143	4'8"	SU108	42"
SG148	4'10"	SU110	43"
SPG151	5'0"	SU43	43"
SG158	5'2"	SPU115	45"

continues

continued

Grands		Verticals	
SPG161	5'4"	SU115	45"
SG168	5'6"	SU117	46"
SPG178	5'10"	SU118	46"
SG185	6'0"	SU120	47"
		SPU121	48"
		SPU123	49"
		SU32	52"
		SU132	52"

Heintzman

Made by Heintzman Piano Co. Ltd, a Canadian company, built in a factory in Beijing, China.

Grands		Verticals	
Model	*Size*	*Model*	*Size*
168	5'6"	110	43"
203	6'8"	120	47"
274	9'	121	47$\frac{1}{2}$"
		123	48"
		126	50"
		130	51"
		132	52"
		140	55"

Kawai

K. Kawai grands are made in their factory in Japan with the exception of their entry-level model, GM10, where the final assembly is done in a Kawai factory in Indonesia. Kawai verticals shorter than 47" are made in their factory in Indonesia. Kawai verticals taller than 47" are made in their factory in Japan (one exception is the new model K2 45" also made in Japan).

Grands		Verticals	
Model	*Size*	*Model*	*Size*
GM10K*	5'0"	K15	44"
GM12	5'0"	506	44$\frac{1}{2}$"
GE20	5'1"	508	44$\frac{1}{2}$"
GE30	5'5"	607	44$\frac{1}{2}$"
RX1	5'5"	907	46$\frac{1}{2}$"
RX2*	5'10"	UST7	46"
RX3	6'1"	UST8	46"
RX5	6'6"	UST9	46"
RX6	7'0"	K2	45"
RX7	7'6"	K3	48"
EX	9'0"	K5	50"
		K6	52"
		K8	52"

Rhythm and News

The initial "K." in front of the Kawai name on their grands bears no significance; it is just tradition, out of respect to the original owner, Koichi Kawai, a grand-piano designer.

Shigeru Kawai

This is an upscale series of limited edition, hand-crafted Kawai grand pianos. They feature the finest of materials and attention to detail. They are crafted in Kawai's factory in Japan.

Grands	
Model	*Size*
SK2	5'10"
SK3	6'1"
SK5	6'6"
SK6	7'0"
SK7	7'6"

May Berlin

May Berlins are built in the Toyama factory in China to Schimmel's specifications, then receive finishing touches in Braunschwieg, Germany. So, do these pianos end up with an Asian sound or European sound? In our opinion, the touch and tone on this line is somewhat in between the two.

Grands		Verticals	
Model	*Size*	*Model*	*Size*
M162	5'4"	M121	48"
M187	6'2"	M126	50"

Palatino

Made by AXL Musical Instruments Co., Ltd. Corp. in a factory in Shanghai, China.

Grands		Verticals	
Model	*Size*	*Model*	*Size*
KP-PGD-46	4'6"	KP-PUP-123	48½"
KP-PGD-50	5'0"	KP-PUP-126	50"
KP-PGD-59	5'9"		
KP-PGD-90	9'0"		

Gebr. Perzina

Perzina pianos are manufactured by Gebr. Perzina at Yantai-Perzina Piano Manufacturing Co., Ltd. in Yantai, China. They are distributed in the United States by Piano Empire, Inc., Santa Fe Springs, CA.

Grands		Verticals	
Model	*Size*	*Model*	*Size*
E160	5'3"	GP112	44"
G160	5'3"	GP118	46½"

Grands		Verticals	
E187	6'1"	GP122	48"
G187	6'1"	GP129*	51"

Pearl River

Pearl River has been building pianos in their factory in Guangzhou, China, since 1956.

Grands		Verticals	
Model	*Size*	*Model*	*Size*
GP142	4'7"	UP108	42½"
GP148	4'7"	UP110	43"
GP150	4'11½"	UP115*	45"
GP159	5'3"	UP118	46½"
GP170	5'7"	UP120*	47"
GP183*	6'0"	UP125	49"
GP186	6'3"	UP130	51"
GP188	6'3"		
GP198	6'3"		
GP213	7'0"		
GP275	9'0"		

Ritmüller

Built by Pearl River in the factory in Guangzhou, China.

Grands		Verticals	
Model	*Size*	*Model*	*Size*
GP142	4'7"	UP110	43"
GP159	5'2"	UP118	46"
GP183	6'0"	UP120	47"

continues

continued

Grands		Verticals	
GP213	7'0"	UP123	49"
		UP125	51"
		UP126	51"
		UP130	51"

Henry F. Miller

Built by Pearl River in the factory in Guangzhou, China. The name is owned by Sherman Clay & Co., a large retailer. They currently wholesale this brand to select other retailers outside their market areas.

Grands		Verticals	
Model	*Size*	*Model*	*Size*
HMG056	4'8"	HMV043	43"
HMG063*	5'3"	HMV045	45"
		HMV047	47"

Samick Music Corporation, SMC

Samick distributes a variety of piano products in the United States. Originally a Korean company, SMC now has factories in Korea, Indonesia, China, and most recently in Tennessee.

Wm. Knabe & Co.

Upscale uprights and grands made in SMC's factory in Inchon, South Korea. Future production in Gallatin, Tennessee, USA, projected by late 2008. Even though these pianos have been built in Korea, the design and material specifications have come from the original American scale designs and therefore sound very American to our ears.

Grands		Verticals	
Model	*Size*	*Model*	*Size*
WKG53	5'3"	WKV118*	46³/₄"
WKG58*	5'8"	WKV121	48"
WKG64*	6'4"	WKV131*	52"
WKG70	7'0"		

Sohmer & Co.

Upscale uprights and grands made in SMC's factory in Inchon, South Korea. Future production in Gallatin, Tennessee, projected by late 2008.

Grands		Verticals	
Model	*Size*	*Model*	*Size*
50	5'0"	43	43"
63	5'4"		
77*	5'9"		
90	6'2"		

J. P. Pramberger

Upscale uprights and grands made in SMC's factory in Inchon, South Korea. Future production in Gallatin, Tennessee, projected by late 2008.

Grands		Verticals	
Model	*Size*	*Model*	*Size*
PS150	4'11¹/₂"	PV110	43"
PS157	5'2"	JP116	45"
JP160S	5'3"	PV118	46"
PS175	5'9"	JP118	46"
JP170L	5'10"	PV121	48"

continues

continued

Grands		Verticals	
PS185	6'1"	JP125	49"
JP190A	6'3"	PV131	52"
JP208B	6'10"	JP131	52"

Kohler & Campbell

Standard K&C verticals and grands as well as some of the Millenium series are made in SMC's facility in Indonesia. Some of their Millennium series verticals and grands are made in SMC's facilities in Inchon, South Korea. Millenium series have an "M" in their model designation.

Grands		Verticals	
Model	*Size*	*Model*	*Size*
KCG450	4'9"	KC142	42"
KCG500	5'2"	KC244	43"
KCM500	5'3"	KC245	45"
KF/CM600	5'7³/₄"	KC647	46¹/₂"
KCG600	5'9"	KC247	46¹/₂"
KF/CM650	6'1"	KC121	48"
KFM700	6'8³/₄"	KMV48	48"
KFM850	7'4¹/₂"	KC131	52"
		KMV52	52"

Samick

All Samick-branded pianos are made in SMC's factories in Indonesia.

Grands		Verticals	
Model	*Size*	*Model*	*Size*
SIG50*	5'0"	JS042	42"
SIG54	5'4"	JS143*	43"

Grands		Verticals	
SIG57	5'7"	JS115	45"
SIG61	6'1"	JS247	46½"
		JS121*	48"
		JS131	52"

Remington

All Remington-branded pianos are made in SMC's factories in Indonesia.

Grands		Verticals	
Model	*Size*	*Model*	*Size*
RG150	5'0"	RV43	43"
RG157	5'2"	RV108	43"
RG175	5'9"	RV118	46½"
RG185	6'1"	RV121	48"
		RV131	52"

Yamaha

For new Yamaha pianos distributed in the United States, all Yamaha-branded grands come from their factory in Japan except their model GB1 (4'11"), where the final assembly is done in a Yamaha factory in Indonesia. Yamaha-branded verticals less than 46" tall were made in their factory in Thomaston, Georgia, USA through March 31, 2007, when the Georgia factory closed. Beginning sometime in August 2007, these models began shipping from Yamaha's own facilities in Taiwan (a Yamaha factory built in 1969) and in Hangzhou, China. In June 2007, Yamaha began distributing the model T118 its new factory in mainland China. Yamaha-branded verticals 48" and taller are made in their factory in Japan.

Grands		Verticals	
Model	*Size*	*Model*	*Size*
GB1	4'11"	M460	44"

continues

Grands		Verticals	
GC1*	5'3"	M560*	44"
C1	5'3"	P22	45"
C2	5'8"	P660	45"
C3*	6'1"	T116	45"
S4	6'3"	T118*	46½"
C5	6'7"	T121	48"
C6*	6'11"	U1*	48"
S6	6'11"	YUS1	48"
C7	7'6"	U3	52"
CFIIIS	9'0"	YUS3	52"
		YUS5	52"

Rhythm and News

Yamaha became a joint venture partner with the established Chinese manufacturer Pearl River in 1995. Together they built one professional-model upright (UP125M1) with the Pearl River name on it. Yamaha also built some Yamaha-branded pianos in Pearl River's factory for distribution in China only. This relationship was ended after 12 years in June, 2007, by Yamaha in favor of its own Chinese and Taiwanese factories.

Cable-Nelson

Yamaha also makes Cable-Nelson in their mainland China factory.

Verticals	
Model	*Size*
CN116	45"
CN216	45"

Young Chang

Young Chang distributes a variety of products in the United States. The company is owned by Hyundai Development Company. They have factories in Korea and mainland China. Distributors in the United States are Young Chang North America, based in Rancho Dominguez, CA.

Grands		Verticals	
Model	*Size*	*Model*	*Size*
YP175	6'1"	YP121	48"
YP208	6'10"	YP48	48"
YP228	7'6"	YP52	52"
		YP275	9' 0"

Bergmann

Pianos built in Young Chang's factory in China.

Grands		Verticals	
Model	*Size*	*Model*	*Size*
BTG150	4'11"	BAF108	43$\frac{1}{2}$"
BTG175	5'9"		
BTG185	6'1"		

Weber Legend

Pianos built in Young Chang's factory in China.

Grands		Verticals	
Model	*Size*	*Model*	*Size*
WG150	4'11"	WGS109	43"
WG175	5'9"	WGS121	47$\frac{3}{4}$"
WG185	6'1"		

Wyman

A line of pianos commissioned and specified by Wyman. Manufactured by the Beijing Hsinghai Piano Group, Ltd., in Beijing, China. Distributed by Wyman Piano Company out of Nashville, TN.

Grands		Verticals	
Model	*Size*	*Model*	*Size*
WG145	4'9"	WV108	42½"
WG160	5'3"	WV110	43"
WG170	5'7"	WV115	45"
		WV118	46"
		WV120	48"
		WV132	52"

Nearly 100 piano manufacturers are currently established in China. Most do not export to the United States, but the numbers are growing!

The Least You Need to Know

◆ Many brands that were once made in the United States are now made in Asia.

◆ Asian pianos first came to the states in the 1960s from Japan.

◆ At first Japanese pianos were great bargains, but they now compete in the price categories of world-class manufacturers.

◆ As with American and European brands, the lines between countries of origin among Asian pianos are becoming blurred, and only time will tell if country of origin will remain a marker of performance value.

14

Are Lower-End Pianos Worth the Savings?

In This Chapter

- ◆ What stencil pianos are and how to spot them
- ◆ When stencil pianos are a good value
- ◆ Student model pianos
- ◆ Pianos from China

If you're on a tight budget when shopping for a piano, then you are probably in the market for lower-priced models. You might also be looking at lower-end pianos if you have doubts that your piano is going to be played frequently enough, or over a long enough period of time, to get your return on investment. Lower quality typically—but not always—goes hand-in-hand with lower prices, so we want you to know what you're getting into if you're out to save a few bucks. In this chapter, we explore lower-end pianos including stencil pianos and pianos from China.

Stencil Pianos: What They Are

Not all pianos are what they appear to be. For decades, some manufacturers have built generic, lower-quality pianos for distributors and retailers with a variety of names stenciled on the front. These are called *stencil pianos*. Often the stenciled name sounds close to that of a more famous and recognizable brand. Frequently these names come from old, defunct American companies that still command some recognition in the marketplace. Names are usually chosen because they sound American or German, even though the piano may be made in Indonesia or mainland China. Unfortunately, many customers are hoodwinked into paying top dollar for lesser-quality instruments and are deliberately led to believe the product comes from Germany or another high-profile location.

def•i•ni•tion

A **stencil piano** is an instrument built by a manufacturer with another brand name placed on it.

Key Note

Important questions to ask when considering the purchase of a stencil piano are: Who made this piano? In what city and country was it made? What is the factory warranty? Besides you, who backs the warranty, should your company fail or I move? To be safe, double-check what you are told.

Typically these pianos are built under contract with a retailer, distributor, or another manufacturer. Often the manufacturer of a stencil piano wishes to increase its market distribution by adding additional brand names under its own auspices without jeopardizing the reputation of the factory name.

Stencil pianos are not intrinsically of poor quality, but they are usually less impressive than pianos bearing the true factory name. The concern with stencil pianos is not that the quality is always bad but that the makers and/or sellers of these pianos mislead customers into thinking they are buying something they're not. The reputations and value of piano brand names are built on decades of consistency in quality, durability, performance, and predictable resale values. It is not uncommon for once renowned, but now defunct, manufacturers to trade or sell their name to the highest bidder. Unsuspecting customers see that name on a piano and assume they are getting great value, when in fact, the actual instrument may or may not be at the level of quality that name implies.

Finding a Quality Stencil Piano

In recent years, Samick Music Corporation (SMC) downsized its Inchon, South Korea, piano factory and moved production of its lower lines of production pianos to

Jakarta, Indonesia. Samick re-tooled the smaller Inchon operation to produce a limited number of higher-end pianos that did not resemble their other lines.

Their lower lines share the characteristics of other Asian pianos with mahogany plywood rims, V-Pro cast plates, and typical high-polish polyester finishes. The special pianos built in SMC's Inchon facility today represent a departure from the norm. The brand names produced there are Wm. Knabe & Co., Sohmer & Co., and Pramberger (see Chapter 13). All three lines feature hardwood rims (maple and/or oak), sand-cast plates, spruce support beams, and premium action components; they are often available in hand-rubbed fine furniture finishes.

Several of the Knabe and Sohmer models feature original American scale designs from the 1920s and 1930s, as well as a faithful use of original materials and parts specifications. We are told that the Pramberger line is an extension of the late Joseph Pramberger's design work. These three lines of pianos do not fit the classic definition of a stencil piano in that they are distinct and varied products from Samick's other lines. Their specifications, materials, fits and finishes, and, more importantly, their performance in touch and tone surpass the Samick-branded instrument line. These are not cheap knock-offs or re-badged inferior instruments by any means.

B-Sharp

Dealers sometimes resort to the stencil piano ploy when they cannot earn authorized representation status of a particular high-profile brand. These dealers buy container loads of Chinese pianos, put German names on them, and try to market them as an exclusive line. Selling this one-of-a-kind, unknown brand name opens the gates for price gouging.

Many stencil pianos being produced today are built under contract by one manufacturer for another manufacturer. And, in fact, the piano may be a decent instrument with a pretty good value. After a few years, it may begin to build a reputation and acceptance in the market place, resulting in a certain expectation of resale value and longevity. As the business climate turns, the contracting manufacturer may decide to award the contract to a cheaper builder. If this transpires, the lineage of that label becomes clouded and is especially problematic when subsequent manufacturers are lower bidders with not only lower profiles, but lower standards of materials and build quality.

In short, tread carefully with pianos of questionable origin. You don't want to end up paying a hand-made German price for a mass-produced piano bearing a German-sounding name that was built in China.

Student-Model Pianos: Myth or Reality?

In the world of school bands and orchestras, instruments are frequently identified by manufacturer, model name, and/or the retailer as being a "student model" or "beginner's model." Many parents shopping for a piano for a young beginner are wary of sinking a lot of money into an instrument and therefore express an interest in a student-model piano.

There are, in fact, no "student-model" pianos. However, lower-end, less expensive pianos are available. Typically, these pianos come from China. Clearly, there are differences in design, materials, workmanship, and performance between these and more expensive models.

The problem with the concept of student models is a matter of semantics, image, and prestige. No piano manufacturer wants to admit that his company makes a student-model piano. All piano makers tout their products as "best quality" and "professional grade." Most piano companies evolved from the hands of the founder craftsman. His pride in his workmanship was the genesis of the company, no matter how big it is today. Even new factories springing up in mainland China without this singularity of craftsman's pride still adopt the concept of touting "best quality" and "professional grade." You will never see company literature or an ad campaign touting, "Company XYZ, the foremost makers of student pianos for the discriminating beginner."

Deciding If a Lower-end Piano Is Right for You

All new acoustic pianos on the market today meet certain minimum standards with a full complement of 88 keys, and are at least 42 inches tall or taller. No longer are 76-note or spinet pianos made today. These substandard instruments were not found to be suitable, even for beginners, by most teachers.

What, then, are the differences between an entry-level Chinese 42" console for $2,000+ and a 48" Japanese professional-model upright for $6,000+? How does a $6,000 Chinese 5'3" baby grand perform against a larger model Japanese grand for nearly triple the price? You may ask, "Do I need to pay for this difference for my beginner student?" To answer this question, we recommend that you analyze your needs by asking yourself these three additional questions:

- Can we comfortably afford the higher-end model option?

- Are the student, teacher, and supporting family fully dedicated and committed long-term to the continued musical growth of the student? (If nobody is serious about the endeavor of piano playing at the intermediate and advanced levels, then advanced capabilities in the instrument are valueless.)

◆ Are we uncomfortable with the idea that we'll have to go through this shopping process again in a year or few years to upgrade to a higher-level instrument?

If you answered "no" to at least two of these questions, then a lower-end purchase might be the best thing for you. It's the more affordable option for now. Just be aware, though, that if the student does continue in piano, you will have to go through the buying process again to upgrade to a better instrument, at even higher prices, down the road.

Comparing Performance Levels of Pianos

As you contemplate whether it's worth the savings to go with an entry-level piano, consider the following comparison points:

◆ A professional-grade instrument produces a fuller and more lyrical sound. Bigger, better tone is like more watts of power in a stereo. You can hear more of the texture and detail.

◆ A professional-grade instrument has a stronger bass response and, therefore, more power.

◆ A professional-grade instrument has a more precise and responsive key mechanism, a characteristic that means better touch.

◆ A professional-grade instrument is more resonant and has more sustain, as well as more keyboard control at soft play.

◆ A professional-grade instrument has more dynamic range capability (louds and softs) and is thus more expressive.

◆ A professional-grade grand is likely to have more pedal function to command.

◆ A professional-grade piano is more stable through environmental changes because of better quality materials and greater precision manufacturing.

The seven differences detailed above are matters of degree. They lead to incremental increases in performance. Some are very subtle and relegated to the finer points of advanced play, but they are discernable and necessary at higher levels. Are these seven qualities important to a student? That depends on the student. Are they necessary for every family? Absolutely not. Are they desirable for those who will progress to the higher levels of performance? Absolutely yes.

> **Key Note**
>
> The characteristics that make a professional-grade piano stand out do decline over decades of play, so a new entry-level piano may actually beat the performance of an old and worn professional-grade piano on many points.

Does this mean that entry-level pianos are junk and not worth considering? No. Many entry-level pianos present good values and years of serviceable use. This point, coupled with a factory warranty on parts and labor for 10 years or more, makes many entry-level verticals and grands good buys for families with beginners.

If you are considering an entry-level grand, dealer preparation would be a key element in this decision. Complete preparation on entry-level grands is critical to any level of consistency and performance. A solid tuning or two, key-action regulation touch-up, and some light voicing to even out the tone can do wonders for these inexpensive grands. Torquing down the plates, seating and leveling the strings, and bedding the action can make these pianos come alive.

Should your family decide, for whatever reasons, to invest in a more professional-level instrument, the one thing we want to help you avoid is paying a professional-level price for an entry-level piano. This is where the unscrupulous take advantage of the uninformed. Study this guide and do your homework so that you won't become a victim.

New Kids on the Block: Pianos from China

As you learned in Chapter 13 in our discussion of Asian manufacturers, Chinese piano makers have hit the scene in a major way in recent years. In the 1960s, we saw the distribution of Japanese pianos blossom in the United States. In the 1970s, it was Korean pianos. In the late 1980s, the Chinese began distributing pianos to America. Beginning as a trickle at first, then growing, Chinese pianos didn't start entering the United States in earnest until the early 2000s. We're focusing on pianos from China in this chapter beyond our mention of them in Chapter 13 because Chinese piano factories are turning out many of the lower-end pianos these days, so they warrant inclusion in this chapter.

Nearly 100 piano factories are operating in mainland China, most of them less than 10 years old. It takes any piano builder years to learn the careful art of working with wood to build instruments that will be consistent, perform well, and last in all climate zones. Most of these new factories still have much to learn about building quality pianos suitable for the demanding American marketplace and our varied climate zones.

Confusion Surrounding Brand Labels out of China

American distributors of Chinese pianos often choose European or American sounding names to place on the front of these instruments. Few Chinese pianos have Chinese-sounding brand names. To compound the confusion, a number of retailers have adopted deceptive sales presentations and pricing strategies that do not fit with the bargain entry-level nature of these pianos.

The most common sales pitch is to claim that Chinese-made pianos have German parts and were built under German supervision in the German tradition. Some may have Delignit pinblocks and/or Rouslau stringing wire from Germany, but this does not make them German by any means. Most true German uprights retail for more than $12,000 with many costing more than $20,000. If a new piano is selling for $3,000, it is most decidedly not German. If a Chinese-built new vertical piano is selling for $12,000 or more, it ought to be considered a felony!

To confuse matters more, a couple of Chinese manufacturers actually have (or at one time had) a single model built in Europe, to which a salesperson can point and thus lead a customer to believe all models of that brand are made in Europe. Ask your salesperson about the specific model you are considering to determine where it's really from.

Brand Names Produced in China

The following is a partial list of Chinese-produced pianos:

Atlas	Hobart M. Cable	Ridgewood
August Hoffman	Hsinghai	Ritmüller
Bergmann	Irmler	Sagenhaft
Breitman	Kelman	Schumann
Brentwood	Kingsburg	Schwechten
Cable-Nelson	Lothar Schell	Sejung
Campbell & Young	Maddison	Silberman
Canary	Marshal	Steigerman
Carl Ebel	May Berlin	Steinberg
Cristofori	Milton	Story & Clark

continues

continued

Dongbei	Moutrie	Strauss
Essex	Nordiska	Suzuki
Everett	Odin	Vose & Sons
Falcone	Offenbach	Vienna
Geo. Steck	Otto Meister	Vivace
Hailun	Palatino	Weber Legend Series
Hallet Davis	Pearl River	Weinbach
Hamilton (some)	Perzina	Wendl & Lung
Hardman & Peck	PianoNova	Wurlitzer
Hayden	Prelude	Wyman
Heinzman	Rawlins & Co.	Xinghai
Henry F. Miller	Young Chang Gold Series	

Of the 65 names listed above, only 8 sound remotely Asian.

When Chinese Pianos Are a Good Value

Despite the concerns around misrepresentation of Chinese pianos, there are some bargains to be had and good values to be obtained from Chinese factories. To find these, be sure you are doing business with a dealer who represents the Chinese-made pianos honestly. Second, try to settle on a piano that has a United States, stateside, distributorship with parts stocked for support. These include:

◆ Pearl River and Ritmüller—Ontario, CA

◆ American Sejung products including George Steck, Falcone, and Hobart M. Cable—Walnut, CA

◆ Nordiska and Weinbach through Geneva International—Chicago, IL

◆ Cable-Nelson, made by Yamaha's factory in China, with warranties and parts supplied by Yamaha America Corp in Buena Park, CA

◆ Young Chang/Bergman/Weber, supported with warranties and parts from Young Chang North America in Rancho Dominguez, CA.

◆ Perzina pianos distributed by Piano Empire, Inc. in Santa Fe Springs, CA, providing parts and warranty support.

◆ Wyman Piano Company in Nashville, TN, provides warranty and parts support.

Stateside distributorships have staging areas for replacement parts here in the United States. This is important because you do not want to wait for your replacement parts to come by boat from China. You will also have some warranty recourse if the dealer who sold you the piano goes belly-up or becomes uncooperative about a pesky and expensive warranty problem (rare, but real).

We have been watching the growth, development, and evolution of pianos from mainland China for more than a decade. The bulk of the products today are vastly superior to those of just a few years ago. Many of the major players in the industry are joint venturing with existing factories. Other mainstream manufacturers are building their own factories in China from scratch to take advantage of the lower labor rates.

B-Sharp

Distributorships for pianos from China are in an almost constant state of flux, so it is difficult to nail down precise information at any given time. Always verify where parts and warranty recourse will come from if you buy a piano made in China.

You might have concerns about sweatshops, child labor, slave labor, abuse, and exploitation of workers in China. While we can't make promises about conditions at every factory, we can tell you that we've heard first-hand accounts from people we know and trust about clean and comfortable company worker housing, regular employee feeding programs, exercise programs, and education programs. Wages in mainland China are shockingly low by our standards, but according to our sources these factories are paying at or above the norm for that area.

Leading Piano Makers Operating in China

Yamaha was one of the first major players to dip into the cheap Chinese labor pool, with a $10 million investment as a joint venture partner with Pearl River in 1995. Today, both Yamaha and Kawai have their own factories in mainland China. For years, Yamaha has been producing Yamaha-branded products in their Chinese factories only for domestic consumption in China.

In 2005, Steinway & Sons announced they had signed contracts with Pearl River in China to build the Essex line of pianos for their dealership network. Essex had formerly been built for Steinway by Young Chang in China. Essex pianos are available from both Pearl River and Young Chang in China, and Young Chang out of Inchon, South Korea.

Geneva International Corp. decided to shift Weinbach (traditionally a sister piano to Petrof, made in the Petrof factory in the Czech Republic) production to Dongbei Piano Co., in China. This is another example of how secondary and tertiary lines of pianos can be broken off or shunted to other factories or manufacturers.

Initially, international piano building in China was for foreign manufacturers to invest in or become joint venture partners with existing Chinese builders. The Chinese government is relaxing regulations to encourage foreign investment. Many piano companies are now building their own manufacturing facilities in China. Only time will tell the tale of their success in Western markets and their long-term durability and serviceability.

The Least You Need to Know

- A stencil piano is an instrument built by a manufacturer that places a different brand name on it.

- Stencil pianos are not necessarily bad, but you don't want to pay European prices for a Chinese-made piano.

- Entry-level pianos can be a way to save money for the short-term.

- Few Chinese pianos distributed in the United States have Chinese-sounding names.

- Having German parts is not the same as a German-manufactured piano.

- Pianos manufactured in China are not necessarily bad, but make sure the piano you choose has a stateside distributorship for parts and warranty support.

15

Judging a Piano by Its Cover: Acoustic Piano Cabinets

In This Chapter

- ◆ Vertical cabinet features
- ◆ Vertical cabinet styles
- ◆ Grand cabinet styles

What matters most in selecting a piano is how it sounds and feels, as well as the quality of the materials and craftsmanship that have gone into it. Nevertheless, you also have to live with the look of the piano, possibly for many years to come. There's nothing wrong with caring about the color, finish, and style of a piano. Whether purchasing for your home or an institution, your piano reflects your own taste and style. When not being played, a piano is a piece of furniture, plain and simple. So it makes sense that you would want a piano that blends well with your overall décor.

In this chapter, we survey current furniture styles for both verticals and grands so that you know what your options are.

Differences in Grand and Vertical Cabinet Options

Upright pianos less than 47" tall are frequently offered in designer-style cabinets to complement period furniture in most American homes. In Europe and in the Far East, cabinet styling of 48" to 52" uprights leans toward a sleek, clean, somewhat utilitarian look.

Grand piano styling has never offered the variety found in vertical cabinets. Some styles echo the period styling of the current era, while others are recreations of styling from days gone by.

Vertical Cabinet Features

Many manufacturers offer two to four price levels in the vertical cabinet furniture style category, and offer distinct scale designs and quality/performance levels for each price point. A few companies offer the same insides, differing only in levels of cabinetry at each price point.

Most entry-level cabinets of the furniture-style category feature several items in common:

◆ Flat lids with squared off edges.

◆ Very plain music racks with little or no ornamentation.

◆ Pull-out, drawer type key-covers or fallboards.

◆ Screwed-on front legs.

◆ Only one or two finishes or styles.

Most standard-line or mid-line cabinets of this category feature these items:

◆ Flat lids with some bevel or profile to the edges.

◆ Some embossing (engraving), shaping, or cut-out designs in the music racks.

◆ Single fold or Boston style (double-fold) fallboards.

◆ Screwed-on front legs.

◆ Frequently, five to six furniture styles and colors. Styles are distinguished only by legs, finish, and music rack change-outs for economies of scale in manufacturing.

◆ Standard models frequently sell for 50 percent more than their budget counterparts.

High-line cabinets are distinguished by:

◆ Boxed in (framed) lids with profiles, beading, or other tooling.

◆ Ornate music racks, often with burled panel appliqués or brass or wire accents.

◆ Single-fold or Boston style fallboards with many now featuring "slow-close" features.

◆ Full-length legs that are doweled into the arm as an integral part of the cabinet design.

◆ A fully-developed style in whichever period type it is designed to reproduce. Cabinet panels may incorporate raised panels, embossing, contrasting wood appliqués, decorative moldings, and tone venting.

◆ High-line models frequently sell for double the price of the budget models.

It's interesting to note the creep in height of this furniture-style category over the decades. In the 1950s the focus was on spinets in the 36"-tall range, but during the 1970s, the category inched into the console designation, with 42" pianos becoming standard. The 1980s saw greater customer sophistication and demand for taller pianos. The category stretched into the 44"-tall realm. Today some companies' highest-end cabinetry boasts cabinets reaching 47" tall. We believe this is about as tall as they can go, as traditional period furniture styling will probably not render authentically in cabinets any taller.

Key Note

Take a good look at your existing furniture in the room where your new piano will be placed. Designers often caution that it is rare to be able to match the style *and* color, so they suggest trying to match one or the other and to consider it a bonus if you can nail both. Other designers strive to make the piano a contrasting focal point.

Vertical Cabinet Styles

American taste in furniture goes in waves and cycles. Crazes for white-washed Southwest finishes or light woods like maple and oak swing back to the darker, more traditional mahoganies and walnuts. As you consider finding a cabinet style that matches your décor, consider that your living room furniture might change several times over the next 50 years, but the piano will likely stay through it all. So your piano's style must be versatile, even neutral, enough to ride out these decorating cycles.

Rhythm and News

In their early days exporting to the United States, both Yamaha and Kawai struggled to render American style cabinets that appealed to American tastes in furniture. Finally, both companies decided to build these cabinets in factories located in the United States. However, after nearly three decades of U.S. production, both companies now have moved the production of these cabinet styles offshore.

Over the years, piano manufacturers have offered several styles. These are summarized below, and photos are provided of the more popular styles.

Continental Style: This style hit the American market with the Japanese pianos of the late 1960s. The continental style or "Euro style" was a fresh, new look for the American market but was common in Asian and European households. The cabinet is sleek with no ornamentation, and its most noticeable feature is the absence of legs. The key-cover lifts to reveal a little shelf that folds down to hold music. This style was slow to catch on but grew in popularity, reaching its zenith in the 1980s. The continental was offered in a variety of finishes, including walnut, mahogany, black (ebony), white, and ivory, with one company even trying pastel colors. Most were sold in the new high-polish, wet-look polyester finishes. By the late 1990s, this style began to decline in popularity.

Continental Style.

Traditional style: This nondescript title has been given to cabinets with rounded spindle legs and somewhat simple cabinet styling. The traditional style has been offered in all major price points and from most manufacturers. Although typically rendered in a walnut or mahogany, this style surged in the early 1960s as the Salem maple craze developed. This style was often re-branded as Early American, with spindles in the music rack as a style element.

Traditional/Early American Style.

Italian Provincial style: This enduring style features square, tapered legs and an angular music rack. These cabinets are frequently rendered in walnut, and the legs may feature carved out panels or raised panels that follow the taper of the leg.

Queen Anne style: This formal-looking style features a cabriole (S-shaped or French curved) style leg. The finial or bottom part of the curved leg shows a round pad or foot. Typically, the Queen Anne leg shows no additional ornamentation. Most Queen Anne pianos are rendered in cherry or mahogany finishes. In recent years, some companies have offered them in oak finishes, as well. Queen Anne music racks showcase cut-outs and flourishes with rounded corners in keeping with this design. More formal styles in darker woods are back in fashion again and selling strong.

Italian Provincial Style.   *Queen Anne Style.*

French Provincial style: This style is one of the more formal styles, boasting some of the most ornate and intricate cabinet work. The French Provincial (FP) style is often confused with the Queen Anne style because both share the cabriole curved leg, but the French style takes detailing a few steps further. The French style ends the leg in a more ornately turned foot, a kind of curly-que. The FP leg is commonly adorned at the top with an appliqué or carving of a shell, grain sheaf, or fleur de lis shape. Music racks possess delicate cut-outs (fret work) with much ornamentation. The fanciest of the French Provincial cabinets are often referred to as Louis XV style and are the most ornate. FP styles are nearly always found in cherry finishes. A few have been offered in an antique white and gold finish.

Country French Provincial style: This style became popular in the late 1970s and is still offered by some manufacturers. It mirrors provincial furniture of those in the countryside of lesser means, who copied designs of expensive furniture from the cities. Country designs feature the same basic shapes but without some of the ornate appliqués and adornments. They also frequently featured lesser woods, such as oak. Sales of this style have slowed down in recent years.

French Provincial Style.

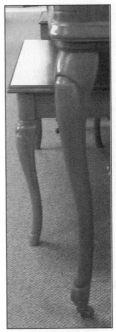

Country French Provincial Style.

Chippendale style: This is the third style that features a cabriole or S-shaped curved leg. Distinctive of the chip style is the finish of the leg at its end. The Chippendale leg features a ball and claw that looks just the way it sounds, like the talons of an animal clutching a ball. Frequently this style features a shell motif appliqué at the top of the leg. Chippendale cabinets are typically rendered in darker mahoganies, cherries, or walnuts. This style is so distinctive that it rarely fits with other styles of furniture.

Mediterranean style: This style also became popular in the 1970s and continues today, though sales have slowed down in recent years. The Mediterranean style features a hexagonal or an octagonal tapered leg. Music racks are moderately styled, often featuring brass or wire. This style is frequently offered in a variety of oak shades.

Sheraton style: This style goes back many decades in the piano world. Its rounded spindle leg features flutes or grooves cut into it. The styling is simple but formal and elegant. Sheraton cabinets are usually rendered in darker woods, such as walnut and mahogany.

Chippendale Style.

Mediterranean Style.

Sheraton Style.

Georgian or Hepplewhite style: This style is often confused with Sheraton because the leg is similar, but it is actually a reverse. The Georgian or Hepplewhite leg is a reeded spindle. Rounded raised ridges, not grooves, are cut into the leg. Again, this formal design is rendered in walnuts or mahoganies.

Georgian or Hepplewhite Style.

The ten styles described here have been found in piano dealers' showrooms for decades. They represent American ideals in furniture style and are offered to complement décor, not detract from it. Although some teachers, professionals, and institutions favor taller pianos over the console category, we believe you should be able to have both a great performing instrument and a wonderful piece of furniture.

Style Embellishments on Uprights

Raised panels are commonly found on vertical pianos as a form of adornment to the flat cabinet panels. By adding a framing look, the panels give the cabinet depth and dimension. This feature is typically found on the high-line cabinets on the bottom and/or top door panels.

Raised panel.

Burl-wood appliqués are panels or added adornments to cabinets made of lesser woods to dress them up and create a fancier look. To make the entire cabinet of burl would be too costly.

Molding appliqués are hardwood moldings applied to the outside of the cabinet to create decorative effects as raised panels, beading, tambours, coves, and more.

Burl-wood appliqué.

Molding appliqué.

Intarsia inlay is a time-consuming method of applying hand-cut small contrasting wood pieces into precisely made cut-outs in the cabinet surface to form intricate designs and flourishes. This old-world craftsmanship is only found in hand-crafted pianos where time and expense are not an issue. Mass-produced pianos sometimes mimic this by using decals of this ornamentation under the finish, though the result is never as beautiful.

Intarsia inlay.

One final design or style in the console/studio category is the institutional cabinet or "school piano" that nearly every manufacturer builds to bid on institutional sales. This design is utilitarian in nature yet has a simple grace. The school piano features a flat panel top whose top board slopes down to a full width music desk. No separate music rack is featured on these instruments. Music lies against the face of the top door itself and is kept in place by a groove or molding fit to the music desk. School cases feature a toe-block design, in which the end of the leg is tied back into the cabinet bottom by a wood strut. Where the leg and toe-block join, double, rubber roller-casters are anchored to facilitate moving the piano.

School-style pianos typically feature locksets for the lid and key-cover to secure the instrument. During periods when furniture styling has shifted to a plainer look, such as with the Stickley, Mission, and Craftsman styles, these designs have gained popularity with home users.

School piano.

Taller instruments, in the "professional upright" series, leave behind styling and focus on function and performance over form. Taller pianos are nearly all angular, boxy, and mostly black and shiny. The tone and volume of taller pianos are incrementally better than they are in the furniture category but are still bound by the physical limitations of all upright pianos.

Grand Piano Cabinet Styles

Some cabinet features evolve as an engineering consideration. A good example of this is the two most traditional grand piano stylings.

First is known as a *Brass-Toe* leg design. Each leg of the piano ends with a brass cap known as a ferrule. This reinforces the end of the leg where a caster or wheel may be attached. It is a signature design characteristic of some manufacturers and is particularly common in Baldwin pianos.

Brass-toe grand leg.

The second is known as a *Spade-Toe* leg design. Each leg of the piano ends in a four-sided angled bulge. This is to reinforce the narrowing end of the leg where a caster or wheel may be attached. It is a signature design characteristic of some manufacturers, especially Steinway & Sons.

The majority of grand pianos sold in the past 75 years have fallen into these two descriptions. However, a few historical cabinet styles are still available from some manufacturers.

Spade-toe grand leg.

Victorian or empire cabinet designs are more often found on grand pianos than on verticals. These styles reflect ornate designs of the 1800s. The leg shapes are large and rather bulbous at the tops and taper down to narrow ends at the bottoms. They may be completely round or in faceted hexagon or octagon shapes as they taper. Often these legs are described as shaped like an ice cream cone. The legs typically end in a round brass ferrule. Along with this leg shape, the style often features an open or *filigree* cut-out music rack. These delicate and fragile racks rarely survive on old pianos. There are companies that specialize in crafting re-creations for rebuilds.

Queen Anne styling is reflected in grand piano cabinets with an "S" shaped cabriole style leg that is typically free of adornment. The leg ends in a soft plain foot, without turn or claw, and typically without caster wheel. Queen Anne styling is nearly always rendered in cherry or mahogany. It is a simpler design to the French styles, Chippendale, or the Victorian styles.

Empire grand leg.

Filigree music rack.

Some manufactures offer grand pianos in French Provincial, Chippendale, and Hepplewhite stylings. These leg styles are the same as those described earlier under vertical piano styles. In grand piano form, often the cabinet rims are sculpted and/or adorned to carry out the styling. The music racks are styled accordingly, as well.

Queen Anne grand.

Shiny or Satin Finish?

Today a variety of piano cabinet finishes are available. Sheens range from flat matte to the wet-look, high-polish finishes. Not all sheens and colors are available in all models and styles.

For the first 260 years, piano cabinets were only available in hand-rubbed satin finishes. These finishes were created using organic lacquers and varnishes. Traditional finishes do wear and weather. We see furniture finishes from the 1940s and earlier that have cracked, checked, dried, and alligatored. However, these finishes can be stripped and refinished.

The Asian pianos of the 1960s introduced a new wet-look, high-polish finish option. The early high-polish finishes were synthetic varnishes such as polyethylene and polyurethane. Today the high-polish finish is achieved through the use of high-tech, polyester. This modern coating is thicker and more wear-resistant than traditional satin finishes. Over 90 percent of grand piano cabinets and vertical piano cabinets over 47" tall are sold in high-polish finishes. These finishes cannot be stripped and replaced, but can be repaired and buffed back to like-new condition many times.

Care and maintenance is counter-intuitive. It would seem that the satin finishes would be easier to care for, but this is not the case. Satin finishes are often softer and have a fine parallel grain where the finish has been hand-rubbed to cut the gloss. Even a feather duster can introduce scratches that run contrary to this grain. Lacquer finishes must be treated as other fine furniture is. High-polish finishes, on the other hand, can be cleaned and dusted with a damp t-shirt.

What about changing the finish or color down the road? High-polish cabinet finishes are basically unstrippable. Whichever color your piano is, if it has a high-gloss finish, the color cannot be changed. The only thing you can change about a high-polish finish is to have it rubbed down to a more satin-like finish by a skilled cabinet person.

Traditional lacquer or varnish finishes can be stripped and the wood restained to alter the color. It is easy to go from wood-look to black, not so easy to go the other way. To strip and refinish a vertical cabinet can run $2,000 at a minimum; grand pianos as much as $10,000 at a minimum. Often, a new piano is a better way to go.

Interior design trends and styles have life cycles that come and go. The styles we've identified are classics that have withstood the test of time. When narrowing your selection, remember trends such as the Marie Callender-look of oak and brass of the 1980s, the Southwest look of the 1990s, as well as the espresso finishes of today. These fads have life cycles much shorter than the life cycle of your piano.

> **Key Note**
>
> Pianos that start off as black typically do not have matching cabinet grade veneers under the finish. When stripped, they may be unsuitable to be refinished in a natural wood color.

The Least You Need to Know

- Vertical pianos under 47" tall are usually available in a variety of cabinet styles.

- Taller vertical pianos have fewer finish and style choices.

- Grand piano cabinets have fewer style options than verticals.

- Choose a style that you can live with for a long time.

- Take a good look at the styling on your furniture at home before you head to the piano store.

- Polyester finishes are more durable than traditional lacquer finishes, but are limited in how they can be altered later.

Part 4

Alternative Pianos

This part is for those of you who want something a little different—cutting edge or a cut above. For you cutting edge types, we explore the fascinating realm of "plugged in" pianos—those that are fully electronic as well as electronic attachments for traditional acoustic pianos. We explain digital, hybrid, and player pianos, and also talk about why a portable electronic keyboard usually won't do the job when it comes to learning to play or playing seriously.

Then, we cover topics for upper-intermediate and advanced players who may be looking for something that's a cut above ordinary. We go behind the mystique of the big brand names and examine whether there really is that much of a difference between a piano that sells for $100,000 and one priced at $40,000. We also cover the risks and rewards of buying a used performance piano.

Chapter 16

Plugging In to Digital Pianos

In This Chapter

◆ Benefits and downsides of digital pianos

◆ Digital piano terminology defined

◆ Deciding if a digital is right for you

◆ How much they cost

Some pianos require electrical assistance. These range from fully electronic digital pianos to acoustic pianos with electronic attachments. In this chapter, we provide an overview and description of digital pianos—the various types, their benefits and downsides, and how to determine if one is right for you. We also define digital piano terminology so that you'll know what your salesperson is talking about.

It's important to note that this chapter goes hand in hand with Chapter 17. In that chapter, we focus on two specific types of acoustic pianos with added digital components—hybrid and player—and the technology that makes them work. We also discuss electronic keyboards in that chapter. Keyboards are not really pianos but are often mistaken for them. We'll tell you more about that in the next chapter. For now, let's just get acquainted with digital pianos in general.

Types of Digital Pianos

A digital piano is a modern electronic musical instrument that functions as a standard piano. However, these pianos have no strings, never need to be tuned, and must be plugged into electricity. Digital pianos feature the full 88 keys in regulation length and width and should have a fully weighted keyboard that replicates the touch and effect of an acoustic piano. A digital piano should feature at least two pedals, if not the standard three. The pedals should perform the same functions they do on a grand piano. Digital pianos are commonly mounted on permanent bases or stands that house the pedals.

> **Rhythm and News**
>
> Acoustic pianos as well as most digital pianos sell with a matching bench as a part of the package.

Digital pianos can also be played silently with the use of headphones, so that only the player can hear the sounds the piano makes. A digital piano can also be connected to a computer, which facilitates interactive software such as arranging and composition or interactive lesson programs.

Most manufacturers of digital pianos divide their product lines into two categories: the solo digital piano and the digital ensemble.

Solo Digital Pianos

Solo digital pianos focus on reproducing *voice(s)*, i.e., instrument sounds, and offer a grand piano touch in the process. All of their processing power is devoted to this voice reproduction. These instruments are more basic than their ensemble counterparts. They can sound like a piano but may have other musical instrument voices (sounds) as well. Voices are often selected by pressing buttons on the dashboard above the keyboard. Voices can often be layered; for example, the piano sound can be played while the string sound is also playing.

> **def•i•ni•tion**
>
> **Voices** on digital pianos represent instrument sounds.

On some solo digital pianos, built-in flash recorders can record a performance and then play it back so the student or performer can critique his or her performance. Some of the newest models feature USB ports for recording to memory sticks. Unlike their ensemble counterparts, solo instruments do not have rhythm or accompaniment capabilities.

Solo Digital Piano.

Digital Ensembles

The digital ensemble category adds drums and rhythm to the mix. Ensembles usually feature some multi-track recording capability and hundreds of sounds or voices, whereas solo pianos feature no more than a few dozen, if that many. Ensembles often feature stored music libraries, karaoke features, and teaching systems. Ensemble instruments are often complex, with large display screens and many buttons. Although not as complicated as the dashboard of a Boeing 747, ensemble display screens sometimes can be that intimidating!

Ensemble instruments can literally sound like an ensemble of instruments playing together. In addition to hundreds of instrumental voices, there are often hundreds of percussion (drum) accompaniments. In addition, most ensembles allow the user to play one finger at a time with the left hand while the instrument fills in the rest of the bass line. Record features usually boast a minimum of eight tracks, allowing instruments to be recorded over each other to resemble a full orchestra. Many units have 16-track recording. Some ensemble instruments even feature microphone inputs and on-screen karaoke functions. Ensembles can be fun for the entire family!

Digital Grand Pianos

Most digital manufacturers make one or two models in the shape of a grand piano. While there are distinct advantages of an acoustic grand piano over those of an acoustic upright, there are no touch or tone advantages in the digital grand over the digital upright. The premium in price will only be for the look of the instrument. Most digital grands represent the top-of-the-line model of that manufacturer. Frequently there is a vertical cabinet version that has nearly all the same specifications for hundreds or thousands of dollars less.

Digital Ensemble.

Rhythm and News

The first truly digital piano was a Yamaha invention that debuted in the United States in 1983, a five-model series called the Clavinova (loosely translated, new piano). It was the first electronic piano to use digital sampling technology, by which the sound of a piano is recorded and translated into code stored on a computer chip, to be recalled when the key is played. Several other manufacturers followed suit within 18 months. Today three manufacturers account for the lion's share of the United States' digital piano home market: Yamaha, Roland, and Kawai.

Benefits of Digital Pianos

It's no surprise that digital pianos have taken off in popularity as they offer some very appealing benefits:

- They never need tuning.

- They do not need regular maintenance.

- The player can practice silently, with headphones.

- They take up less space.

- They are easy to connect to a computer to use learning, writing, and arranging/composing programs.

- Highest quality versions feature a grand piano-type of sensitive repetition touch.

- Kids often see them as "hipper" than traditional instruments and less threatening.

- Customers can often take them home in the box, thereby avoiding delivery expenses.

- Built-in features, such as metronomes, transposers, recorders, instrument voices, and multi-track recording make digital pianos more interesting and useful to many families than their acoustic counterparts.

Now that we've pointed out the benefits, let us look at some of the downsides of digital pianos. You will need to weigh each of these factors in your decision process.

Downsides of Digital Pianos

The picture isn't all rosy with digital pianos. The following characteristics represent their downsides:

- Like computer equipment, they depreciate in value quickly and dramatically.

- Some argue that they are not as good as "the real thing" in touch and tone.

- All but the most expensive ones come in lack-luster cabinet enclosures (barring a few low-quality brand names that focus on looks, not touch or tone).

- Some teachers do not recommend digitals and will not teach students with them.

- Digital pianos are probably not the best choice for advanced classical piano students, as larger grand pianos still have greater sensitivity, variation, dynamic control, and tonal color.

The Terminology of Digital Pianos

Just when you thought you'd mastered piano terminology from our chapters on acoustic pianos, comes a whole new set of words to know. Here are some of the terms you might hear in a digital piano sales presentation or when reading digital piano literature:

- **Velocity sensitive** refers to the effect of attack on the key. If you play the key harder, the instrument plays louder, while an easier keystroke plays softer. Many keyboards do not have this critical feature. On the other hand, nearly all digital pianos have this feature.

- **Fully weighted touch** refers to the resistant feel of the keys. Acoustic piano keys have a weighty (52+ gram *down weight*) resistant feel, as well as a feeling of the hammer moving toward the strings. An accurate reproduction of this touch is critical, especially for beginners. Cheaper digitals accomplish this feeling of touch by adding springs to the back of the keys. Better, more realistic units use actual weights in the mechanism.

- **32, 64, or 128 note polyphony** refers to the number of musical events that can be sounded simultaneously, a bit confusing since you have only 10 fingers. The significance of polyphony comes when you step on the right pedal, the sustain pedal, and drag your fingers along the keyboard. In musical terminology, this movement produces a *glissando*. When you get to the 32nd key with 32-note polyphony, the first note will drop out, and so forth up the scale. Reaching the point where notes drop out is a rare occurrence and a somewhat obscure need, especially for beginners. However, on some digital pianos, two voices can be selected to sound at the same time. For example, you may select a grand piano voice and a string voice to sound at the same time. Thus, you could play 20 musical events at the same time if you used all ten of your fingers. Again, this is not a big concern for the beginner.

def•i•ni•tion

Down weight refers to the grams of weight or pressure necessary to press a key down.

B-Sharp

Salespeople often confuse customers when talking about polyphony, making it sound so important, when in fact, it has *nothing* to do with the quality of sound in the reproduction of the voice selected.

Increased polyphony really comes into play during playback of a multi-track sequence or recording. With several tracks or layers playing at the same time, you might need increased polyphony numbers to accomplish this playback. Again, this feature is not necessary for beginners.

◆ **Graduated hammer weighting** is a relatively new buzzword term and feature. Manufacturers are changing the weight behind the key-action in four or more sections, with the heavier keys on the left or bass side and the lighter ones on the right or treble side. Acoustic piano hammers are larger on the bass and gradually become smaller at the treble end. This differential is balanced by the weighting of the keys. We are both pretty well experienced in evaluating touch on both digital and acoustic pianos, and the differences in touch-weight across the keyboard are nearly imperceptible to us. We, therefore, believe that when salespeople include this factor in their presentations, they are making much ado about nothing. We're more concerned about the consistent weight and response of the action or keys across the scale. If the digital action feels and responds like a decent acoustic grand piano, it is good. If it does not, it is not good.

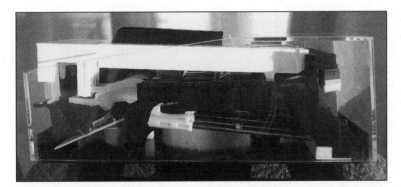

A typical digital action mechanism weighted from beneath the key.

A higher-end wooden digital action mechanism that has keys that lift a hammer-like mechanism above the key (similar to an acoustic grand).

◆ **Built-in teaching systems** through the use of blinking lights above the keys are available on some digital pianos. Some brands have keys that light up. Regardless of the process, there is no substitute for a quality private teacher and a traditional teaching method for learning to play the piano. The learner needs to associate the written notes on the music with the keys on the piano and the proper fingers to play those notes. But some digital pianos also have displays showing the notes on a screen. Flashing lights alone cannot teach hand and finger position.

Key Note

Having said that built-in teaching systems cannot really teach piano, we also believe that anything that encourages more members of the family to play the piano is good for the entire family and does support learning.

◆ The **connectivity** of the digital piano to use in conjunction with computer and learning programs is dynamic in the learning process. Again, this combination of computer and digital piano is not encouraged as a substitute for a real teacher and live lessons. However, as a supplement, these programs are terrific in keeping beginners enthusiastic and energized. Every hour you or your child sits and plays adds up to proficiency at playing piano. This ability to connect to a computer is typically accomplished through USB or MIDI ports.

◆ **Sampling technology** is the method a manufacturer uses to record and store the sounds of instruments on the computer chip(s) inside a digital piano. Current sampling technology is much wider and deeper than when it was first developed and has resulted in really good authentic-sounding pianos. Each company touts its patented process and has endowed it with elaborate names or acronyms. The proof is how it sounds, not how they do it.

Recording on Digital Pianos

Even entry-level model digitals are equipped with a simple one-button rehearsal record, a typically volatile memory recording that disappears when the instrument is turned off. In addition, the first recording is lost when the next song is recorded. Permanent recordings must be made to removable media, which may be in the form of a computer floppy disk (the most common), digital camera-type memory cards, "thumb drive" USB memory sticks, CD, and soon probably DVD. The last two methods are overkill as the MIDI files recorded are very small in nature. The greater capacities of CDs and DVDs are unnecessary for this kind of recording.

At the time of this writing, we are able to confirm only two brands that will translate the MIDI files on the fly and record standard audio to a CD file. This feature is available on the top two models of Kawai. Yamaha accomplishes this through a USB stick. More companies will likely be offering this feature in the near future. Note that several brands offer an "optical out," which can be attached to a CD burner.

Are Digital Pianos Right for You?

Digital pianos are your gateway, or user interface, to the power of the computer in music. Some terrific learning programs are designed to be interactive with the digital piano. When you press the A key on the piano, the A key goes down on the computer monitor as well. Interactive! Most of these learning programs are designed for kids. They are wonderfully instructive and lots of fun for adults as well. Once the software is loaded onto your computer, you type in your name, and the program takes you right back to where you left off in the preceding practice session. Hence the entire family can use the program with an account for each member. These learning programs do not require terribly sophisticated computers. You may already have an old computer in the garage that will work with them.

> **Rhythm and News**
>
> Marty's experience as a piano technician and a dyed-in-the-wool "piano man" kept him from embracing digitals as a recommendation for his clients until just the past few years. He is on the bandwagon now and, much to his surprise, has won several sales contests, one national, in this product category.

Digital pianos are not for every family and every need. They are, however, very much mainstream today. New digital sales constitute at least a third of the piano business today. Some statistics show that digital pianos are outselling acoustic pianos nationwide. Nearly every college and university is teaching basic piano proficiency to music majors in laboratory setups with digital pianos. Most teachers who have attended recent conferences and symposia have been exposed to the latest digital models and are embracing them in their own private teaching. Frequently, they will teach on their grand piano for the first 30 minutes then move a student to the digital with headphones for an additional 15 minutes to rehearse and record their lesson songs. So, acoustic or digital? You decide for yourself which is best for your family's needs.

One concern we hear repeatedly from customers is, "How durable are digital pianos?" It is unclear exactly how long current digital pianos will last. We have seen dozens in institutional service for more than 20 years that are still going strong. The newest generation of digitals should last as long or longer.

> **B-Sharp**
>
> A few "hold-out" teachers simply will not recommend or endorse digital pianos of any brand or model. As purists, they will recommend only acoustic pianos. Check with your teacher about his or her preferences before plunking down the money for a digital.

Which Digitals Are Best?

Over 25 years ago, Yamaha invented the category of digital piano with their *Clavinova*; they are joined today by Kawai and Roland as the top three digital piano manufacturers in the field. We have experience with all three and feel great confidence in all of them.

Each company has its own theory about how to organize the dashboard and operating system. Yamaha digitals record the sound of a Yamaha concert grand. Kawai digitals record the sound of a Kawai concert grand. We cannot confirm what piano Roland records into their digitals, but the sound is good. The sampling technology of the three companies is different. You should find the comparable model in each brand, listen to the tone yourself, and play with the controls.

What Digitals Cost

Good digital solo pianos start at $1,500, while ensembles typically start at $3,000. Digital product lines are engineered by the major manufacturers, with "step-up" selling features added at each price point. As you move up the line in price, more watts of power and size and number of speakers are added. More sound or voice choices are added, as are more elaborate recording capabilities. Connectivity is enhanced in the form of microphone inputs, audio and video outputs, and USB ports. Often there are three or four levels of sophistication and realism in the key-action mechanism itself that manifest as step-up features.

Before paying for the added features, try to focus on the ones you feel you will most often use. Always evaluate the grand piano sound and its feel as the most important considerations.

Key Note

If you're unsure whether or not the sound of a digital is good, play a few notes on a recognized brand of grand piano, then play the same notes on the digital. Do they feel and sound similar?

Regardless of which add-on features you choose, price is where digitals really shine. Families with beginners on a budget under $2,000 will receive more performance and consistency for their buck in a digital than they will in an older, worn-out used spinet or console. For folks who live close to neighbors in apartments and condos, the silent headphone play is a tremendous feature. For college music majors, the digital connected to a computer is nearly a requirement for writing, arranging, and composing course work.

Digital pianos continue to get better and cheaper for the same features. Typically many features in the $3,000 range on the 2003 model trickle down to the $2,000 range on the 2005 models, etc. Manufacturers usually do not release new models every year. Often it takes two or three years before new models come out.

As you survey the cost of digital pianos, be aware that digital piano warranties are shorter than acoustic piano warranties. Lower-end digitals often come with a 1-year parts warranty, with 90-days labor, carry-in service. Better quality digitals come with three-year parts warranties and one-year labor warranties. The best warranty on digital pianos is a five-year on parts and a five-year labor warranty, in-home service.

Adding on Composition Software

The last two decades have seen a dramatic evolution in writing, arranging, and composing software. Just as with word-processing software, composition software has grown more powerful and yet more user-friendly.

You can find elementary programs starting at just under $50 and some power-user programs in the $500+ range. These programs, when connected to a digital piano, will notate your playing and allow you to note-edit the music in the computer, transpose your creation, cut and paste recurring phrasing, title and label your composition, and print the sheet music on your printer.

The Least You Need to Know

◆ Digital pianos have 88 keys that should have the touch and feel of an acoustic piano.

◆ Digital pianos are separated into two categories: the solo instrument and ensembles, which feature rhythm and accompaniment.

◆ Practicing silently with headphones, connecting to a computer, recording capability, and other built-in features are benefits of digital products.

◆ Downsides include rapid depreciation and lack-luster cabinets; some teachers believe they have a less than adequate touch.

◆ Families with lower budgets will get more performance and consistency from a digital piano than from an old worn-out used piano.

Hybrid Pianos, Player Pianos, and Keyboards

In This Chapter

- ◆ How hybrids work
- ◆ How player pianos work
- ◆ Comparing multi-media systems
- ◆ A few words on electronic keyboards

Now that you have an overview understanding of digital pianos from Chapter 16, we'll take a look at some specific types of pianos with digital components: hybrids and player pianos. (If you haven't read Chapter 16, we urge you to do so as it's an important foundation to the information in this chapter.) We also discuss electronic keyboards, which might seem like a form of digital piano but actually are not pianos at all.

Hybrid Pianos

Hybrid pianos are acoustic pianos that have a simple digital piano component, which comes in the form of a box attached to or sitting on top of the piano, or may be built into the cabinet itself. This component allows the player to flip a lever or engage a pedal to silence the acoustic piano and allow the digital piano to take over. A player can enjoy the feeling of an acoustic piano with its hammers moving toward the strings and its wooden keys, yet can play silently, hearing the music only through headphones. The digital piano part of the instrument is usually limited to only a few voices. However, some can have a tone module added to produce more instrument voices. It's the best of both worlds!

Hybrid pianos evolved in the 1950s when some manufacturers attempted to blend the electronic organ with an acoustic piano, but they've never really taken off as a popular product line. Many manufacturers have marketed the hybrid with only limited success in the United States.

Before you purchase a hybrid instrument, consider buying two separate instruments for about the same price. You can have that beautiful piece of furniture, the acoustic piano, in the living room and have a digital piano in the office or game room to hook up to the computer for learning programs and for writing, arranging, and composing music using computer software. But should your personal situation dictate that one combined instrument is preferred or necessary, then the hybrid is a great solution.

Player Pianos

Player pianos are pianos that play by themselves; that is, a player mechanism moves the keys move up and down. Usually, the player mechanism is installed in an acoustic piano, although, digital piano manufacturers have sold models that move the keys, too. If you are a nonplaying family, you will get ten times the fun and usage out of your new acoustic piano when a player is attached to it. Five basic player piano types have been developed over the past century: paper-roll, cassette players, floppy disk players, CD players, and multimedia players. We'll examine each of those here.

Paper-Roll Players

These pianos are the earliest form of player piano and actually use a perforated paper roll as the device to trigger the keys to move up and down. Early versions did not replicate expression or volume, though later "reproducing pianos" did. Air pulled in through the perforations in the paper rolls activated pneumatic plungers that played the keys. The reproducing players had three to five additional rows of holes that varied the vacuum to the pneumatics to create volume changes.

Paper roll players were popular in the 1920s and 1930s but production ceased in the '30s. Paper-roll pianos had a curious resurgence and rebirth in the late 1970s through mid-1980s, with a few companies making antique reproduction-looking upright cabinets, complete with lighted stained glass windows in front.

B-Sharp

We do not recommend paper-roll player pianos from the 1920s and '30s for serious piano students today. Even with some restoration, these instruments are over the hill and rarely play with sensitivity and consistency.

Cassette Players

Developed in the 1960s, player mechanisms used cassette tape players encoded with information to make the piano play. Electronic signals were passed from the tape to electronic *solenoid plungers* that played the keys. Additional code was routed to the plungers, which allowed dozens of levels of volume in the attack of the key. These systems were very expressive compared to their predecessors. However, numerous problems associated with the tape players plagued owners and dealers. The tapes themselves often stretched and corrupted the code.

Cassette players are no longer made, but you may run into them on the used market. It is difficult to find the cassette tapes and even harder to find repair people to work on them, so this would not be a wise used piano purchase.

def•i•ni•tion

A **solenoid plunger** is an electronic piston that lifts the back of a key from underneath to make the note play.

Floppy Disk Players

Still found today, floppy disk players have a drive that uses a standard 3.5-inch floppy disk. The disk's encoded information drives solenoid plungers under the keys. Floppy disks can also contain files that imitate other instruments, thus creating a piano with orchestral accompaniment playing at the same time. Speakers are used to play the orchestra backgrounds, which may or may not be imbedded in the floppy disk files. Orchestra backgrounds come in the form of MIDI files that trigger a sound card in the player mechanism, much the way music is played back on a computer. Believe it or not, most companies still offer systems that include floppy disk players, though most of the time they are packaged with a CD player as well. The digital format used for encoding the playback information takes little space (a floppy can hold up to 3 hours of music) and therefore does not require larger types of data storage. Because floppy disk systems are combined with CD systems, the cost is usually just a few hundred dollars more than the CD-only system, but they often have additional features including ports to connect to a computer.

CD Players

The most common player system found today, compact discs are encoded with a digital signal that tells the piano which key to play (driven by a solenoid rail), how hard to play each note, and at what velocity the hammer should strike the key. Unlike floppy disk models, CDs can contain audio files as well, for "live" performances of symphony backgrounds and even vocals (singers) that play out through speakers. (Floppy disks are not large enough to contain audio files and therefore cannot play singers' voices.) Basic, compact disc player systems sell at prices from $5,000 to $8,000 (these are "out the door" prices, not full retail), depending on the features included. Note that this is the price for the player system and does not include the cost of the piano.

Multimedia Players

Multimedia systems use floppy drives, CD drives, hard drives, compact flash drives, and in some cases, USB ports. You can actually load and store songs onto the hard-drive memory, which makes it possible to listen to hours of music without having to get up and change discs. These systems often have record features that allow you to capture, store, and replay your own performance. The most sophisticated of these systems even offer karaoke features and built-in digital piano (hybrid) features.

Modern player systems use solenoids to lift the back of the keys from underneath, thereby giving the impression that the keys are magically playing. When the back of a key—the part you can't see—is lifted, the front of the key—where your fingers touch—goes down. (Think of the motion of a teeter-totter). In addition, most systems include one or more speakers to play orchestrations. On vertical pianos, a speaker is usually set next to or near the piano, while in grands, speaker(s) are mounted to a beam underneath the piano.

How to Compare Multimedia Systems

Today the major players in player pianos are Disklavier by Yamaha, PianoDisc, PianoForce, and QRS Pianomation. Of these, only the last three are available as an after-market installation. In other words, the last three companies' player systems can be installed on nearly any piano. Spinets and certain consolettes are not able to support player systems, but most other pianos can.

Each company offers a variety of options. And, sales reps for each company will present theirs as the best system on the market. We urge you to make your own comparisons. Listen for how quietly the piano can play. Listen to the music—is it musical or mechanical sounding? Can you hear the player mechanism thumping or just the music? Use our shopping form in Appendix B to help you evaluate the player system.

B-Sharp

Multimedia player systems sell between $8,500 to $25,000, depending on their features; this is in addition to the cost of the piano.

Multimedia Systems by Manufacturer

All player system manufacturers offer multiple models of their systems. In this section we take a look at what each of the major manufacturers offers and what their specific models can do.

QRS Pianomation

The oldest of the player companies still alive today, QRS started in 1900. QRS has a vast library of music available from CD and floppy versions as well as their old paper rolls. QRS's systems are modular in design, which makes adding additional components easy. Each system comes with an infrared remote control, user's manual, and three sampler CDs.

2000C

This a basic playback system that uses a wireless transmitter to drive your piano from an existing CD player and an existing sound system in your home.

◆ No hardware is visible on the piano.

◆ Uses your existing CD player and sound system.

◆ Downside: Competing wireless frequencies in your home may interfere with the wireless system.

CD2000+

This is a basic, reliable playback system that reads QRS CDs via a box attached to the front edge underneath the piano (hereafter referred to as the "front-end" box).

◆ Utilizes prerecorded CDs.

◆ Has a two-digit LED display to help users navigate without the remote.

◆ Downside: Front-end box is larger than some models.

Petine

The Petine model is QRS's most popular system, combining a CD player with a compact flash reader.

◆ Flash reader allows easy software updates as well as a large storage capacity.

◆ SyncAlong CDs can be played on this system. SyncAlong combines an over-the-counter CD with encoding to make the piano play the piano part of the songs on the CD.

◆ Is record ready, which means that a recording system can be added without changing the front-end box.

◆ A microphone can be plugged into the system to amplify the user's voice.

◆ The front-end box is relatively small and can be attached almost anywhere along the piano.

◆ Can play MP3 files if they are saved on a CD or compact flash card as well as prerecorded QRS CDs.

◆ Downside: Cost is greater than some systems.

Ancho

This is QRS's most advanced system.

◆ Offers compact flash and CD formats.

◆ Is record-ready.

◆ Has internal memory and a mic input as well as an onboard sound card for producing orchestral backgrounds from MIDI files.

◆ Can also play MP3 files on a CD or compact flash.

- ◆ The front-end box has a 20-character alpha-numeric display and data dial control for navigating without a remote.

- ◆ Offers MIDI in and out so the unit can be connected to a computer.

QRS add-ons (at additional cost) include PNOScan, which is an optical sensor recording system. All the pedals as well as the keys can be equipped with optical sensors to replicate authentic playback. Beware of promises of DVD performances coordinated with the piano playback, however. Currently, this option is for demonstration purposes only. Focus only on what's actually available now, not what features are on the horizon.

Rhythm and News

Salespeople carrying competing brands will point out that QRS plays back only 80 of the piano's 88 notes. Those who do carry QRS will point out that competitors' systems require cutting off part of the legs of your piano to fit in their 88-note playback. Most songs don't play the top four notes of the piano or the bottom four, so most people will never notice that those notes do not playback.

Salespeople might also mention "levels of expression." This term refers to how many levels of volume are available on each note to playback a song. Have the salesperson turn on the system and show you its range from loud to soft or vice versa and listen to the louds and softs within a song. All of the current models have good levels of expression. Older, used models you might run into play only loud and louder.

PianoDisc

PianoDisc player systems have been on the market since 1989. Every PianoDisc system offers 88-note playback with 127 levels of expression. PianoDisc features its SilentDrive technology in all models. They offer several levels of player systems from the entry-level PianoCD system to their top of the line Opus 7 system.

PianoCD

This model plays specially formatted CDs.

- ◆ The slim front-end box measures only about $1^1/_4$ inches thick.

- ◆ One of the least expensive models on the market.

- ◆ Downside: System is not flexible or easily upgradable.

228CFX

PianoDisc's more sophisticated 228CFX system offers more flexibility than their PianoCD system.

- ◆ It can play 3.5" floppy disks as well as CDs.
- ◆ Offers hard disc storage space as an optional add-on.
- ◆ Offers MIDI in and out so the unit can be connected to a computer.
- ◆ Can have a record strip added.
- ◆ Downside: Front-end box is larger than other models.

iQ

This system can be driven from many external devices.

- ◆ Can be controlled by an MP3 player, iPod, or computer.
- ◆ Electronics are hidden within the piano.
- ◆ Can interface with their Sync-A-Vision system, which adds a visual element.
- ◆ Downside: Technically-challenged individuals will find this system intimidating.

Opus 7

PianoDisc's top-of-the-line system.

- ◆ Forty hours of free PianoDisc music are included with this system.
- ◆ Includes Internet connectivity.
- ◆ Includes a wireless, touch-screen tablet, eliminating the need for a front-end box.
- ◆ Downsides: Not all broadband connections are supported nor are all network-enabled devices.

PianoDisc offers a variety of optional add-on features, including their QuietTime system, which allows the user to mute the acoustic piano so that a piano sound is only heard through headphones. The company has a large library of songs to choose from, and their PianoSync technology also plays your piano with some over-the-counter CDs.

Some competitors point out that PianoDisc's solenoids are shorter than those of their competition and can become *pitted*, especially in coastal environments, because they are not protected by a special coating. We have only encountered this with systems located in coastal areas.

def•i•ni•tion

Pitted refers to small depressions that occur in the surface of the solenoid plunger due to oxidation or rust.

PianoForce

PianoForce is one of the newest player systems on the market. Although PianoForce does not have its own library of music, the system plays Yamaha's and QRS's CDs. It should be noted, however, that while it plays most of these companies' CDs, it is not guaranteed to play all of them.

Ensemble CD

This piano player system offers sophisticated technology at an affordable price. It also plays very expressively.

◆ The front-end box is extremely thin and can be mounted nearly anywhere around the perimeter of your piano.

◆ Can automatically calibrate itself, which keeps it playing as sensitively as possible.

◆ Comes with five free CDs and has over 500MB of memory space to store a large internal music library.

◆ Has a USB port to utilize external storage devices.

◆ Plays MIDI and MP3 formats on CDs as well as other player piano formats and also supports QRS's over-the-counter-type CDs synchronized with the piano music files.

◆ The onboard sound generator can play MIDI background orchestrations.

◆ Downside: Because this system is new on the market, we have no long-term observations to determine its longevity.

PianoForce also offers a WiFi module to connect to the Internet to download music. And, it can be set as an alarm clock if you would like to wake up to your piano playing your favorite music. The system also has two mic inputs for those who like to sing.

Live Performance LX

Live Performance LX is a relatively new product on the market. We recently were able to review this product briefly, and have also heard good things about it from people in the industry. It is available for installation on existing pianos.

- Features high-resolution control over the player solenoids for superior play-back.

- Offers an amazing 1,020 dynamic levels for each note and 256 pedal positions.

- Plays other brands' formats of prerecorded music but will not play encrypted CDs (those that cannot be duplicated by the public).

- Downside: More expensive than some other systems.

Yamaha Disklavier

Yamaha Disklavier is only available preinstalled on Yamaha pianos. It is not available as an aftermarket installation. Disklavier offers several levels of player systems. A limited number of vertical pianos offer the Disklavier system. The key and pedal sensors are optical and do not interfere with the touch of the piano. In addition, this system has Yamaha's XG tone generator for producing background orchestral sounds.

Mark III Series Upright Piano: DU1A

This system is featured on a 48" vertical piano, model U1.

- Can play back vocal and instrumental tracks.

- Has a CD drive as well as a floppy disk drive that plays MIDI formats as well as prerecorded CDs.

- Allows you to play over-the-counter CDs with Yamaha's encoded disks, which play the corresponding piano part.

- Features SmartKey technology, which acts as a teaching guide to help you play songs note-by-note while the system fills in a professional arrangement.

- Can be played silently with headphones.

- Offers speaker jacks so you can plug in your own powered speakers to play recorded backgrounds.

- Can record yourself and play it back.

- Downside: More expensive than other systems.

Mark III Series Playback Grand: DGB1

Yamaha offers this basic player system on their 4'11", model GB1.

- Features CD and floppy formats.

- Has MIDI jacks and a direct computer jack.

- Pedal system plays back sustain and soft pedals.

- 16 MB total flash internal memory.

- Built-in speakers.

Mark IIIB Series Grands: DGC1B and DC2B

This player system is offered on a 5'3", model GC1 and a 5'8", model C2.

- Has a 64MB internal memory for storing your music.

- Comes with 528 songs (about 30 hours of music).

- Offers PianoSmart and SmartKey technologies.

- Records and plays back.

- Can play back vocal and instrumental tracks.

- Has a CD drive as well as a floppy disk drive that plays MIDI formats as well as prerecorded CDs.

- Internal sound module allows other instrument sounds to be played along with the piano, including string sounds, chorus, guitar, etc.

 B-Sharp

No matter which multimedia system you are considering, get a full demo of the features included and find out which ones come at an additional cost.

Mark IV Series Grand Pianos

This system is revolutionary in that it is computer based and always upgradeable. It is available on every model of Yamaha grand, except the 4'11" size.

- Low-profile front-end box features a USB port in addition to CD and floppy drives.

- The remote is WiFi and features a full-color touch-screen. In addition, it has a standard QWERTY keypad.

◆ The Quiet Mode feature allows the user to play silently through headphones.

◆ PianoSmart and SmartKey are both featured in this system.

◆ Videotaped performances can be synchronized and immortalized by the Mark IV. You can watch the video playback as your piano plays the performance live.

◆ Can be connected to Yamaha's website to download music directly into the player system.

◆ Can access Disklavier Radio, which offers music on 11 different stations 24/7, much like satellite radio.

◆ 80-gig hard drive can store hundreds of hours of music.

◆ Allows you to create your own playlists.

◆ Can transpose music up or down so you can sing along through the microphone inputs. You can even enjoy karaoke by connecting the Mark IV system to your TV.

◆ Downside: More expensive than most systems.

Manufacturers' Websites for Multimedia Systems

Be sure to look at the manufacturer's websites to make sure the systems you're considering offer music and features that you're interested in. The websites are:

www.QRSMusic.com

www.PianoDisc.com

www.pianoforce.com

www.live-performance.com

www.disklavier.com

Browsing product specifications on the web is an important supplement to what you'll hear in a sales demonstration.

Keyboards

A keyboard is a portable electronic device that usually does not have the regulation size and full complement of 88 keys. Keyboards rarely have a true weighted key mechanism that mimics the touch and effect of an acoustic piano.

A keyboard may work with batteries and/or an AC adapter. Nearly all keyboards have headphone jacks for silent play and some additional connectors for optional sustain pedals, volume pedals, in-puts, out-puts, and microphones. Keyboards typically are not sold with a stand or a bench; these are optional at extra expense.

Our use of the term "keyboard" should not be confused with other categories of instruments with similar appearances. There are stage pianos, MIDI controllers, and music workstations. Each of these more expensive *slab-type cabinets* has specific applications to performers, music arrangers, and composers. They involve additional expense for capabilities that are not necessary as a practice instrument for piano lessons or simple play.

def•i•ni•tion

Slab-type cabinet keyboards are rectangular instruments typically about 3 to 4 inches high and about a foot deep. The length varies with the number of keys offered, from as small as 2 feet long to as much as 4½ feet in length.

Best Uses for Keyboards

Portable keyboards can bring music into places that will not support traditional acoustic pianos or true digital pianos. Because of their portable nature and ability to run on batteries, or often 12-volt DC car lighter plugs, they can be used in RVs and trailers to make music and have fun on the road. They can bring music into schools, small churches or Sunday schools, and music therapy settings for the disabled. They can bring music to shut-ins or those in retirement communities or recreation centers. Keyboards can be fun and exciting for young and old alike to play with and make music, but one cannot learn how to play piano on a keyboard.

When Not to Use Keyboards

Our opinion, and that of many piano teachers, is that keyboards are not suitable instruments for serious piano students. Following are some of the reasons for this conclusion:

◆ Most keyboards do not have the full set of 88 keys.

◆ Most keyboards do not have key sizes of regulation length and width.

◆ Most keyboard keys do not have a resistant feel (weighting) or the feeling of motion from the movement of a hammer toward the strings. Many keyboards attempt to offer some kind of key resistance with springs. This is not to be confused with a true weighted action found in digital pianos. Touch training begins with the first lesson, so this feel is important.

◆ Many keyboards do not have velocity-sensitive mechanisms that make the instrument play loud when struck hard and soft when struck lightly. This loud-soft dynamic range is one of the essences of modern piano music. Mastery of this should come early in the lesson process but cannot with most keyboards.

◆ Most keyboards do not have the three pedals that function like those of an acoustic piano.

◆ Most keyboards' sound systems do not deliver an accurate reproduction of the tone of a decent acoustic piano. Remember, ear training begins with the first lesson.

Keyboards are usually small and portable and are not suitable for learning how to play the piano.

These deficiencies make keyboards an unsatisfactory substitute for a piano for anyone who wants to learn to play the piano. Every hour a student practices lessons on a keyboard, he or she is developing bad habits that will have to be unlearned later. Touch training and ear training are subverted by the touch (or lack thereof) and sound of the keyboard. Much of learning piano is rote muscle memorization. If you are learning on keys that are not regulation size, where does that put you when confronted by a real piano?

So why would anyone buy a keyboard for a piano student to practice on? Price and space. Many families with young beginners do not want to risk a large investment on an acoustic or digital piano when kids can be fickle about sticking with lessons. Parents, we urge you to resist this temptation! This toe-in-the-water approach frequently becomes the reason why a student fails at lessons. If you simply cannot bring

Key Note

The poor touch and sound of keyboards that leads most piano teachers not to recommend them for lessons also often leads them not to recommend digital pianos either. True digital pianos, however, have excellent touch and sound, so this fear of digitals for students is sometimes unfounded.

yourself to arrange the furniture in your home to accommodate the space required for a piano or even a digital piano, then you might want to encourage your child to learn to play another instrument.

The Least You Need to Know

◆ Hybrid pianos are acoustic pianos with simple digital piano attachments or digital features built-in.

◆ Player pianos are typically acoustic pianos that play without a person touching the keys.

◆ Player pianos no longer use old-fashioned paper rolls; today they use electrical solenoids to play the keys and floppy discs, CDs, or internal hard drives to store the music.

◆ Multimedia players offer the most options of the player systems for family fun and entertainment.

◆ Keyboards are portable and rarely have 88 regulation-size keys, and the keys do not have the realistic touch of a piano.

◆ Keyboards are not recommended for piano students learning to play.

Chapter 18

Upscale Pianos for Upscale Players

In This Chapter

- ◆ Pianos for more advanced players
- ◆ How to select a performance piano
- ◆ The differences between a $40,000 and $100,000 piano
- ◆ The pros and cons of used performance pianos
- ◆ Trading in your old model

Much of this book focuses on advice for the first-time buyer or for the buyer of a piano for a beginner, whether it's a first purchase or not. That doesn't mean, though, that experienced players don't have questions and needs, too. So we've devoted this chapter to those of you who play the piano at upper-intermediate levels or above and who would like to upgrade from your current instrument.

What the Advanced Player Needs and What It Will Cost

Before we discuss how you're going to find the right piano for your more advanced level of play, we need to let you know that we're basing our advice on certain assumptions:

- ◆ You are a serious student or professional.

- ◆ You are dissatisfied with the performance of your current piano.

- ◆ The performance of your instrument is important enough for you to make a sizeable investment.

- ◆ Only the performance values of a grand piano, rather than a vertical, will satisfy your needs.

- ◆ The instrument will be for your home or for your teaching or personal recording studio.

Following the logical assumptions above, our discussion will focus on grand pianos from 5'10" to 8' in length. Baby grands are not going to cut it for your advanced needs, so we'll focus on pianos no shorter than 5'10". Nine-foot concert grands rarely appear in homes and studios because of space and budget, so we'll cut off our range at 8 feet.

What's it going to cost you? It is unlikely that any of the Chinese or Indonesian pianos will offer the advanced performance levels you desire, so we can rule those out. At a minimum, the top of the Korean limited edition lines might work for you. Both Japanese lines fit this category. High-end, limited edition European pianos are certainly enough for most advanced players. And any of the current American-built grands may satisfy your needs. Therefore, our price category will extend from just under $20,000 to $100,000. Your search will expose you to all of the world's greatest brands and best models. What an exciting journey!

Identifying Your Selection Criteria

In this rarified category of performance-level pianos, concerns about country of origin, warranty, construction, quality, and features become peripheral because all pianos in this category are going to be top of the line on those factors. Only four significant factors come into play as you make your decision: size, cost, touch, and tone.

So before setting out on your journey, identify your selection criteria by measuring your space for size and acoustics, assessing your finances, and determining what you want in the touch and tone of your next piano.

One way to know what you want in your next piano is to assess what your current piano is not doing for you. What are you unhappy with in the touch, tone, sustain, pedal response, or dynamic range? Try to get very specific. "I want a heavier touch" may not be specific enough for your plan. "I want a touch that allows me to control the rapid passages that are written at pianissimo in a certain nocturne." Now we are getting closer.

"I want a bass that growls when I get on it and purrs when I caress it." "I want a clearer, bell-like tone without any metallic edge to it." "I want a rounder, hollower, woodier, warmer tone." "I want more over-all power and a more percussive attack." "I want more precision and finesse." "I want several levels of pedaling that make an audible difference and are controllable." "I want more projection in the tone." "I want a more compact and present tone." "I want a piano with a voice that can match the mood in my playing." These descriptors are all ethereal in nature and cannot be measured by criteria other than your own ears and hands.

> **Key Note**
>
> This is a personal decision for you, so trust your own judgment about the piano that sounds and feels right for you. You have the experience and the ear to make a good choice without anyone swaying you.

An exercise that's helpful to perform on your old piano before you go out to shop and compare is as follows. Find three pieces or parts of pieces that call for fast and slow play and that travel nearly the breadth of the keyboard. Select pieces that challenge your technique but that you feel you have mastered. Choose passages you know well and that come easily to mind, thereby allowing you to concentrate on the process and the results, rather than the notes. When you play your pieces, note to yourself how many levels of dynamics or volume you can achieve. Can you achieve five or six clear and discernable levels of volume? Can you control 10 or 12? Make note of this exercise's results as you'll be doing the same when you try out pianos at the dealerships.

Shopping for Your Upscale Piano

The nice thing about shopping for an upgrade is that, in most cases, you already have a piano, so you can take your time in finding a new one. You do not have the urgent need that the majority of piano shoppers have. If you live in or near a major urban area, you are lucky, as you will have a wide selection within a short distance. If you are out in the country, you'll have to plan day or overnight trips to travel to dealers and to allow yourself enough time to play several brands and models.

B-Sharp _____

You are used to the sound of your own piano. Make sure you recognize this fact when you suddenly like the tone of a test piano; make sure your judgment is not positively influenced simply because its sound is familiar.

At the stores, play as many of the marques and models as you can. Keep a diary and make notes as you move from one instrument to another. If you are graduating from an upright piano to a grand, your first sensation will be the action repetition difference and the leverage in the keys. Grand piano key-action mechanisms facilitate note repetition down deep in the key. You will be able to play more rapidly, more smoothly, and more expressively than on an upright.

Each time you sit to play a new brand or model, play the same three pieces you played in the exercise on your own piano, and then record the results and your impressions in a notebook or diary. Push the envelope in your test drives to see the number of levels of expression. Push yourself on the rapid passages. What can you accomplish on this test instrument that you cannot at home? Listen to the sound coming back at you from the rest of the room. Listen to the sound coming from just behind the music rack. If you have the piece memorized, you can fold down the music rack and really listen while you are playing. Play loud. Play the softest you can and still control the keys. Most pianos play well at _forte_. Fewer are controllable at _pianissimo_. Listen to the tone color change as you work through the dynamic spectrum. Test out the sustain by holding several notes and timing the decay. Make notes! Make notes! Make notes!

Each time you review a piano, have the salesperson play for you at the end. Stand back a few feet in the same physical relationship to each instrument, close your eyes, and just listen to the tone. Try not to listen to the playing or the musicianship, just hear the sound of the pianos. Make more notes.

We assume that because you are in this upper performance level, you are familiar with voicing and regulation (if not, they are defined in Appendix A). Do not select an instrument on the promise of a dealer to make it "your" piano by custom work, post-delivery. Understand that minor post-delivery voicing and regulation alterations are expected and should be included with the purchase of an upscale piano, but they cannot change the inherent tone and physics of a piano. These customizing alterations are incremental in nature, i.e., small percentages, and should be mostly to get the right fit with your actual room acoustics. We want you to fall in love with your new piano before you have written the check and it is delivered, not feel like you want to break the engagement afterward!

If you encounter an instrument you believe has potential for your serious consideration (right size, price, and first impression) but you feel it is enough out of tune or regulation to spoil your consideration, ask if the instrument can be serviced so you can return in a few days and review it again. Most shops will accommodate you for instruments that are obviously out of proper condition. Just don't ask for custom voicing or for lightening or hardening the entire action!

If pricing is not posted, ask for the MSRP on the units you feel are appropriate and note these figures in your log. Some stores may offer you a sale price on the instrument as well. Try to get both numbers. Remember, you can expect 15 to 30 percent off the MSRP. (Limited edition, hand-crafted pianos may not be as deeply discounted, however.) Further negotiations on discounts and trade-in allowances should wait until you have narrowed the field of choice to four or fewer. There will be plenty of time to make deals with your final selection.

Behind the Brand-Name Mystique

Many people shopping for performance pianos have dreamed their entire lives of owning a certain brand, and sometimes even a certain model of piano. They have gotten caught up in the image of a particular piano as an icon and may buy it simply because of that one factor. After having it delivered and serviced, they are sometimes very disappointed with it. This disappointment stems from a few factors.

All manufacturers go through ups and downs in their evolution. Piano companies are no different. Brand X may have been a powerhouse in the industry in the 1940s, but today it may be at its nadir.

Rhythm and News
Comments on blogs and other web forums about pianos often propound the idea that selecting a piano should take months and months and that dozens of instruments should be played. We disagree with this advice for the bulk of piano shoppers. Even for the upscale shopper, there is a danger in over-diligence. Your impressions of pianos fade and blur with time, and the "perfect piano" you saw last month may be sold while you deliberate.

Some brands carry with their name a real up-scale cachet pride-of-ownership aura. While the brand may still remain a great status symbol, it may not measure up to your specific and personal needs at this time in your playing or for the future.

We encourage you to devote little focus to brand and model name, beyond size and budget considerations. Your focus should be entirely on performance and the way each piano you review measures up to your needs.

In this section on piano icons, we want to restate a Chapter 6 admonition: don't buy a piano over the Internet, sight-unseen, and without your technician's survey, especially if it is one of the revered piano icon brand names. Just because it is a Steinway & Sons or a Bechstein or a Bösendorfer, does not guarantee a good piano and a good value.

The $100,000 Piano vs. $40,000 Piano: Worth the Difference?

In the higher-level pianos, the big issues for consideration have already been lopped off. You won't have to worry about whether each note plays properly or whether the piano is going to fall apart in a year. Instead, your choices now come down to incremental increases in sensitivity, repetition, tone color, sustain, and all the qualities that facilitate greater expression.

If you were a professional racecar driver, you and your team would gladly pay another $100,000 for just 2 or 3 percent more horsepower, even though you are already driving a 600+ horsepower rocket ship. The same rationale holds for the competitive edges a professional musician might seek, or for the player of means who wants to express him or herself without limit. Performance and tonal differences are very subtle at this level and frequently not evident without an hour or more of play. In a typical selection scenario, this consideration makes it difficult to make a quick choice.

If we rule out, for this discussion, exotic veneers, inlays, styled legs, and other stylistic differences, and focus on traditional ebony polished cabinets, the differences come back to the time spent, materials selected, scale designs, and the craftsmanship. These considerations are the determining factors in all pianos, but they are even more critical at higher levels. These factors are what impact size, cost, touch, and tone.

In most pianos with selling prices less than $40,000, manufacturers must make compromises in certain areas. Once we cross the $40,000 divide, many of these compromises are now unnecessary, and manufacturers can fully self-actualize in producing elegantly performing instruments. More time is spent in selecting and matching components, fine regulating, and fine voicing. Materials can be the best of their category cosmetically, tonally, and structurally. The elegant nuances of the physics of perfected scale designs can now be truly realized and appreciated. Only the top journeymen craftsmen are allowed to assemble higher-end instruments. Each instrument becomes a symbol of the true craftsman's life's work.

As useful musical instruments, higher-end performance pianos frequently outlast their mid- and low-end counterparts by as much as three times. Often, high-end performance pianos have enough lasting intrinsic value that the cost of later rebuilding and restoring them makes sense.

Ultra premium pianos are all about the details. Sight down the lid of a 7-foot Bösendorfer high-polish finish; then sight down the lid of a 7-foot Chinese piano. They are wholly different animals. Check out the plate finish on a Bechstein and compare it to the finish on a lesser piano. Play some runs and scales on a Bösendorfer, and then play them on a lesser piano. Of course, one would expect the more expensive pianos to play better, look better, and sound better for the difference in price to be worthwhile.

Reasons for ownership of upscale pianos come from a variety of directions. Pride and prestige of ownership is a driving factor for many buyers of venerated brand-name icons. Some buyers will settle for nothing but the best in everything they buy. These and other factors drive a significant number of upscale piano purchases and are not to be denied or ignored. But for the advanced player, performance is king.

Performance considerations in pianos over $40,000 are incremental in nature and in some cases, very subjective. It is this subjectivity that drives diversity in the marketplace at this high level. Only by playing several pianos in this category will you be able to decide which ones challenge your technique and inspire you to play more expressively. If performance is your number one consideration, only you can determine the value in these differences.

Risks and Rewards of Used Performance Pianos

The biggest source of used performance pianos is performance venues, such as colleges and universities, public rooms, recording studios, and teaching studios. It is much rarer for high-end instruments to come onto the secondary market from personal home use than it is for uprights and smaller, cheaper grands. Therefore, when performance pianos come available, they are often worn way beyond their certifiable serial number age. One must assess the remaining useful musical life and the cost per year. This is a situation where you absolutely *must* retain a competent, disinterested third-party piano technician to survey any used piano you are seriously considering. The dollar stakes are higher in the performance-piano arena.

For your performance needs, we simply do not recommend any used instrument of any brand more than 25 years old. Neither do we recommend any "reconditioned" or "rebuilt" piano. You are seeking sustain, tone color, consistency in the keyboard, precision in the touch, and infinitely controllable dynamics. In pianos, these are all qualities that fade with age. Unless you are on the senior side of senior citizenship, we want you to have more than just a few good years with your next piano.

The Least You Need to Know

- Grand pianos 5'10" to 8' meet advanced players' needs and cost at least $20,000 new.

- Touch, tone, size, and cost will be your determining factors when comparing professional-level pianos.

- On each piano you are considering, play the same three pieces to note how many levels of dynamics you can control.

- When you are finished playing, have your salesperson play so you can stand back and listen.

- Don't get caught up with brand-name icons. Trust your eyes, ears, and fingers.

- Don't buy used performance pianos more than 25 years old, and watch out for ones worn beyond their years.

Part 5

For Richer or Poorer— Striking a Deal and Going Home

You've nearly come to the end of your piano shopping journey, and the start of your piano playing adventure. You've learned just about everything there is to know about your piano choices and are closing in on the one that's going home with you.

In this part, we help you figure out how you're going to pay for your new piano and what goes into pricing negotiations, what deals are out there for institutions purchasing pianos, what the warranties will and will not cover, and what's involved in moving and storage.

Chapter **19**

Paying For Your Piano

In This Chapter

- ◆ Ways to finance your piano purchase
- ◆ What you can expect to negotiate on price
- ◆ Trading-in your old piano
- ◆ Piano appreciation and resale values

When you've found an instrument that you're serious about buying, you'll need to turn your attention to the money part of the process. Throughout this book, we've touched briefly on the topics of pricing and value of pianos, but here we give you more details about the financial aspects of closing the deal.

We begin with the basics of how you're going to pay for your piano, then look at pricing negotiations and how much you might receive for your trade-in (if you have one). We'll also explore how and why pianos appreciate as well as take an historical look at price increases in pianos.

Options for Financing Your Piano

In the past few years, extraordinary finance packages have been offered by dealers. "Zero percent" financing for 6, 9, 12, or even 18 months has emerged. Some of these packages are subsidized by manufacturers, while some of the low/no interest financing is "bought down" by retailers. A dealer "buy down" means that the dealer is paying the difference between the low- or no-interest program and the standard finance rate. Usually, any dealer buy-down cost on financing is put back into your purchase price. If you can comfortably pay in full, find out if there is a discount for doing so. You might get to put that dealer buy-down amount in your own pocket. If not, and you do not mind tying up some of your credit worthiness for several months and filling out a lot of paperwork, use the dealer's free money.

If you do not plan to pay off the instrument during the zero percent interest period, it may not be the best option. Most piano finance companies charge a higher interest rate for these option plans than for their regular term financing plans.

Often if you miss your payment by one day, piano finance companies will levy interest retroactively to the date of your purchase. Often these zero percent deals matriculate into high interest loans after the zero percent term has expired and you have not paid off the account.

B-Sharp

Don't be lured in by zero percent interest financing unless you know the details. Be very careful about the due dates on payments and payoffs.

Piano financing falls in the category of personal and furniture loans. Average bank rates are usually in the 11 to 15 percent range for these kinds of loans. When finance rates are pitched at much below this, someone must pay the difference. Usually, it is you, the customer. Expect slightly higher interest rates for digital electronic products. This higher rate is because of the high depreciation rates balanced against a potential for repossession, usually 1 to 3 percentage points higher than acoustic piano financing.

Regardless of how you pay for your piano, make sure you have asked the salesperson about your options, and then select the payment method that best meets your needs.

Pricing and When to Negotiate

Many of the larger manufacturers publish a Manufacturer's Suggested Retail Price, or MSRP, which is like the window sticker price on a new car. Customers rarely pay this price, but it is a place to start. As you settle down to one or two instruments on your short list of consideration, you and your salesperson will need to start getting serious about discounts.

Start with the list price. Establish whether the salesperson's/dealer's starting price is the real MSRP or something else. Often dealers will attempt to start higher than the MSRP to give the appearance of larger percentage-off discounts. The street price for most new pianos is somewhere between 15 and 30 percent off MSRP. There are exceptions to this in both directions. Your ability to work a deal by negotiating down from the MSRP is more effective than bargaining up from a dealer's wholesale cost because accurate information is rarely published and nearly every dealer cuts a unique wholesale deal based on a number of variables.

> **Key Note**
>
> It's okay to ask for ballpark discount prices, but don't start the bargaining process in earnest until you are ready to finish it in one visit.

As you start to work toward a discount, keep in mind that handcrafted, limited edition instruments are typically not discounted as heavily as mass-produced pianos. Special edition (one-of-a-kind) instruments are also not discounted as heavily. Of course, all used instruments are one-of-a-kind by definition. And there is no MSRP on used pianos.

School loan pianos (even with new warranties), closeouts, discontinued models, slow-moving models, and shop-worn floor models may be discounted more heavily.

You might be tempted to offer to pay cash in the hopes of striking a better deal, but only small sole proprietors respond to cash offers. They may skirt the books and offer deeper discounts for cash. But most businesses would rather have a valid personal or cashier's check than cash. Large cash deposits at banks require much time and paperwork. The buy rate on credit card transactions is between 1.5 and 2.5 percent for most volume companies. Many dealers will gladly pass this savings on to the buyer paying with a check. That small amount may not be worth it for you, however, if you'd rather get your frequent flier miles or cash-back feature on your credit card instead.

These are just guidelines. Your ability to negotiate, your dealer's immediate needs for cash flow, and the dealer's inventory situation will determine your final price. Keep in mind, too, that negotiating a great deal and then expecting the dealer to honor it six weeks later is often unrealistic. So you need to be prepared to act on the final price given.

Key Note _____

Some phrases that signal your earnestness and should help get you the best discount are:

◆ "Can we sit down at your desk and work some numbers?"

◆ "I'm ready to buy now if your deal is good enough."

◆ "Is it time to bring in your boss or call the owner?"

When you are at the salesperson's desk, make an offer. Start with an offer about 40 to 45 percent off the MSRP. Ignore the rhetoric from the salesperson and focus on the process. The next price must come from the salesperson. True negotiation is a give and take from both sides. You will have to come up on your price, and the salesperson will have to come down on his or her price until you meet somewhere along the way. The "line in the sand" ultimatum type of bargaining seldom works from either side. Also, there is nearly always a higher authority the salesperson can turn to for approval on a lower price.

Trading in Your Old Model

While considering your payment or financing options and talking pricing, you might also have an old piano to factor into the deal. Let's look at how the dealer will decide what your trade-in is worth and what information you need to provide the dealer to facilitate the transaction.

Determining the Value of Your Trade-In

Every used piano has a wholesale value (the cost at which dealers buy a piano) and a retail value (the cost at which the dealer will sell a piano). This is similar to the high and low blue book values on cars. Values are adjusted for regional differences, amount of inventory in the area, and level of dealer competition in the area. If we were to show a particular used piano to five industry professionals from the same market area, their values would usually be within a few dollars, but if we showed the same piano to a professional from an outside market, the value could vary by as much 10 to 15 percent either way.

Some dealers and customers want to work with a high resale figure. For example, a customer is looking for "feel good" dollars for his mother's beloved spinet. Some dealers and customers, on the other hand, want to work with the lowest possible selling price of the new piano and the barest wholesale value for their trade. (There may be a sales-tax advantage in some states as to which way the deal is actually written.) Most deals are a compromise somewhere between these extremes.

Key Note

Call a few piano stores to learn the approximate value of your piano if you were to sell it, before you head to a piano store to trade it in.

Trade-In Information the Dealer Needs

Be sure to take your trade-in information with you to the dealer. It is best if you can take your original paperwork to the store. If not, write down the brand name, model number, and serial number.

Here is what you need to bring with you to the dealer:

◆ **Make.** The brand name should appear on the face of the key-cover, embossed in the cast iron plate, on a decal under the strings on the soundboard, or on the back of the piano on a name-plate or sticker.

◆ **Serial Number** (typically four to seven digits and some with letters). In vertical pianos, this number is usually located under the lid near the tuning pins, lettered onto the cast-iron plate, embossed into the wood in a window of the plate, on a name-plate inside or on the back, or embossed into the wood on the back of the piano. If you can't locate this information, measure your vertical from the floor to the top. Note the style of legs (curved, square and tapered, round and tapered, etc.) and the finish. Take a picture of your piano if you can.

On grand pianos, the serial number is found lettered onto the cast-iron plate in front of the tuning pins, embossed onto the wood of the soundboard on the left side, embossed onto the wood of the inner rim underneath the piano, or embossed onto the wood on the inside of the key-slip wood just in front of the keys. If you can't locate it, close the lid of the piano and measure the longest length from the very front to the very back. You may need to use a vertical stick or ruler to identify the front edge of the piano because its location is lower than the lid edge. Again, note the leg style and finish (shiny black, satin black, brown walnut, mahogany, etc.)

B-Sharp

If you can't find the actual model and serial number, you won't receive the highest possible trade-in value.

- ◆ **Size.** If your trade-in is an upright, the height measurement from the floor to top of lid represents the size. If it's a grand piano, the size is measured from front to back. The size is critical to the dealer in determining the category of your trade-in piano.

- ◆ **Model designation,** typically a combination of letter(s) and number(s). This designation is commonly found somewhere near the serial number. However, the dealer may be able to determine the model from the age and size of the piano, along with a visual description. The specific model can peg certain features that can influence the value.

- ◆ **A visual description** of color, leg shape, carving or absence thereof, as well as the condition of the finish, are important in determining your trade-in's value.

> **Key Note**
>
> All dealers have a book of serial numbers listed by manufacturer. They can look up your make and serial number to determine the year your piano was made.

In addition, know the answers to the following questions: How long has it been since your piano was tuned? Have you had any major restoration work done? Do you have any family photos with the piano in the background that you can show? (Before you leave the house, take a shot or two of your piano with your cell phone or on a digital camera that you take with you.) Where is your piano—in the living room, garage, storage? If in storage, do you owe any balance on the storage charges or is the account paid up?

The more information you can provide to salespeople, the less money they have to reserve for surprises. Most seasoned salespeople or sales managers can figure a trade allowance without seeing the piano.

On a trade-in with a value of several thousand dollars, someone knowledgeable from the dealership will likely be dispatched to see your trade before the deal is consummated. Don't be insulted; it is just good business on their part. We can't tell you how many "Steinway & Sons" trade-ins have turned out to be Starrs, Starks, or Steinlagers.

Piano Appreciation: Does It Really Happen?

It is comforting to know that a piano is one of the few things you can buy for your family that, 10 years from now, will likely be worth *more* than you paid for it. We don't, however, recommend that you begin buying pianos to build an investment portfolio for retirement. "Investment" is probably not the best term to use when discussing pianos.

Economists view an investment as a tangible thing used to generate income, such as a factory machine. Financial managers view an investment as money deposited into an institution, like a bank, a negotiable stock or bond or mutual fund, and other financial instruments. Clearly a piano is not the kind of asset that generates income, the way a machine builds widgets. And, clearly, no one recommends creating a retirement portfolio by buying up pianos. However, the purchase of a piano for your home and family carries the potential for a greater residual value years down the road than do other large purchases, such as a big screen TV, spa, personal watercraft, motorcycle, boat, high-end stereo equipment, pool table, or china hutch. This is not a reason to buy a piano, but it is comforting to understand its longevity and lasting value.

Here are two facts: Pianos don't get better with age. Pianos go up in value over time. These two facts appear to be contradictory, but they are not. The first fact is concerned with the piano's musical value. As a musical instrument, a piano's tone and touch decline with time. The second fact has to do with the piano's resale value. Because manufacturers increase the prices of new pianos nearly every year, the resale value of your used piano to a private party eventually goes up, too.

Rhythm and News

For several years, your author Marty was actively involved in buying used pianos for several retail locations. It was part of his job responsibility to have his finger on the pulse of what the market would bear on a variety of brands and models. He has purchased hundreds of pianos from private parties for re-sale in retail stores. With the length of time we have had in the business, we have a great deal of perspective on the topic of pianos as a valuable investment. This is not just conjecture on our part or sales hype!

Acoustic Pianos Appreciate In Value (Almost) Always

Piano salesmen often tout the appreciation value of acoustic pianos, but it's more than just hype. It's typically accurate. For the past several decades, new piano retail selling prices have been doubling approximately every 15 years. A new piano of a particular brand and model that costs $10,000 today will likely be selling new for $20,000 in 15 years.

This increase in value creates a prime market for the resale of your 12-year-old used piano. Pianos last for decades. Manufacturers rarely change designs and often maintain model designations for decades. In good condition, recently (15 years or less) used instruments sell for as much as 70 percent of the price of a new, like model, thus creating a market for the piano you paid $10,000 for, 15 years ago, to sell today for $13,000 to $15,000 as a used instrument.

When Acoustic Pianos Depreciate

When manufacturers go out of business, the values of their used instruments decline, and appreciation slows. When manufacturers completely redesign and redesignate their line, the values of the older models decline, and appreciation slows. When manufacturers change ownership, the value of their used pianos is affected. When entire categories go out of fashion, like the square grands of the 1840s to 1890s, tall uprights of the 1920s to 1930s, and spinet pianos of the 1940s to 1970s, the category can take a nosedive and depreciate.

A depreciation-appreciation-depreciation cycle exists for all types and genres of acoustic pianos. The retail resale value of a mainstream average used piano takes a dip below the original purchase price for the first three to five years, just as it takes new price increases to counter the stigma of used versus new. In years 6 to 15, the value will rise above your purchase price and hug the street price of a new unit at about the 70 to 75 percent level. This rise begins to level off at about years 16 to 25 and will not keep pace with new prices. The years after 25 will see a gradual decline in the value of the instrument relative to the price of like new, but the value will rarely drop below the original purchase price.

Higher end pianos may enjoy a longer rise and level phase. Budget, low profile pianos may suffer a shorter stint at each of the three phases. The year estimates in the cycle may vary slightly for brand and region, but the theory is sound and highly supportable. This analysis is thrown off by a few years if the original buyer paid too high a price to start with. We are also assuming a private party to private party resale. If you sell to a dealer, he will want to buy it at a wholesale value. We are assuming original purchase prices to be in the normal margins realm of American piano retailing for the brand considered.

Appreciation Rates

All pianos appreciate in value at nearly the same proportional rate. This might sound like heresy to high-end manufacturers and aficionados of the top-tier brands, but our extensive experience has demonstrated that all piano prices continue to rise at about the same proportional rate across the board when judged at five-year periods, or longer.

Steinway & Sons has always been used as the benchmark for this discussion. The appreciation of Steinways has been studied and journaled several times against blue chip stocks and other investments. The reason the dollar value of Steinways and other high-end instruments rises to such astronomical amounts so quickly is that they are so expensive to start with.

Here's the math to illustrate this point:

◆ In 15 years, a $50,000 piano will likely be worth $70,000 as a used instrument. This is an increase of $20,000 over the original purchase price and a 40 percent rise in value.

◆ In 15 years, a $5,000 piano will likely be worth $7,000 as a used instrument. This is only a $2,000 increase over the original purchase price, but still the *same* 40 percent rise in value.

The proportionate rate of increase for both pianos is the same.

Rhythm and News
Frequently, we hear stories from customers about less-than-satisfying resale situations. We have also read blog posts that pose serious doubts regarding used piano values. Our information is based on the mainstream, most common scenario of a private party to private party sale of a piano that is over five years old. We never suggest that private party used piano sales are easy or quick. There are also some security issues with strangers and cash handling, as well as time-management issues with appointments. It is definitely more convenient to sell to a dealer, but it won't garner the top dollar you might get selling it on your own.

Conditions For and Against Good Appreciation

The formulas presented above regarding how much a piano is likely to appreciate are based on some assumptions:

◆ The piano has been kept in top condition by regular tuning and other recommended maintenance.

◆ The instrument is being resold to the end-users, i.e., a private-party buyer.

- Selling a used piano to a dealer or other re-seller encounters the wholesale-versus-retail differential. Dealers need to make a profit. For a used piano, dealers will often pay less than half of what they expect to sell it for, minus any necessary reconditioning needs. Dealers always must pay a price meaningfully lower than they can buy the same model new at wholesale from the manufacturer.

- Reselling a piano less than five years old will always return disappointing results.

- Reselling a piano in a distressed or duress situation, which involves liquidating the instrument in a big hurry and forcing acceptance of the first offer, will always return disappointing results.

- Reselling stencil pianos, off brand names, discontinued/defunct brand names, or odd cabinet designs or colors will often bring disappointing results; hence our recommendations to buy recognizable brand names and mainstream models and colors.

- Reselling a piano where the original purchase price was materially above the market price at that time will make it difficult to meet these projections.

There are two additional caveats we need to mention. First, retail prices on new pianos continue to rise uniformly across the country on an annual basis. We can document this. What is hard to document is the resale of used instruments and the relationship of the selling price to that which was paid when the instrument was new. Our experience has been in a major metropolitan area including Los Angeles, Orange, San Bernardino, and Riverside counties in Southern California. This area encompasses a massive *BPI* or *Buying Power Index*.

def•i•ni•tion

Buying Power Index (BPI) is an index that weighs population, effective buying income, and retail sales to measure a given market's potential.

Clearly a private party wanting to sell a 52" polished mahogany off-brand vertical piano in rural Vermont will have a harder time finding a buyer and getting the desired price than someone selling the same instrument in midtown Manhattan. The further you are from the core of a major metropolitan area, the harder it will be to sell your piano at the price it should command.

There are also regional biases about brand names and countries of origin. The popularity of Japanese and Korean pianos came much later in the Midwest than it did on both coasts, for example. We suspect that it will be easier for a private party wanting to sell a used Baldwin or other domestic piano to find a buyer at the right price in Tulsa, Kansas City, or Omaha, than to resell a brand from Korea, China, or Europe.

Weekly we talk to parents who are reluctant to plunk down the $2000+ for a decent instrument for their eight-year-old child. They are afraid that the child will quit and their $2,000+ is wasted. The best part of this discussion is that if the worst case happens and the child quits piano lessons, they can just wait enough years, then sell the piano and likely recoup 100 percent or more of their original investment.

Examples of Pricing Increases

We can document what has happened to new piano prices over the past 40 years. When Marty started in the business, a new Steinway B model grand sold for under $20,000. Today it shows for over $60,000. A new Kawai 5'10" sold for just under $5,000; today it shows for over $20,000.

With raw data from Don Kobida at ANCOTT Associates, an industry pricing guide, we have put together some representative samples of piano selling prices over the past 20 years. We have included two American brands, Steinway & Sons and Baldwin; two Japanese brands, Yamaha and Kawai; as well as one European brand, Schimmel. For each, we have selected one popular grand size and one vertical size. The raw data come from the ANCOTT spring/summer database for each respective year. The prices in our table reflect typical "street" or actual selling prices. We applied traditional discounting to ANCOTT's Average Suggested Retail prices (sort of MSRP figures). Not an exact science, but consistent across the table.

Piano Selling Prices

Brand / Size	1986	1990	1995	2000	2005	2X Y#	% Up
Steinway							
6'10.5" Grand	$27,180	$31,158	$39,960	$48,510	$57,870	17	113%
46.5" Vertical	$7,376	$8,892	$11,790	$14,760	$17,640	14	139%
Baldwin							
6'3" Grand	$11,739	$13,890	$17,642	$23,152	$39,345	15	235%
45" Vertical	$2,654	$3,246	$3,816	$4,128	$6,688	17	152%
Yamaha							
6'1" Grand	$10,322	$12,315	$17,918	$21,968	$23,543	14	128%
48" Vertical	$3,559	$3,758	$5,018	$5,993	$6,075	22	83%

continues

continued

Piano Selling Prices

Brand / Size	1986	1990	1995	2000	2005	2X Y#	% Up
Kawai							
6'1" Grand	$8,141	$9,821	$17,168	$20,093	$22,043	10	171%
49" Vertical	$3,559	$3,575	$5,018	$5,693	$5,993	23	83%
Schimmel							
6' Grand	$13,064	$14,816	$23,344	$27,664	$33,904	12	160%
48" Vertical	$5,272	$6,336	$9,264	$10,464	$12,144	14	130%

Note that the price of new pianos has increased an average of 138 percent over this 20-year span. According to the Bureau of Labor Statistics Consumer Price Index (a kind of cost of living yardstick), the index has increased about 85 percent in the United States during this same period. This means that a $1,000 item in 1986 would be an $1,850 item in 2006. Clearly piano pricing is out-pacing the general U.S. economy.

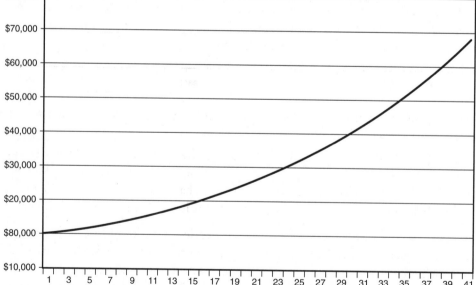

New piano price growth representation over a 41-year period.

Typically, prices on used brand-name pianos, in good condition and less than 20 years old, run between 70 and 80 percent of the lowest "down-in-the-mud" price for a new one in that market region. For example: a brand X grand that lists for $25,000 and can be bought new at deep discount for $17,000 today would typically determine the price for a 15-year-old model at $13,000. The original purchase price, 15 years ago, would likely have been about $8,500. This is nearly a 53 percent growth in 15 years or about 3.5 percent per year.

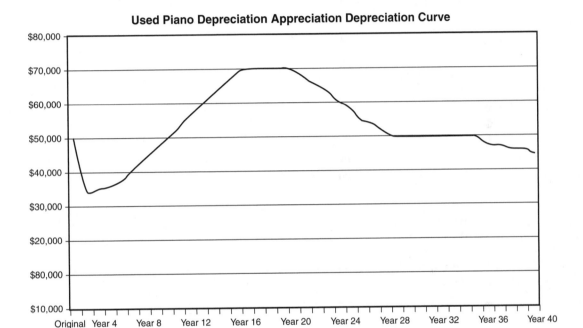

Depreciation-Appreciation-Depreciation cycle of a piano once it is purchased.

It is true that there will come a time when the physical and musical decline of the instrument will not allow it to keep up proportionately with the inflation of new pricing. Nothing good lasts forever. Pianos that have been well maintained and are between 10 and 50 years old generally sell for at least what they cost when new.

We have seen much counterpoint to these theories on various blogs and chat rooms regarding piano values. There are naysayers who regularly present scenarios to debunk what is pretty common thought on this topic. Situations in which a couple who bought a new piano at retail two years ago and want to sell their piano back to a dealer

B-Sharp

This discussion refers only to acoustic pianos. Digital products do not appreciate in value.

will be disappointed at the huge "depreciation" it suffers. This scenario ignores the common assumption of new-versus-used in the first five or six years, and it also ignores the relationship between wholesale and retail pricing. We believe that the new-versus-used graph curves begin to parallel between six and eight years and that you must sell to an end user (private party) to break even. After that, with moderate play and regular routine maintenance, it should be all gravy until year 25 or so.

The Least You Need to Know

- Don't be lured by 0 percent interest until you know the details.

- Expect to pay between 70 percent and 80 percent of the Manufacturer's Suggested Retail Price (MSRP) for most new pianos.

- Don't negotiate until you're ready buy.

- If you have a trade-in, take as much information about your piano as possible to the store, including the brand, model, serial number, and a photo to get the best possible allowance.

- All acoustic pianos appreciate in value under normal circumstances. Digital pianos do not appreciate.

- Acoustic piano prices have increased an average of 138 percent in the last 20 years, while the general U.S. economy has increased only 85 percent during this period.

Chapter 20

Special Considerations for Institutional Purchases

In This Chapter

- ◆ Institutional discounts and school loan programs
- ◆ How to plan before you shop
- ◆ Features of institutional pianos
- ◆ Pros and cons of digital pianos for institutional use
- ◆ Pianos for teachers, hotels, concert halls, houses of worship, and more

Are you shopping on behalf of a house of worship, school, college or university, community center, hotel, music school, public or commercial space, recording studio, concert hall, or other performance venue? If so, this chapter is for you. Much of the advice offered in Chapter 19 about striking a deal as you close in on a purchase applies to you as well, but there are special considerations for institutional piano shopping. Here you'll learn about institutional discounts and school loan programs as well as how to assess which instrument best suits your needs and how to organize the buying process.

Discounts to Institutions

Most major manufacturers offer their dealers wholesale discounts on instruments ordered specifically for a bona fide institution. These discounts typically allow the retailer to bid competitively for institutional business outside the scope of a typical retail sale.

Many dealers have a dedicated staff whose primary job is to solicit institutional business, prepare bid proposals, work with committees, receive and file purchase orders (P.O.s), handle deliveries, and coordinate post-delivery servicing.

As you approach these dealer reps, be aware that institutional prices cannot be given over the phone. The protocol is for the institution to mail, e-mail, or fax a bid request for a specific make and model. The request must be made on an official institution's or organization's letterhead if sent by mail or fax. This identifies the request as genuine. Then a formal bid is constructed and transmitted back to you. Institutional pricing is traditionally below retail sale pricing and is not offered to the general public. Here's why:

◆ Institutions frequently purchase multiple instruments.

◆ Institutions are often nonprofit in nature and support music education and/or piano performance.

◆ Institutional placements offer the manufacturer's brand and logo increased public visibility (free advertising of sorts) and an unstated endorsement of the brand by the performers.

◆ Institutional sales are often openly bid and, by necessity, represent a low margin of profit, but at the same time offer extra incremental business with high-profile visibility.

Private party sales, and even sales to teachers, cannot meet these requirements. Most retail sales today are predicated on a certain percentage off the Manufacturer's Suggested Retail Price (MSRP), reflecting a certain minimum profitability factored into a retailer's business plan. Typically, bona fide teachers do a little better than the person off the street. This is why we encourage institutional pricing to remain confidential. Knowledge of these prices only frustrates the retail buyer or teacher trying to match or beat a school deal he or she has heard about.

Organizing the Process of Buying an Institutional Piano

Often, institutional purchases are decided on by committees deputized by an organization to shop for a piano and make a recommendation to the organization's board of directors. It is not uncommon for folks who have absolutely no experience with music, pianos, or piano shopping to find themselves "volunteered" for one of these committees.

Whether you find yourself as a first-time buyer or have done it before but would like to have a better process this time, we offer several suggestions:

◆ Spend some time brainstorming with the entire committee to establish your needs regarding size, performance level, furniture style and color, and budget for the project. It is important that all members of the committee understand the parameters of *exactly* what they (or you) are shopping for. This will keep everyone on the same page as the process evolves.

◆ Decide within the entire committee if the organization will consider a used piano purchase. (Some public entities are prohibited from buying used.) If yes, what is the maximum age to be considered? Our recommendation is 10 years or less for a used piano.

◆ Establish one central contact person to whom all information collected will be given and who will serve as the committee's spokesperson and dealmaker.

◆ Call ahead to dealerships you plan to shop, and inquire as to who will handle institutional sales. If you can, set a firm appointment to see that person. Give a brief description of your needs. The salesperson may need to bring together a selection of products, tune and service instruments, double check current institutional pricing, and more prior to your visit.

◆ Identify yourselves when you arrive at the dealership and ask for the person with whom you made the appointment.

◆ Focus only on those instruments that fit your agreed-upon parameters for the organization's needs.

◆ Don't expect a retailer to hold merchandise for you with or without a deposit while you and the committee continue to shop. On the other hand, you can expect a retailer to accept a $500 nonrefundable deposit to hold an instrument that the committee is sold on, to enable an organization check to be cut and delivered for the balance, or a purchase order to be issued.

If you have a plan such as the steps we've laid out here, and stick to that plan, your process should go smoothly and have a positive outcome.

Institutional Instruments

Which types of instruments are suitable for institutional use? Nearly every manufacturer designs at least one vertical piano model for institutions. These models feature heavy-duty double casters that facilitate room-to-room movement, as well as locksets for the lid and key cover to secure the instrument. They also feature heavy-duty construction in the cabinet and an absence of frills. Often, they include full-width music desks to facilitate the use of full scores and binders of music.

Another attribute of institutional pianos is leg styles that are called toe-block, wherein the floor end of the leg ties back into the bottom of the cabinet with an additional block of wood. This extra block prevents the leg from breaking off when the piano is moved from room to room. Typically these designs are in the 44"- to 46"-high studio piano category, a height that makes them suitable for seeing over while rehearsing with performing groups. Institutional pricing in this category typically runs from $3,000 to $5,000. Steinways run three to four times more in this category.

The toe-block helps support the leg.

Toe-block

Grand pianos for institutional use come in many more choices. It is in this category that completing a needs assessment by the committee is the most beneficial. The two characteristics most often focused on are volume/tone and touch performance.

The committee's first consideration should be the size of the room, the acoustic properties of the room with people in it, and the musical demands on the instrument. There is a great difference between the need for chamber music in a 15' by 20' parlor with carpeting and an 8-foot ceiling and the needs of a gospel church that seats 800.

One common mistake in institutional grand piano purchases is that the customer or agent thinks too small. When larger pianos are advised by a salesperson, many committees believe they are trying to be up-sold. We have seen dozens of 5-foot baby grands in institutional settings that have literally been beaten to death. For example, the church pianist, who is supposed to lead the way, has had to compete with hundreds of inspired singers on their feet. This is not the best setting for small or poorly crafted grands. One well-cared-for 7-foot grand of good quality will outlast 2 or 3 baby grands in this kind of setting. It is easier for a pianist to attain a desired volume by playing the larger-size grands. Years of easier play means the instrument will last longer. There will also be fewer unbudgeted crisis repairs, such as broken strings and action parts.

If a grand piano is intended as a design effect for the foyer of an outside office, the size or quality will not matter. It is here that experienced institutional salespeople can help you. The more information you can give them about your specific needs, the better they can help and advise you.

 Key Note

Depending on the intended use, a larger, more expensive grand piano will actually save money and last longer in the long run.

Who Will Play the Piano?

The committee's next consideration is about who will play the piano. What kind of music and at what level? Clearly, professional-level playing demands professional-level piano performance, no matter what the genre is. If your organization regularly has professional-level entertainment, you should provide an instrument of that caliber. If your organizational needs involve having a member get up and play for the sing-along part of the monthly service club luncheon meeting, then your needs are down the performance ladder a bit.

Volume and projection are a function of size in grand pianos. Sophistication in performance is a function of several other variables, such as scale design, materials, and craftsmanship. Both considerations drive pricing. The level of sophistication in performance drives the price higher than volume and projection. Several Chinese 7-foot grand pianos can be bought at institutional pricing for less than $15,000. Most professional-level performance, 7-foot grand pianos sell for more than double that amount. Steinway & Sons sells for quadruple that amount in this category.

Consider a Digital Piano

Frequently, institutions overlook the entire category of digital pianos in their deliberations. This is unfortunate because the newest generation of digital pianos has much to offer institutional use:

◆ Frequently sanctuaries, classrooms, and public halls are not climate-controlled when not in use. Temperatures and humidity are driven in wild swings to accommodate room usage. This fluctuation in temperature wreaks havoc on acoustic pianos.

◆ Digital pianos are engineered to be maintenance free. Often, organizations do not budget for needed piano tuning and regular maintenance, so this can be a particularly handy feature.

◆ Digital pianos are easily patched into existing sound reinforcement equipment and do not require microphones to be amplified. This procedure can create a cleaner sound without the problems caused by additional cables, microphone stands, and feedback.

◆ Digital pianos can do double duty with their other instrument sounds to present organ effects and contemporary piano sounds. These sounds can be multitracked to present ensemble effects to complement any program. Contemporary praise and worship programs are geared toward bass, drums, and other accompanying instruments. These programs are a natural for the modern digital ensemble.

◆ Digital pianos can record and play back prerecorded performances, thereby offering a plan B when the pianist is ill or doesn't appear at showtime.

◆ Digital pianos can give big grand piano sounds in a much smaller footprint than an acoustic piano, especially when tied into the house PA system.

◆ Top-of-the-line digital pianos can come in grand-piano-shaped cabinets to deliver the look of a grand in addition to the performance.

◆ Many higher-end digitals outperform lower-end acoustic pianos in touch, tone, and volume.

Before your committee rules out the feasibility of a digital instrument, get a full demonstration and see for yourself. You may be able to save thousands of dollars and get a lot more value for the money you do spend.

Pianos for Hotels and Other Commercial Venues

Hotels, as well as public and commercial buildings, may want to consider player pianos. Often, pianos sit without being played for days and weeks at these types of facilities. A player grand located in the lobby or near a bar can encourage patrons to linger and buy more drinks. Live piano music always adds to the ambiance of upscale settings. Player pianos provide live entertainment without the presence of an actual pianist. And having a piano on hand to be rolled into a banquet hall or suite can command additional rental revenue.

Pianos for Recording Studios

For most established recording studios, the cost of a new grand piano is secondary to the specific acoustical properties and/or the profile that a particular brand name projects to prospective artists. Typically, grands less than 6 feet in length are not considered for recording purposes. The expense is amortized over several years and recouped in just a few high-level sessions.

Pianos for Concert Halls

The needs of a concert hall depend on its size. Large venues require no less than a 9-foot concert grand. More intimate settings may embrace pianos between 7 and 9 feet. Nearly every concert hall will have at least one *house piano*. Often high profile artists will bring in their own instrument or one from an outside source. Steinway, Yamaha, and Kawai maintain banks of *concert and artist, or C & A, pianos* for this purpose.

def•i•ni•tion

A **house piano** is a piano owned by a performance venue. House pianos may or may not be properly maintained for high-level concert performance. **Concert and artist, or C & A, pianos,** are 7-foot and 9-foot grand pianos designated by manufacturers for loan or rental usage by performers in concert or recording venues.

Pianos for Teachers

Some institutional pianos are to be used as teaching instruments. If the majority of those who will play the instrument are at the beginning and lower-intermediate level of play, then the performance characteristics are not too critical. On the other hand, if the focus is to challenge these players to greater levels of performance, then the instrument needs to be up to the task. Grand pianos must always be the first consideration for any teacher with the space and budget to support it. Often tax advantages for private teachers help offset the cost of a performance instrument.

Unfortunately, the professional demands and brand affinities of piano performance professors do not always dovetail with music department budgets. Often compromises must be made to fill everyone's needs. As a result, music departments often purchase smaller grands than a professor might prefer or opt for a lower-profile brand name. If you are the professor in question, identify your specific performance requirements and make them known. The better prepared you are to communicate your preferences, the more likely you will get your needs met.

Universities rarely buy grand pianos that are less than 6 feet in length, even if they will be crammed into professors' private teaching studios. Most recital halls demand 7-foot grands. Nearly every concert venue demands a 9-foot concert grand piano. Each of these size categories has dynamic tone and projection characteristics that must be considered. Rarely will you find brands other than Yamaha, Steinway & Sons, or Kawai represented in these settings.

Public schools purchasing pianos for classrooms are looking for durability, price, and, finally, performance. The purchasing departments are focused on getting the lowest price on a piano that fits the bid specifications set by the committee. Often brands of lesser quality are substituted as long as their specifications fit the list given to the purchasing department. School committees or music department heads must stress the need for a specific brand and model to meet their musical needs if they are to receive what they have shopped for and decided on.

School Loan Programs

School loan programs have been in effect for nearly 25 years. Manufacturers such as Yamaha and Kawai, working with local dealer sponsors, have put thousands of professional-grade pianos into colleges and universities. A school loan is a kind of partnership between the school, the manufacturer, and the retail dealer sponsor. The location of the school, the size and profile of its music program, the number and mix of its instrument needs, and most importantly, the projection of future sales for the dealer are factors in securing a school loan.

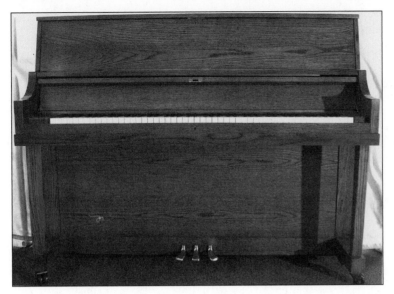

Institutional vertical piano designs incorporate features useful to institutions such as full-width music desks and locking features.

An essential component of these programs is that schools budget to buy a small percentage of the instruments loaned each year. After a few years, many schools become self-sufficient in their instrument needs and only must replace instruments because of attrition. Some music departments gain a higher profile and recruiting strength by becoming known as an "all brand X" school.

For the typical retail dealer, the number of institutional sales each year is a very small percentage of the total number of instruments sold. On these few deals, the margin of profit is low. The value to the manufacturer and the retailer is the outside exposure of brand names and the tacit endorsement of those who play them.

The Least You Need to Know

♦ Institutions usually receive discount prices below those of the general public or even teachers.

♦ Needs assessment is critical for institutional committees.

♦ Bigger grand pianos can last longer and be cheaper over time than smaller grand pianos.

♦ Digital piano features are often a good match for institutions.

♦ Player pianos may bring additional revenue to hotels.

♦ University loan programs may be available to schools that meet certain criteria.

Chapter 21

From Showroom to Home: Living Happily Ever After with Your Piano

In This Chapter

◆ Manufacturer and distributor piano warranties

◆ What warranties don't cover

◆ The downside of dealers' warranties

◆ How often you should tune and service your piano and what it will cost

◆ What you need to know about moving and storage

With the substantial investment you'll have in your piano, you'll want to make sure that you know how to keep that investment safe and in good working condition. In this chapter, we'll help you understand different types of warranties offered on pianos so that you'll know what kind of long-term service you can expect should anything go wrong, or just for routine servicing. Then, we'll take a look at maintaining your piano, including how often it needs tuning and other ways to care for it. Finally, we'll help you learn what you need to know if you have to move or store your piano.

Manufacturers' and Distributors' Warranties

Every new piano comes with a warranty. All warranties, however, are not created equal. First you should determine who (what business entity) is warranting the product. Warranties are issued either by the manufacturer to the end user (you) or by a regional distributor of the product to the end user. Since the majority of instruments today are made off-shore, it is easier to deal with a distributor than with someone in a factory located in Timbuktu.

Whichever of the two styles of warranty you receive with your new piano, your first line of defense, in the event of a problem, is with the authorized dealer from whom you purchased the piano. The dealer acts as an agent for the manufacturer and/or distributor. The dealer is responsible for making you happy with the instrument in the event repairs are necessary under warranty. They do the work; then they bill the distributor or someone higher up the line. You should not have to deal with that aspect of a warranty. In the rare event of an uncooperative dealer, you can, of course, turn directly to the issuer of your warranty for relief. Manufacturers and distributors do not like unhappy owners of their products, so they will listen to you!

What's Covered (and Not) in Manufacturers' Warranties

Manufacturers' warranties (sometimes called factory warranties) typically cover defects in materials and workmanship for 10 years. However, warranties do vary. Ask your salesperson for the details on your piano. Because a piano bench is included with nearly every new piano purchase, the bench is also warranted, though rarely for more than one year. Disputes do arise about what is and is not a warranty issue. For a little fun, we thought we'd include some of the things that warranties do *not* cover:

◆ Scratches, dings, and dents in the finish that are discovered more than a few days after delivery.

◆ The three dents in the side of your new bench after it is tipped over onto the pedals.

◆ Fading of that deep mahogany finish after it has sat in a bay window in direct sunlight.

◆ The disastrous results when a husband buys a beginner's piano tool kit and re-regulates his new piano's action.

◆ The use of a sprinkler key and pliers to "touch up" the tuning.

◆ The damage when mice build condos in the upright piano.

◆ The mess resulting from when the family cat leaves a roasted chicken carcass on top of the beams under a grand piano.

◆ Tuning stability in your vacation home in the desert, in which the temperature was 110 degrees when you arrived, and you flipped on the AC to bring it down to 70 degrees in less than an hour.

◆ The cabinet damage and internal chaos resulting when your son-in-law drops the piano off the moving truck's tailgate.

Believe it or not, these have all happened in real life! We've heard these actual stories, and dozens more like them, from customers.

New product warranties come in two types, limited warranties and full warranties. While there are always dozens of details in the fine print of every warranty, the significant difference between these two types is that the full warranty is transferable to subsequent owners within the term of the warranty. The limited warranty is typically for the original owner only.

Most new-piano warranties stipulate a term for parts replacement costs and a term for labor costs. The standard new, acoustic piano warranty is a limited warranty for 10 years on parts and labor. The shortest warranty on a new piano that we know of is that of Steinway & Sons, with a five-year warranty. Clearly, most Steinway purchasers are little concerned about quality issues and warranty protection. The longest warranty in our records accompanied some stencil pianos from Korea that offered a lifetime limited warranty. This was in an era when Korean pianos were at the bottom of the barrel in quality, consistency, and durability! Interestingly, in relation to the gobs of pianos sold during that period, few warranty claims were made against those pianos.

New-piano warranties do not include expenses for tuning and regular piano maintenance, such as regulation adjustment, voicing adjustment, cleaning, or cabinet touch-up and repair post delivery. These types of expenses are equivalent to oil changes and tune-ups on cars. You have to foot the bill for these.

B-Sharp

When you buy a new piano from a dealer *not* authorized to sell that brand, you, in effect, void any manufacturer or distributor warranty that comes with the piano! Companies are very fussy about this practice. You may be promised some kind of dealer warranty, but any dealer who consistently bootlegs pianos for which he is not franchised will not linger long in that market, and you will be left without a valid warranty.

Most Typical Problems with New Pianos

In our experience, the most common complaints reported on new pianos within the first six months of ownership are the following:

◆ The customer never received his initial in-home (warranty) tuning.

◆ The piano has sticky keys and/or sluggish action.

◆ The piano has squeaky pedals.

Most dealers provide an initial in-home tuning for the piano after delivery. Although not required by most manufacturers, it is usually offered by reputable dealers. The ideal period for this initial tuning is from three to six weeks after delivery. Some dealers insist that the work be performed within this period. New instruments require a certain settling in or acclimatizing period to settle down from the move and stabilize with your home's temperatures and humidity.

The second issue, sticky keys, usually arises when a customer insists that a piano be delivered in a box, without its being prepared at the dealership. Sometimes, not always, this is a sign that, prior to delivery, the dealer did not adequately prepare the new piano technically. Usually a qualified tech can quickly identify the parts in the mechanism causing the symptom and ease and/or lubricate those parts. If this is done correctly and thoroughly, sticky key problems should not return. Technically, sticky keys is not a warranty issue, but many dealers will send a technician to resolve this issue if it occurs within the first few weeks of purchase. Sticky keys can also arise when a child spills a soft drink onto the keys. (This is never covered by warranty.)

B-Sharp

Check into the initial in-home tuning offered by your dealer. Some dealers will honor this service only within a certain time frame after delivery. If you are required to call and set up this service, make sure you do so within that period.

Squeaky pedals or excessive pedal noise is another common complaint, also often arising from lack of preparation by the dealer. This malady is easily fixed. The exact cause of the symptom must be divined by the tech, who will then perform the proper adjustment and/or lubrication. Again, though this is rarely a warranty issue, a dealer will often send a technician to fix the problem if it occurs soon after delivery.

Before you buy a piano, ask about the dealer's policy on prepping and tuning the piano prior to delivery. Most reputable dealers prefer to solve problems before delivery. It is much more cost effective to prepare pianos and correct their problems in the dealer's shop, rather than in the customer's home afterward. Most larger dealers understand this concept. However, it should be noted that because many dealers receive calls from customers looking for fixes that are not warranty issues, a dealer may have you call the technician who tuned your piano and schedule an appointment at your expense. If the technician determines it is actually a warranty issue, then the technician will bill the store. If not, you will pay for his service call.

Pros and Cons (Watch Out for the Cons!) of Dealer Warranties

Occasionally some dealers offer additional warranties to their customers, covering items that are not covered by the manufacturer or distributor warranty. Sometimes, larger dealers sell extended warranties to offer an additional period of protection after the manufacturer or distributor warranty expires. You should think twice before paying for this additional protection, because things usually go wrong in the first 120 days after delivery, when the piano is under the manufacturer's warranty. After that, problems will likely not manifest until the later years of the piano's musical life expectancy and would be beyond both manufacturer (or distributor) and extended protection.

Dealers often offer warranties on used pianos. Typically, used pianos are at an age beyond the original manufacturer's warranty. Usually, the manufacturer or distributor warranty protected the original owner only. By definition, most used pianos will lack any manufacturer or distributor warranty protection. Most reputable dealers sell decent used pianos with a standard 10-year parts replacement warranty. This protection is provided by the dealer to the customer. It does not cover labor charges, unless so stipulated. Most dealers offer this warranty to satisfy any uneasiness about buying a used instrument. They know that most of the time nothing goes wrong. They also know that when it does, parts are much cheaper than the labor to install them.

B-Sharp _____

Dealer warranties not backed by a manufacturer are only good if the dealer cares about his reputation and longevity in the business.

Dealer warranties are only as good as the reputation of that dealer and only as long as that dealer stays in business under his business name entity. Smaller and less scrupulous piano dealers make a career of supposedly going out of business and resurrecting themselves under a new business name. This action stiffs all customers holding dealer warranties under the old business name.

The Care and Feeding of Your Piano

Okay so it's not a potted ficus tree needing water and fertilizer and just the right amount of sunshine. But your acoustic piano is more alive than you might think. You now know that a piano is an amazing amalgam of moving parts that change over time from normal wear and tear, and you know that the materials pianos are built of, particularly the wood, react to temperature and humidity fluctuations. So your piano does need ongoing care in the form of tuning and regular maintenance. Tuning and regular maintenance are not covered under most warranties, so these are things you'll need to plan and budget for.

Determining How Much Maintenance Is Needed

Before we look at what goes into regular maintenance and how much it will cost you, let's explore the conditions that require only routine maintenance. These are:

♦ The piano is experiencing normal home use (no more than 10 hours of play per week).

♦ Your player(s) is/are in the beginner to upper-intermediate level range, not advanced.

♦ No one in your family has perfect pitch (a "born with it" thing that is very rare).

♦ You are starting with a decent quality new piano.

♦ Your home is not subject to wide and rapid swings in temperature and humidity, such as a vacation home in mountains or desert, or a home at the shore with sliding doors open wide much of the time.

All of these factors influence wear and tear on even great instruments. If you don't fit one or more of these requirements, you will likely need more maintenance sooner. However, significantly less play than indicated above will not push back the clock on every recommended service.

Our recommendations below also assume that you are buying an instrument that at least one member of your family intends to play regularly. Our service recommendations are based on the assumption that you want to maximize the performance value of your piano for the years you own it, and that you want to promote its longevity so that its useful musical life will be there for generations to come.

Planning and Budgeting for Tuning and Service

You should budget several items for your piano. First, plan to have your new piano tuned two or three times a year for the first several years. After that, you can probably back down to once or twice a year. In the early years, the strings have more elasticity. Each time it is tuned the strings lose some elasticity, making the piano more stable with each subsequent tuning. A typical tuning runs about $100. Some high-profile tuners charge more; some charge less. All will charge more if they have to raise the pitch on a piano that has not been tuned for years.

Next, you should plan to have your grand piano cleaned in the action area and under the strings every 5 to 10 years, depending on the dust level of your environment. Excessive dirt, grime, and grit can creep into friction areas and cause excessive and premature wear. This condition shortens the life of some components. A good cleaning, when scheduled with a routine service trip, should cost an additional $150.

Small regulation adjustments are commonplace with competent tuners. They do a little each visit to take up wear and correct touch issues. Your budget should allow your piano to be fully regulated every 10 to 15 years. With over a dozen adjustments for each of the 88 keys, plus adjustments to the damper and pedal assemblies, the process takes several hours and may cost as much as $500.

Small voicing adjustments are also routinely performed by competent tuners. They make small adjustments each visit to even out the tone across the scale. All pianos become brighter and harsher sounding with time and hours of play. Hammers develop deep grooves where the strings are struck, and the consistency of the felt hardens with time. A complete set of hammers with installation and initial voicing is expensive. To preserve your original hammers and the original performance and tone of your instrument, you should budget to have a complete hammer shaping and voicing every 15 to 20 years. This procedure will take several hours and may run $500.

On a decent quality new piano, these charges will amount to about $6,000 over 20 years. This averages to about $300 per year—less than you spend on scheduled maintenance of your car, and a piano will last for multiple generations, all the while appreciating in value.

We have seen hundreds of woefully neglected instruments, many of which were 40 to 60 years old and likely tuned only once or twice in their entire lifetimes. Sometimes, with extensive and expensive care, they can be brought back to being some form of useful musical instrument. If you are shopping for a decorating accessory (stage prop), and no one will ever play it, feel free to ignore the advice above. We do encounter shoppers for PSOs (Piano Shaped Objects) on an occasional basis! But, if you want your piano to last for generations as a useful musical instrument, not just a prop, we recommend following the guidelines for regular maintenance.

Ouch! That Was My Toe! Moving Pianos

When moved, vertical pianos fare better than grand pianos because they do not have to be dismantled. They can be moved in an upright position. Still, vibrations and bumps occur as the piano is moved in and out of the house and in and out of the truck, not to mention the rumble along the highway. All these movements take their toll on a piano's tuning and can loosen screws or glued-together parts. Temperature and humidity changes during the process work hard to destabilize a piano as well. Be prepared to allow your piano to settle for at least a couple of weeks before you have it tuned and serviced at its final destination. Have the technician check all action screws on the first visit and adjust where necessary.

B-Sharp

Moving pianos is not all about muscle. Seasoned piano movers have specific equipment and know how to use leverage in the process. Upright pianos can weigh as much as 600 pounds and are awkward. Grand pianos can weigh over 1,000 pounds and should *never* be moved by nonprofessionals.

Grand pianos must be rolled onto their long sides and placed on special padded, grand-moving boards. The lid is strapped shut for protection. The legs and the pedal lyre are removed and strapped to the curved side (now the top) during the move. This process looks barbaric to the uninitiated, but don't worry, it's the only way to move the beast! Pianos are positioned against the inside walls of the moving truck and strapped down to secure them. You can't have them wandering around during the trip, although some have, with ghastly results.

Because a grand piano must be moved on its side, parts that are designed to swing up and down and to be supported when at rest, now must hang unsupported and sideways. The longer the piano stays on its side, the more the parts inside will begin to sag and drift out of alignment. Grands must be moved on their sides, but they don't have to be stored on their sides, though most storage companies do tend to store them that way.

Being in the industry for so many years, we've heard dozens of horror stories about pianos that have been dropped and damaged by careless movers. It happens, but fortunately, it is rare. In our experience, less than 1 percent of piano moves result in significant damage, defined as more than $500 to fix. We've also found that less than .1 percent of piano moves result in damage that causes a total loss of the instrument.

Key Note

If you don't have to move a piano, don't. If you don't have to store it, don't. Both take a toll on tuning stability and regulation adjustments. There is always a remote potential for mishap as well.

While major damage is rare from moves, minor mishaps are quite common, particularly with grands due to their size, weight, and necessary handling. It is nearly impossible to move a grand piano without putting at least one mark somewhere on the cabinet. There is simply too much handling and manipulation involved with soft and reflective finishes to avoid a scuffmark, pad mark, strap mark, pressure mark, or color off an edge or corner. In most moves, you, the owner, won't even notice.

This small stuff is impossible to document when used pianos are moved because used pianos already exhibit wear marks. This is not a mover's responsibility; it is normal wear and tear. However, if you should receive a new piano with cabinet marks, contact your selling dealer for touch-up relief.

Storing Your Piano

Life brings unexpected situations to households. Damage from natural disasters, plumbing problems, and localized fires can sometimes require storage of household goods (including your piano) while repairs are being made. Temporary living situations may require storage of big household items. New flooring installation can require pianos to be stored elsewhere temporarily. Any situation that requires storing your piano out of your home should be given serious consideration.

Renting your own storage space to store your piano for several months is not cost effective. You will have to pay the movers to drop it off, then again when they pick it up and make the final delivery. The alternative is to make use of a professional piano storage company; many larger piano-moving companies also offer piano storage. They will charge you the moving fees, an in-and-out fee, and a monthly storage fee. The fees will depend on the mileage, size, and weight of the instrument, and length of time the piano is stored.

Key Note _____

Whenever possible, store pianos in a climate-controlled environment. Store grand pianos on their feet, not their sides.

Nearly all of these companies store grand pianos on their sides, and most of these facilities are not climate controlled. Many are not even insulated. Most have concrete floors. Often companies hoist vertical pianos onto pallet racks several feet off the floor. Although this looks dangerous, pianos stored up in the air are less susceptible to moisture that may creep in from the concrete floor.

Clearly the environment found at most piano storage companies is not good for acoustic pianos. The longer a piano stays in this environment, the more it will deteriorate. If you have a valuable grand piano that you must store for longer than six months, do what you can to store it with family or friends in a home where temperature and humidity will be more regulated.

Even if your grand piano is stored for only six months on its side, plan not only to tune the piano after it is returned, but also to have the action regulated, as it will undoubtedly have sagged out of alignment. Furthermore, plan to let the piano acclimatize to your home for at least a month after its return before having it serviced.

The Least You Need to Know

- Every new piano comes with a warranty, but you should determine who is actually warranting the product—retailer, distributor, or manufacturer.

- Warranties do not cover scratches, dents, fading, abuse, or neglect.

- Typical standard new acoustic piano warranties are limited warranties for 10 years on parts and labor.

- Before you buy, ask the dealership about their policy on in-home service and tuning after delivery.

- By regularly maintaining and tuning your piano, you will help it last a very long time.

- Store your piano in a climate-controlled environment whenever possible.

Glossary of Piano Terms

action   All of the linkage between the key and the hammer striking the strings. Traditionally made of hardwood, plastics are used in some Yamahas and Kawais.

agraffe   Brass piece that spaces and frets off strings. Usually found in grands; screws into the plate.

aliquot   Steel-bearing piece that frets off treble strings in some grands.

aluminum extrusions   Shaped bar stock that is squeezed through a die. In pianos, these extrusions are typically used for action rails.

at pitch (or at concert pitch)   When a piano's key, specifically the A note above middle C, makes a tone at 440 Hz or cycles per second. Concert pitch has evolved from as low as 380 Hz in the 1600s to the modern standard of 440 Hz today.

Boston fallboard   Hinged key-cover on uprights that folds down twice.

bridge   Hardwood ridge that strings bear down on soundboard to transmit sound.

bridge pins   Steel pins inserted in top of bridge that strings bear upon.

cabinet   The outside of the piano; the part you see when the piano is closed.

Capo D'Astro bar   Horizontal bar cast into plate that bears on strings in treble section.

cast iron plate (also known as the harp)   Gold painted iron support in modern pianos.

closing   The act of gaining a commitment to purchase. *The closing* refers to the paperwork, signatures, and payment part of the process.

coils   Tightly wound and uniform wraps of string wire around tuning pins.

concert and artist pianos (or C&A pianos)   Seven-foot and nine-foot grand pianos designated by manufacturers for loan or rental usage by performers in concert halls or recording venues.

console piano   An upright piano measuring 40" to 43" high.

dampers   Wool felt pads that sit on top of the strings to stop the tone when the key is released.

digital ensemble piano   A subcategory of digital pianos that often features rhythm, drum kits, karaoke, teaching systems, multi-track recording, and more.

digital piano   An entire product category that typically features the full 88 keys at regulation size and fully weighted, with a variety of voices or sounds. Typically mounted on a permanent stand with three pedals and includes a bench.

digital solo piano   A subcategory of digital pianos that focuses on the primary voice or voices selected. There are no drums or accompaniments.

down bearing   Downward force of the string tension on the bridge and consequently on the soundboard. Assures energy transmission from the bridge to the soundboard.

down weight   The grams of weight or pressure necessary to press a key down.

drawer fallboard   Pull-out type of key cover. Two-hand operation.

duplex scale   Odd lengths of strings behind the bridge that are encouraged to ring sympathetically to enhance treble response. Other scales mute these lengths off with cloth webbing string braid. A design characteristic only, not a sign of quality or performance.

ear training   A term given to the aspects of beginning piano lessons that focus on teaching the aural aspects of learning the pitches or sounds of the notes, how they relate to each other, and how to regulate volume at the keyboard.

fallboard   Key cover on the piano.

flitch   A flitch of veneer is several sheets or rolls of veneer that all come from the same tree. This is important in matching grain character and color when crafting cabinets.

flooring company   A lender that specializes in financing inventory stock for retailers. Typically retailers pay interest only for several months or until an instrument is sold, then pay off the remaining balance.

forte   A volume descriptor for loud play.

full warranty   A warranty covering parts and labor for term without restrictions to ownership, i.e., it is transferable.

fully weighted touch   Refers to the resistant feel of the keys. Acoustic piano keys have a weighty (52+ gram down weight) resistant feel, as well as a feeling of the hammer moving toward the strings.

grand piano   A piano standing free of the floor on three, four, or six legs, and is 4'7" to 10'2" in length.

hammers   Wool felt pads that hit the strings to begin the sound.

house piano   A piano owned by a performance venue. House pianos may or may not be properly maintained for high-level concert performance.

in regulation   Regulation is a process in which a technician makes a dozen or so critical adjustments to each of the 88 key mechanisms. The goal is to bring each key mechanism to factory specifications and to have all the key mechanisms consistent with each other. When this process has been completed satisfactorily the piano is said to be in regulation.

in tune   A piano is considered to be in tune when its concert A note delivers a tone that is at 440 Hz or cycles per second, and the tone of the rest of the scale of the piano is consistent with itself.

keyboard   As it relates to acoustic pianos, the keyboard is the user interface of the instrument, the keys themselves, as a subassembly. As it relates to digital products, it may describe a category of small portable keyed instruments that sit on a table-top or on a folding stand. These typically do not have the regulation number of keys and the regulation size keys. Some folks mistakenly lump all electronic keyed products, including digital pianos, under this confusing title.

key buttons   Hardwood reinforcements on keys where rail pins enter.

key-tops   The plastic coverings over the wooden keys that used to be made of ivory and ebony. Some pianos still use ebony wood on the sharps.

limited warranty   A warranty covering the original owner only. Other restrictions may apply.

medium-density fiberboard (MDF)   High quality, fine grained, particleboard frequently used in upright piano cabinets. It is chosen for its stability and flatness under veneers.

model number   Descriptive combination of numbers and letters unique to each manufacturer that usually denotes the size, cabinet style, and finish of the instrument. Often, a model with three numbers represents the centimeters of height or length of the piano. (Example: Model 122 often means the piano is 122 cm tall, or 48".)

music desk   Shelf that holds the music rack.

musical instrument digital interface (MIDI)   Standardized computer connections that enable synchronized communication between computers and digital pianos.

nail-down   A term given to an instrument that is placed on the sales floor, not to be sold, but to sell off of.

piano   A volume descriptor for soft play.

pin block   Laminated hardwood block in uprights that tuning pins are driven into.

pitch   The frequency (cycles per second) of the sound. *See also at pitch.*

plate pins (also called hitch pins)   Steel pins inserted in the plate that strings tie off to.

practice mute   Found in uprights. Activated by lever or middle pedal. Provides muffled softer play for practice purposes.

pressure bar   Steel bar on uprights that frets off the strings just before the tuning pins.

professional upright   A vertical piano measuring 47" to 53" high.

purchase order (P.O.)   A written order for and commitment to pay for goods and services for an institution. It is a binding official document.

rebuilt piano   A used piano rendered to like-new condition. Rebuilding typically includes a new cabinet finish, plate regilded, new strings, new hammers, new dampers, replaced or repaired action parts.

reconditioned piano   Piano cleaned, adjusted, and lubricated. Broken parts repaired and replaced. Tuned, regulated, and voiced.

refurbished piano   Somewhat nebulous term, often used to mean reconditioned.

regulation   Adjusting of the key-action assembly, damper assembly, pedal functions, and string seating and leveling to promote performance and consistency. *See also* in regulation.

registered Piano Technician (RPT)   A member of the Piano Technicians Guild (PTG) who has passed a rigorous testing and certification program for most aspects of piano technical and tuning work.

restored piano   Nebulous term, often used to mean reconditioned or rebuilt.

serial number   Discrete and sequential number given to every piano as production is completed. In uprights, it is usually found printed onto the plate near the tuning pins or embossed into the wood or nameplate on the back of the piano. In grands, it is usually found near the front under the music desk printed onto the plate near the tuning pins. Nearly every retail dealer has a book that sources this number to a year of manufacture.

shaping   Process of filing hammers into a proper shape to produce the best and most consistent tone.

side bearing   The force of the strings as they zigzag through the bridge pins. Assures energy transmission from strings to bridge.

single close fallboard   Key-cover pulls forward and down in one smooth movement.

slab-type cabinet keyboards   Portable rectangular electronic instruments typically about 3 to 4 inches high and about a foot deep. The length varies with the number of keys offered, from as small as 2 feet long to as much as 4 feet in length.

sostenuto pedal   Middle pedal on performance grands that captures and sustains notes selected before pedal is depressed. Found on a very few upscale uprights.

soundboard   Thin sheet of spruce wood under the cast iron plate. It is the amplifier/speaker of the piano. Most boards have planks that are edge-glued. Some soundboards have multiple layers.

spinet piano   An upright piano measuring up to 39" high.

stencil piano   Traditionally, the term for a piano that is made as a house brand or a private label instrument. The brand name on the front of the piano is not the same as that on the front of the factory. For example, Company XYZ wants to carry a private label so it contracts with a manufacturer to make pianos that say Company XYZ on the front. Several Chinese manufacturers make private label pianos. Frequently stencil (private label) names are contrived to sound like a famous maker like Steinway & Sons. Other stencils are contrived to sound German with the eye toward deception as to origin and hence price. Not all stencil pianos are meant to deceive buyers, however. Some manufacturers have contracted with another manufacturer to build an instrument with design and material specifications that are different from the building factory's regular models. These exceptions do not fit the traditional definitions of a true stencil.

stock keeping unit (SKU)   A system for identifying and tracking individual discrete models and finishes.

studio piano   An upright piano measuring 44" to 46" high

sustain (loud) pedal   Right pedal that lifts the entire damper assembly to sustain the tone.

touch training   A term given to the aspects of beginning piano lessons that focus on the tactile issues of learning and playing the keys and learning to play the levels of dynamics (louds and softs).

tuning   Precise adjustment of the string tensions to proper pitches and consistencies by turning the tuning pins, using a tuning hammer. This is done aurally or in conjunction with an electronic tuning device (ETD) that shows graphic representations of pitch. These ETDs may also store tuning properties of dozens of specific pianos for future reference.

tuning hammer or lever   A device with a handle that holds a socket-wrench type tip on it that fits over the tuning pins. Pitch is adjusted by turning and setting the pins; movements are minute and hammer technique is critical.

tuning pins   Steel pins approximately $2^1/_2$ inches long and $^1/_4$ inch in diameter found near the top of a vertical piano and toward the front of grand pianos. Piano strings are wound around the tuning pins and the pins are driven into the tuning block. The tuning pins hold tension on the strings. This tension is adjusted up or down during the tuning process.

una corda (soft) pedal   Left pedal on grand pianos that moves hammers to play two strings instead of three.

v-bar   Ridge cast into the iron plate on upright pianos to fret the strings just before the pressure bar.

velocity sensitive   The effect of attack on the key. If you play the key harder, the instrument plays louder, while an easier keystroke plays softer. Many keyboards do not have this critical feature. Nearly all digital pianos have this feature.

vertical pianos   Instruments that measure about 5 feet wide (left to right) and about 2 feet deep (front to back). Their flat back is usually placed against a wall. Also known as upright pianos.

voices   On digital pianos, voices represent instrument sounds.

voicing (tone regulating)   Process of shaping, hardening or softening hammer felt consistency to adjust tone.

wrest plank (pin block)   Laminated hardwood block in grands, running left to right inside the case that tuning pins are driven into.

Shopping Comparison Forms

When shopping for pianos, you will see many different brands and models in various dealerships over several weekends. It can be difficult to keep all the features, specifications, and pricing straight in your mind, and the notes you may jot down hurriedly while listening to a salesperson might not be much help later. To help you organize all the information you'll be taking in, we've included here shopping comparison forms for your convenience. Copy these pages to use when visiting different dealers, or take this book with you. We recommend filling out a form for each instrument you have serious interest in while you are still at the dealership (or any shopping location). This will make your deliberations back at home much easier.

How to Use the Shopping Comparison Forms

There's a different form for the four types of products you might be shopping for—vertical pianos, grand pianos, digital pianos, and player piano mechanisms. Each of the forms contains a list of options or features to check off and comment on. These are features commonly presented in piano demonstrations related to tonal production, mechanical functions, and cabinetry. Just because a given feature appears on our list does not make it a must-have in your piano. Some very fine instruments may or may not have features found on our lists.

Note that one of the forms is for the player piano category and addresses only the features of the player mechanism. Your first and most important consideration is the piano the system will be installed in, so you'd use one of the other forms for that selection. Then, you'd use the player piano form to compare your options for that mechanism.

If you are unsure about some of the industry terminology we use in these sheets, please check the glossary provided in Appendix A.

After filling in these forms, it's a good idea to visit manufacturers' websites to verify the information you received from the salesperson, since some salespeople may be new or untrained. Some may have been given erroneous information by their managers or the manufacturer's rep, and some manufacturers change specifications without notifying those who represent their products. So, it doesn't hurt to double-check the information you put down on your comparison forms before making a decision.

Vertical Piano Shopping Comparison Sheet

Dealership: _____

Manufacturer: _____ Model: _____ Finish Color: _____

New or Used: _____

Height Measurement: _____

Country of Origin: _____

MSRP Price: _____ Posted Sale Price: _____

Warranty: _____ Parts: _____ Labor: _____ Transferable: _____

Who will service the warranty if dealer goes out of business? _____

Number of Post-Delivery Tunings Included: _____

Minor Regulation and Voicing Adjustments Included: _____

Full Perimeter Cast Iron Plate (Harp) or Standard Plate: _____

Single Layer Spruce or Laminated Soundboard: _____

Number of Back Posts and Width and Depth Measurements: _____

Agraffes: _____ Practice Mute Function: _____

Ribs Notched Into Liner: _____

Key Cover Type   Double-Fold, Drawer, or Single-Fold _____

Slow-Close Safety Feature: _____

Integral Leg or Screw-On Type: _____ Toe-Block Leg End: _____

Key Cover and Lid Lockset: _____   Boxed Lid or Flat: _____

Split or Grand Style Lid: _____

Comments On Touch and Tone: _____

Grand Piano Shopping Comparison Form

Dealership: _____

Manufacturer: _____   Model: _____   Finish Color: _____

New or Used: _____

Length (Front to Back) Measurement: _____

Country of Origin: _____

MSRP Price: _____   Posted Sale Price: _____

Warranty: _____   Parts: _____   Labor: _____   Transferable: _____

Who will service the warranty if dealer goes out of business? _____

Number of Post-Delivery Tunings Included: _____

Minor Regulation and Voicing Adjustments Included: _____

V-Pro Plate or Wet Sand-Cast Iron Plate: _____

Single Layer Spruce or Laminated Soundboard: _____   Duplex Scale: _____

True Sostenuto Middle Pedal or Bass Sustain Middle Pedal: _____

Key Cover Slow-Close Safety Feature: _____

Key Cover and Lid Lockset: _____   One, Two, or Three Lid Props: _____

Support Bar on Fold-Back Fly of Lid: _____

Moveable or Fixed Music Desk: _____   Bevel Cut Lid Edge: _____

Spade Toe, Brass Ferule Leg End, or Period Style Decorative Leg: _____

Single, Duet, Padded, Hard-Top, Adjustable Bench Included: _____

Comments On Touch and Tone: _____

Digital Piano Shopping Comparison Form

Dealership: _____

Manufacturer: _____   Model: _____   Finish Color: _____

New or Used: _____   Country of Origin: _____

MSRP Price: _____   Posted Sale Price: _____

Warranty: _____   Parts: _____   Labor: _____   Transferable: _____

continues

continued

Warranty Carry-In, To Where? _____   Or, In-Home Service? _____

Who Will Service The Warranty If Dealer Goes Out Of Business? _____

Regulation Size 88 Keys? _____ True Weighted or Spring Weighted? _____

Graduated Weighting Across the Keyboard: _____

Total Watts of Power? _____   Number and Size of Speakers: _____

Number of Voices? _____   Ensemble (w/Rhythm) or Solo Piano: _____

If Ensemble, Number of Rhythms or Styles: _____

Built In Teaching Function: _____   Built In Music Library: _____

Built In Karaoke Function: _____   Vocal Effects and Harmonies: _____

Dealership Software Support: _____   Product Support Line: _____

Size and Type (LED, SCD, Color) of Control Screen: _____

1-, 2-, or 16-Track Recording Internal: _____   Disk/CD Drive: _____

Connectivity ports—Headphone(s), USB, MIDI In Out Tru, Line In Out, Video Out, Micro Phone, Internet: _____

Comments on Cabinetry Appearance and Design: _____

Comments On Touch and Tone, Ease of Operation, Dashboard Layout: _____

(Does It Sound and Feel Like A Quality Acoustic Grand Piano?): _____

Player Piano Mechanism Shopping Comparison Form

Dealership: _____

Manufacturer: _____   Model: _____

MSRP Price Including Installation: _____   Posted Sale Price: _____

Warranty: _____   Parts: _____   Labor: _____   Transferable: _____

Warranty Carry-In, To Where? _____   Or, In-Home Service? _____

Who will service the warranty if dealer goes out of business? _____

Floppy Disk, CD, DVD, MP3, USB formats: _____

Number and Wattage of Powered Speakers (Typically backgrounds are monaural): _____

Whose Software Will REALLY Work Best? _____

Size of the Catalogue: _____

Dealership Software Support: _____   800# Product Support Line: _____

Remote Control Infrared (line of sight) or WIFI (throughout the house): _____

Size and Type (LED, LCD, Touch Screen) of Control Screen: _____

Recording Capability? _____   To What Type of Medium? _____

Is There A Hard-Disk Software Library Storage Option? _____ How Large? _____

How Much Music (Software) Is Included? _____

Can Other Instrument Voices Be Accessed Through The System? _____

Will all 88 keys play back? _____

Will All Three Piano Pedals Continue To Function In Manual Mode? _____

Will All Three Piano Pedals Function in Player Mode? _____

Is There a Silent Mode To Use With Headphones? _____

Are There Any Video Capabilities? _____

Connectivity ports—Headphone(s), USB, MIDI In Out Tru, Line In Out, Video Out, Microphone, Internet: _____

Comments on Ease of Operation: _____

Index

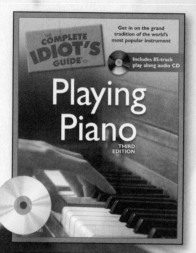